CRIMES OF PASSION

With thanks to Arlette Farge

CRIMES OF PASSION

Dramas of Private Life
in Nineteenth-century France

Joëlle Guillais

Translated by Jane Dunnett

Polity Press

Editorial office:
Polity Press
65 Bridge Street, Cambridge CB2 1UR, UK

Marketing and production:
Basil Blackwell Ltd
108 Cowley Road, Oxford OX4 1JF, UK

ISBN 0 7456 0641 5

British Library Cataloguing in Publication Data

A CIP catalogue record for this book is available from the British Library.

Typeset in 11 on 12pt Caslon Old Face
by Hope Services (Abingdon) Ltd
Printed in Great Britain by
T.J. Press Ltd., Padstow, Cornwall

Contents

PROLOGUE   The Moignon Case: Incest and Fratricide   1

Part I   Crime and the Criminal

1 **Image and Reality**   15
A Man's World   16
The Marginal Criminal   17
Domestic Violence   19
A Question of Honour   23
The Civil Status of Criminals   31

2 **The Cry of Rebellion**   38
Fathers as Murderers   39
The Unemployed as Murderers   46
'Down with the Versaillais, long live the
    Communards!'   49

3 **The Path to Crime**   55
Commonplace Othellos   55
The Crisis Point   62
Committing the Crime   68

Part II   Tales of Men and Women

4 **The Break**   73
A Question of Money   73
The Vulnerability of Men   84
Unrequited Love   88
Adultery   95
Marital Hatred   105

5   **The World Upside Down**   113
      The Working-Class Woman as Martyr?   113
      Portraits of Women   127
      The Freedom of Middle-Class Women   134
      Old Mistresses   142
      Ménages à Trois   149
      Husbands who have Grown too Old   156

    PART III   Society's Attitude towards Crimes of Passion

6   **To Kill for Passion**   167
      Sentencing According to the Individual   171
      The Beginnings of Criminology   177
      Criminal Men and Women   182
      The Desire for Criminal Suppression   188
      1930: A Dangerous Madman   197

7   **The Reality of the Assize Courts**   202
      The Victim   202
      Committing the Crime   215
      The Three Acts of the Court-Room Drama   218

    CONCLUSION   229

    Notes   233

    Bibliography   240

    Index   246

L'âme d'un historien est celle d'un lecteur de faits divers.
(The soul of an historian is that of a reader of short news items.)

Paul Veyne

Translator's Acknowledgement

Translation is for discussion

Newmark, *A Textbook of Translation* 1988

Translating a book can often feel like taking monastic orders, and so any opportunity for discussion is gratefully seized upon. I wish to thank the friends who allowed themselves to be used as sounding boards and shared my enthusiasm for this project. In particular, I am greatly indebted to Karen Fontanive for her help and encouragement and for her relentless pursuit of meaning. The many stimulating discussions I had with Professor Peter Newmark were invaluable; I would like to thank him for reading much of my draft translation. And lastly, I warmly thank my mother, Pamela Dunnett, for her unflagging support and her keen ear for infelicities.

Jane Dunnett
London, June 1989

Prologue

The Moignon Case: Incest and Fratricide

Pierre Moignon not only killed his sister Antoinette; he loved her. Furthermore, he had no compunction in admitting to this unnatural passion before his judges. His private diary bears witness to the intensity of this love. He did not even seek to conceal it from his neighbours; indeed, he confided it with some relish and with no sign of embarrassment. No one denounced their relationship; no one shunned these illicit lovers. People judged but did not condemn them; there was much indignation, and, even though insults and gossip were rife, people still spoke to them. This indulgent attitude contrasts with the behaviour of the respectable people who were later to revile the accursed couple and to refuse to listen to their story.

This story of love, incest and death did not, in fact, attract as much publicity as the major criminal cases of the time. The bourgeois press, stunned and scandalized, elected to remain silent in the face of such a monstrous act. If silence triumphed over the appeal of sensationalism, it was because of the nature of such love. *Le Figaro* preferred to take refuge behind the official version. 'The tale of this brother and sister is almost impossible to recount. Our readers must therefore be satisfied with the bill of indictment.' The newspaper *L'Evénement* justified its position: 'We will, you appreciate, be sparing of words and descriptions; indeed, we were somewhat loath to involve ourselves in this story.' On this occasion one could not openly savour the sombre spectacle afforded by the event, for this man who had shed blood was damned; his transgression only too blatant. It was felt that silence, a sense of propriety and censure would dispel the evil. This singular reaction was indicative of the fear and hostility aroused in the bourgeoisie when faced with the violation of social laws and sexual taboos. Nevertheless, they were fascinated and wanted to hear more. Such openly flaunted propriety was not without ambiguity, since a very detailed summary was none the less presented to readers.

Apart from the sensationalism and scandal attached to this case, it is worthy of

1

special attention, for, far from being unusual, it shares many features that are common to all crimes of passion. Pierre, a rather spineless individual who broke the accepted code of conduct, was rejected by the society which had already excluded him. Without work, a failure, he found himself faced with insuperable financial difficulties, further compounded by his history of conviction which was duly noted in his worker's record-book. Pierre felt trapped as he constantly found himself in situations that were to lead towards his inexorable fate. Already on the fringe of society, he worsened his isolation by channelling all his emotions into an impossible and illicit relationship. In addition, towards his sister he displayed violent jealousy, which aroused in him a state of acute suffering, commonly experienced by people before they commit a criminal act. As a woman, Antoinette was representative of her time: she took advantage of the freedom enjoyed by a working-class woman, having made clear from an early age her intention of living as she pleased. Realizing that her marriage was a mistake, she made the best of the situation by having numerous affairs with men she liked. The circumstances of their lives were now ripe for Pierre and Antoinette to be brought together.

Pierre was born in 1842. At the age of twelve he lost his mother, left his religious boarding-school and started an apprenticeship with his uncle who was an engraver. Like all apprentices, he was badly treated; unable to bear the taunts any longer, he finally ran away. In 1860 he was sentenced to six years' hard labour for robbery with breaking and entering, and was sent to Guyana. After his release he led a life of adventure first in British Guyana, then in the Antilles, and was in no hurry to return home, especially as he barely had the means to pay his fare.

Did Pierre remember his younger sister, who was only four years old when they were separated? Antoinette was brought up at first by the nuns of Saint-Séverin near the Musée de Cluny, and later by her aunt who taught her the craft of silk winding. Then she returned to live with her father, who in the meantime had remarried. She showed no enthusiasm for her job. According to her father,

My second wife tried in vain to reason with her, but she continued to do exactly as she pleased. Then she started to make waistcoats. She also enjoyed the dances which she used to go to with her fellow workers. She used to come home late but never stayed out at night. I don't think she had a lover. All the same, I was scared that she wouldn't turn out right because of her ways. That's why I married her off so young.

In 1867, at the age of seventeen, consenting and carefree, Antoinette married Monsieur Jaffeux, a barrel merchant, who was thirteen years her senior. According to the evidence given by her husband, their marriage was based on reason, rather than passion:

2

My wife and I, we had known each other for a long time, my parents came from the same village. My wife was very young, she was probably about four or five when I saw her for the first time. At that time I was eighteen and two years later I was to go to Africa as a soldier in an artillery battalion; I remained there for seven years without returning to France. During this time the young girl who later became my wife had grown up. I saw her at her father's house in the rue des Meaux where he lived until two years ago. During this period, Mademoiselle Moignon was working at her aunt's; she had been brought up by her father's sister, Gabrielle, and since her behaviour appeared to be perfectly normal, I asked her to marry me. This event took place on March 2nd 1867, as I said before. During the period preceding the wedding, I only ever saw my future wife at her father's and I never took any liberties with her at all; she seemed both well-behaved and hard-working. When I got married I knew that Mademoiselle Moignon's brother had had a conviction . . . This did not make me change my mind about marrying his sister since each individual is responsible for his own faults.

According to Jaffeux, questioned during the preliminary investigation into the case, theirs was a happy household after the birth of their little girl. This, however, was not the view of Antoinette's father:

Right from the start they complained: she, that her husband gave her no money to live, and he that his wife wanted to go out dancing, something which he found boring. I knew that she used to spend time in the cafés at Châtelet where there was musical entertainment in the evening, and that she had various acquaintances. Referring to these people, my daughter used to say: 'I'm enjoying myself, daddy.'

One witness added: 'Her husband complained that she sometimes spent the night out and that she didn't bother about housework.'

Being indifferent to reproaches, Antoinette did not hesitate to go out alone. During one of these gay evenings she met the young Auguste with whom she fell madly in love. Nothing more has been heard of him. Mathieu Fontaine and Victor Sébastard, on the other hand, were more talkative about their affairs with the unfaithful young wife.

Mathieu Fontaine, aged twenty-seven, a minor customs official in Paris, residing in the rue de Charenton, explained:

I met the Jaffeux woman shortly before the war in the widow Lambert's restaurant, in the rue de Rambouillet, where Jaffeux's wife was working as a waitress. Anyway, I knew her well enough by sight to recognize her in the neighbourhood of the aforementioned street where she lived, I think. We became close almost immediately. Madame Jaffeux was very attractive, her manner encouraging, and it was not long before she gave herself to me . . . During the time I was doing my military service – the period which I am referring to—she wrote to me seven or eight times and I learnt from her that she was also corresponding with a soldier stationed on the Rhine. But I don't know how it turned out since I broke with her over two years ago. I might add that I was even more keen to stop seeing Madame Jaffeux after hearing of her relationship with Sébastard which had started when I was in the army.

At the end of his statement Mathieu's recollections became somewhat vague; he described a lively woman: 'I never heard Madame Jaffeux complain about her home life; in fact she laughed rather than complained about the pain which she felt.'

Victor Sébastard, a thirty-three-year-old bachelor who was head clerk at the Paris–Lyon–Méditerranée railway, remembers Antoinette, whom he had also met in the restaurant of the widow Lambert, very vividly:

Shortly afterwards I fell ill and had to stay in bed, although it was nothing serious. Jaffeux's wife used to bring me food from the restaurant. At that time I was living in the rue de Charenton [like Mathieu Fontaine]. After I got better Madame Jaffeux went on coming to my house as a charwoman. She used to talk about her home and about the fact that her husband did not like her to spend money. She also told me that one day he had been so angry he had smashed a pitcher and a bowl by throwing them at her face.

Referring to a certain Auguste, he said:

Apparently, this relationship created in her a genuine passion which continued even during her affair with Fontaine and which she never stopped talking about. She also told me that she was unhappy from the start with her husband, who, as I said earlier, used to beat her and deprive her of necessities. One day after he had returned home completely drunk she had run away to take refuge with Auguste and she stayed with him for a fortnight.

It is not clear if Antoinette's husband preferred to keep quiet or was really unaware of his wife's infidelities. At the trial he avoided this question:

I was living happily and peacefully with my wife when Pierre Moignon came to live with us last March or maybe April [1873]. I had given in to his father's entreaties by allowing him to stay with us and to sleep in our bedroom, on a mattress which we lifted off our bed at night. He spent his time reading or going for walks. He lived on the 15 or 20 francs which his father sent him every week.

In Jaffeux's lodgings, which consisted of a single room, the brother and sister spent all day together in great intimacy. Moreover, no one was shocked by this cohabitation, which was perceived as a sign of mutual support. Before long, their ambiguous behaviour started to excite the curiosity of their neighbours: 'They stayed cooped up indoors until midday, and went out when they felt like it.' Then rumours started circulating about this strange household. These rumours were fully justified since Pierre, who was a former convict, not only continued to live off his family after his return to France, but also loved his sister and passionately desired her.

The evidence of the neighbours and of Pierre, and the letters he wrote to his sister, make it possible to piece together this love story. Pierre was very possessive and was fiercely jealous of Antoinette's old lovers; yet he was completely indifferent to his brother-in-law and clearly did not regard him as a rival. His jealousy was such that he forced Antoinette to break with Victor Sébastard, who stated:

Last April, she told me her brother was coming back. She had always described her brother as having been jealous of her ever since childhood, and as having constantly plagued her, without however, telling me what his motive was for being jealous and pestering her. She told me that he followed her everywhere in the street. It was at her suggestion that I decided to leave her, and I did so without regret.

Antoinette, however, had second thoughts and tried in vain to re-establish her relationship with her lover. Pierre, who was suspicious, went through her possessions and found the letters that Mathieu Fontaine had written to her. He immediately showed them to a neighbour and complained about his sister's misbehaviour. He was embittered and created a jealous scene with her, destroying the letters in front of her. Pierre wanted his beloved to be surrounded by emptiness; above all, he wanted to keep her to himself. He found Antoinette's absences the most difficult thing to bear: 'He never left her; one day he lost sight of her in the street and came back looking like death, and asked us if we knew where she was.'

In July 1873 Jaffeux, who had come into a small inheritance, went to Auvergne to settle his affairs; he was joined by his wife a month later. Pierre remained alone in Paris and found his sister's absence very painful. He sometimes confided in a neighbour: 'Moignon was terribly impatient. He would pace up and down like a madman, complaining all the time about not seeing his sister and saying that "if she is away for much longer, I don't know what I'll do".' Solitude, distance and the uncertainty of the future tormented Pierre and increased his jealousy. In order to find peace, he recorded his various states of mind in a private diary which was meant for his sister:

Dear sister, I have just left you, I am going home, it's five-thirty. I'm already bored; I'm trying to eat but I can't. Something is missing, can you guess who? It's six o'clock, and I go out to distract myself, but it doesn't work. I go as far as the Bastille and then I go home. It is seven o'clock, I go to bed and take some serial stories with me, but it's impossible for me to read. I don't know what I'm reading, you are constantly in my thoughts. I throw the stories on to the floor, blow out the lamp and try to sleep; I can't, I have a fever which keeps me awake until three in the morning. I eventually fall asleep. It's seven-thirty when I wake up. I get up and I don't see you, dearest heart, I realize you're not here and I run out of the room and go as far as the Champs-Elysées, passing by the Halle. Oh darling, I'm so fed up, I keep thinking that all the women who are carrying children are you, I hasten to catch up with you, and then realize my mistake, remembering that you are three hundred miles away from me. So I go back home; it's seven o'clock, I eat a little and light the lamp and try to read, but it's no use, so I blow out the lamp and I fall asleep with you in my thoughts. During the night I wake up and I try to find you with my legs, but I only find the wall. I have to open my eyes to believe that you are not there. Then I go back to sleep and I wake up at six o'clock. I've been dreaming about you and my first thought is to look under the door to check if there's a letter from you, but there's nothing, so I can't stay in bed any longer. I run out of the room, today is Thursday and she still hasn't written to me. I'm already afraid that you're forgetting me. Here I am running around the streets of Paris, but I don't see anyone, and there is nothing to take my mind off things. I am thinking of you.

So I go back to the house in the rue de Charenton. When I reach the place du Marché I look at the time: it's three minutes to two. I go down the rue Dugommier to pass Victor Sébastard's house. I bump into a man who looks radiant and is whistling; I say to myself, perhaps he is happier than me, maybe he has a received a letter from her. I imagine that in this letter you say that everything you have written to him is a sham, that you were forced to write because I was keeping watch over you, but that on your return you will shower him with caresses to make him forget all this. So I become incensed, I don't even know where I went. I wanted to die. Antoinette, forgive me, if only you know how much I love you and how I'm suffering! Jealousy makes me talk like this. Oh! come back quickly, I beg you, I'm losing heart, and I'm scared that I'll go mad.

It is seven o'clock and I go out. When I get to the Seine, the wind starts to blow wildly, and it is raining. I have to go home and so I sit down and go on with my diary. Afterwards, I read a little and then I go to bed. It's eight o'clock darling, I think that I'll get a letter from you tomorrow morning. It's Friday and I've just got up; it's five-thirty and I walk up and down the room waiting for the postman. At last, at ten past seven, the concierge brings me a letter and I hurry to open it; I read it, but there's nothing in it about you, not a word of consolation, not a word of love, I think you don't love me any more as this is not what you promised me. You told me that you would tell me how many times you had been happy and where you were at the time. Come now, dear Antoinette, I think you are forgetting me, write all these things to me. I need consoling. I am going to go up to La Villette to take the shawl to your sister-in-law. When I come back, I'm going to write to you and also to the old man.

Pierre wrote her a frenzied declaration of love, but he did not dare send it to her. Antoinette was surprised at his silence. Before long, Pierre wrote and expressed his feelings of anguish and his terrible jealousy of Sébastard:

Dear Antoinette,

You are cruel to say that I'm not writing. You must understand that if I haven't written to you, it's because I had my reasons. The reason is that I had no money to put a stamp on your letter and, also, because you don't tell me anything in your letter. You say that you have done it twice, that's your business. If I mentioned it, it was because before leaving, you yourself said: 'I will even tell you how many times I go to paradise.' You are going to leave your little girl, well I'm pleased on the one hand as you'll be freer, but who will you spend your free time with? I remember you said that he told you to leave her with a wet nurse and that he would pay her every month. So I think that everything you do is directed at him, and yet you know that I would give my blood, and even my life, for you. Father was right not to send me the money he had promised because on your return you would only have found a corpse. You're all I have in the world, if only you knew how bored I am with you so far away. I tore up my day-to-day diary as I was afraid it might be found by your husband or some stranger. It might have compromised you. Come back soon. . . . I'll finish by embracing you with all my heart as I wait for the joy of giving you a huge kiss on your saucy little mouth.

Pierre scoured the whole of Paris in search of a job, but without success. It was difficult to avoid his fate:

Dear Antoinette,

I received your letter of the 8th, which I had been impatiently awaiting as I didn't know what to make of your silence. I was happy to learn that everyone is well, except for you, but the fact that your milk has dried up is nothing, it will only last a few days and you will return to Paris fresh and healthy. As for me, I'm quite well at the moment. The fever has stopped since yesterday. I'm going back to the Grève[1] tomorrow but I'm not very hopeful about finding a job as the number of apprentice bricklayers increases daily after the bad weather we've had here in Paris – there's rain every day and it's starting to get cold. I'm happy to hear that your business has been dealt with and that you will soon be back. On Saturday and Monday I received a visit from uncle Aumas who asked me why you hadn't been to see him. I know he has received the ham and the lard which you both sent him. I send you my warmest kisses.

Your loving brother

With the money that he had inherited, Jaffeux decided to set himself up in business. He suggested that his brother-in-law work for him. Pierre eagerly accepted; he would not have to leave Antoinette. Only one thing cast a shadow over his happiness, and that was the imaginary or real existence of a rival. At the risk of losing himself or losing her, he asked her to choose:

Dear Antoinette,

What you wrote to me has filled my heart with joy about making barrels with your husband, because then I could see you every day, I would live with you, but what upsets me is that it won't make you happy. But if you love me a little, as I believe you do, then you should be glad, for I suppose that I shall work in town. I won't be able to see you when I like, as I won't always be free. Whereas if I work with your husband I'll have the pleasure of seeing you every evening, of talking to you, of reading something to you, and of taking you to the theatre or to a dance if you like, during the long evenings of winter. I'll always be here, waiting for you, unless you mean to carry on seeing Victor which I beg you not to do, for I am capable of doing anything to prevent you. I don't know what this man has done to me, but something nasty would happen to him if you were to see him again.

If you plan to see Victor again, I do not wish to make you unhappy, so I'll go to London and I'll try to forget you if I can. You must remember the novel which I read to you: *Huminda et Sylvain* – in spite of the love of his wife, Sylvain died for love of Huminda. I'm like him. I will never love another woman, for you have lit a fire in my soul which can only be put out by death. So you must see, you must see, you must judge, examine your heart; if you want me to go far away from you, I will go away out of love for you, but far from you, I won't live long. Oh! dear Antoinette, if only you could read my heart. I am crying as I write this, for I am afraid that I have pronounced my own sentence. I would be so happy to live near you. Come now, I am waiting for my sentence, speak to me frankly, I will sacrifice my love for you, and I will accept the judgement I receive with courage and resignation. So choose between Victor and me. I await your reply with impatience.

Your brother

Behind the emotions, one can detect a tone of blackmail and see the power that Pierre exercised over his sister. At the trial, however, he maintained that not only was Antoinette willing, but she provoked him first: 'I wasn't the one who pestered my sister. She was the one who started to follow me. My brother-in-law even said to her: "Why are you always following your brother?" According to her husband, she apparently said that she was frightened he might do something dangerous and that she was following him because of that.'

These statements shocked the judges, but also unsettled their convictions to a certain extent: 'Did your sister wish to make you her lover?' 'Yes sir. One morning she got into my bed. Who would have resisted?' 'You killed your sister and her memory will not leave this court-room unblemished, but out of modesty you could have spared her the dishonour of certain remarks. You yourself are gratuitously sullying her reputation.'

The rare occasions on which Antoinette confided in her neighbours are not very instructive as regards her feelings towards her brother. Antoinette carried her secret with her, and the ambiguity of the situation remains. The statement made by Madame Foucault maintained the equivocal nature of the relationship:

Without being able to give a definite verdict on the truth of their intimate relationship, I must admit that there was something funny going on between them – you could tell from their looks and from the way they often stayed out until midnight or one in the morning. I wanted to talk to her about it, but she denied the facts, and told me that it was really her brother who was pursuing her relentlessly but that she always resisted. Once when I was in Madame Valentin's room, I heard Madame Jaffeux saying: 'Leave me alone you pig, you brute, you're hurting me,' and she repeated this several times.

In court, the evidence she gave was rather different: she accused Antoinette. 'Did you not notice relations between the brother and the sister?'

Yes, Madame Petiot had talked to me about it, and I had even told Moignon not to behave like this and that the police would stop him. He had replied: 'Oh! don't worry about anything.' At first I thought it was Moignon who was pursuing his sister with his unremitting attention, but later I saw that she was running after him just as much as he was running after her. When his sister was away from Paris, he became very agitated and worried. He said he could see her everywhere and that all the women that he saw in the street reminded him of her.

Was this female rivalry or a true picture of events? It is hard to establish what Antoinette's role really was.

According to Madame Valentin's statement (her room was next to the Jaffeux's), Antoinette tried to resist: 'My brother slapped me, he's never pleased. Yet I do everything I can for him, but he'd like me to give him my arse.' The ambiguity of this statement did not escape the judges, who insidiously distorted its meaning: 'The comments that Madame Jaffeux made to her neighbour lead one to believe that the accused did not merely want to have sinful relations with his sister, but also wanted to satisfy unnatural desires.' The investigating magistrate pressed Madame Valentin: 'Did you ask her to explain what she meant?' 'No, she wanted to complain to the police commissioner, but on her way there she thought better of it and came back.' Should this hesitation be put down to fear and modesty? This is unlikely, since it was very common to call on the authority of the police commissioner to settle conflicts in domestic life, even the most intimate ones. No, it was simply because she did not want to harm her brother.

The unlawful couple did not seek to conceal themselves. It is true that their living conditions were not conducive to intimacy; open doors, frequent visits, and the concierge's surveillance all provided opportunities to be observed. This is supported by a number of testimonies, such as that of Madame Michaux, a neighbour who lived on the same floor:

I never heard anything but I was in the know about certain things . . . Apart from what I have just said about the nocturnal comings and goings of the pair, I once found both of them lying on the mattress that was on the floor and where Moignon slept, but maybe this didn't mean anything. I remember now that on the occasion I am referring to, Madame Jaffeux's door was open and it was she who had called me, saying: 'Come and see how comfortable we are.' Madame Jaffeux was in the middle of feeding her baby, while her brother was reading – as Madame Foucault, who had also seen her in that position once, told me. I therefore regarded Madame Jaffeux as unscrupulous.

Madame Petiot, who was a barrel merchant, was much better informed. This is the scene which she witnessed:

I knocked and entered briskly without waiting for an answer as I was quite friendly with her. I found Madame Jaffeux and Moignon in a position . . . Well, I said to them, with all due respect: 'You're real pigs.' Later, Madame Jaffeux asked me what I had thought of her at that moment. I told her what I thought and she retorted: 'Then you must be saying that because you're jealous and you love my brother.'

As soon as Jaffeux returned to Paris, he started work and gave Pierre a job:

I had arranged with Moignon that he would help me in my barrel business in return for 15 francs a month with bed and board and his laundry done for him. On the following Thursday, October 4th, Moignon willingly agreed to help me and he drove the horse cart; he did so again the following day, but suddenly, on the Saturday morning, just as we were setting out, Moignon said that he wouldn't work. I replied that I couldn't keep him if he didn't work, and that as from the following Monday, he would have to sleep elsewhere. My wife came to the yard to work with me, in place of Moignon. That evening he didn't come back; my wife didn't seem sorry to see her brother leave and she said it was right that he should go as he didn't want to do anything. On the same day I had bought some new bootees for my wife. The next morning, on Sunday, at about six o'clock I went to work in my yard; it's quite usual in my line of business.

Meanwhile, Pierre went to collect his clean linen from Madame Foucault. He referred to his sister's behaviour and added that he would kill himself if his sister carried on: 'I asked him what it was that she was doing. "She is making three men unhappy: her husband, her lover and me. If she carries on, I'll do a mischief – it's three months now that I've been more unhappy than for the past twelve years elsewhere".'

At about nine o'clock in the morning, Pierre went back to his sister's. An argument broke out. When he saw the new boots he threatened her: 'Oh! I see! They're for visiting your lover; but you won't use them.' She went one better than him and asked him who was going to prevent her. 'Someone who is not afraid of you – no, not afraid of you or the others.' With that, he left his sister and went off in search of a revolver with which to kill himself: 'I couldn't find any work, and so at first I wanted to go back to the galleys, and then I thought of killing myself.'

At eleven o'clock, he was back in the rue de Solanges and quarrelled again with Antoinette, who refused to take his threats seriously. She in turn provoked him by being defiant. At this stage in the criminal's excited state, a movement or a word can trigger off a heated exchange:

I thought she looked sad and so I said to her: 'What's wrong? You should be happy to see me go.' She was looking at me. 'Will you go and see your Sébastard?' 'Of course.' I threatened to avenge myself on her if she did not choose between him and me. She scoffed at me, saying that I was too much of a coward to stop her from doing what she wanted to do, and she added that she could have me arrested, under article 47 of the Penal Code concerning convicts who had illegally returned from banishment. She wanted to have me arrested for the benefit of her lover. What she said incensed me – I was beside myself. I remembered my revolver and I fired.

Jaffeux came home and found Antoinette dying; a few hours later she was dead. The autopsy showed that she was two months pregnant. In the meantime, Pierre, who had discarded his weapon and left it in the bedroom, acquired a second revolver and headed in the direction of the Bois de Boulogne. When he reached the fortifications he went down into the ditches and, after burning his sister's letters, he fired two shots at himself, one in the head and one in the heart.

Pierre was misguided enough not to die from his wounds. The judges, who were sceptical, listened to his explanations: 'As my sister was dead, I no longer had anything in the world. The fear of being tracked down by the police had nothing to do with my decision and I freely tried to kill myself.' 'It's very easy to fake suicide.' 'I was revolted with myself.'

Pierre was sentenced to death, but the verdict still seemed to be too lenient to expiate a crime of this nature. Journalists were carried away with the desire for revenge and so they vilified his portrait by maligning his feelings. One journalist wrote: 'Cayenne pepper had given the wretch's senses all the agitations of boiling oil; he was no longer a man, he was a jackal.'

Moignon's crime should not be interpreted as a mere crime of passion, the

11

final aberration of a man who is heading towards his downfall. Before wanting to destroy himself, Moignon had taken his revenge on a society that shattered his life and refused to give him the hope of rehabilitation. He was isolated behind a wall of impotent silence created by misery and social exclusion, and so his crime took the place of speech. When he was arrested, Pierre suddenly recalled his childhood; his mother was the one responsible for all this chaos. 'How do you expect me not to have grown up like this, with the kind of examples I had before my eyes: at the age of seven, when I came back from school and went into my parents' room, I found my mother straddling a bloke who was sitting in a chair.'

Woman – the eternal Eve! Besides, was not Antoinette also responsible for their relationship, and even for their death? Through her, Pierre was accusing society. Society made no mistake about it. This monstrous crime, because it was incestuous, provoked not only horror but also terror. Would it not be a social punishment to give birth to such a criminal? This was a supposition that was keenly felt, and even stated publicly. One journalist, in discussing Pierre, wrote: 'He is one of the Atreidae lost through the ages, a wandering Jew of incest, the double incarnation of Onan and Oedipus; a monster . . . who sometimes reappears in our civilized societies, which he terrifies by his crimes which offend nature, by his loves and by his vile lewdness.' He asserted the timelessness of crime and the futility of fighting against this 'scourge': 'Each time we are astonished, as if this scourge were something new. We swear before our ancestors that history never before had to record such a calamity; then, before long, we hand the responsibility over, saying it is a punishment from above or a revenge from below.'

The notion of permanence is clear. However, each society perceives the crime differently. The attention and the attitude towards it are always peculiar to a social and historical context. Furthermore, its forms vary across time: the motives, the aspects, and even the ways of killing are not repeated. It is precisely because the nineteenth-century crime of passion does not resemble today's crime of passion that it seemed important to set it down in history and to tell its story in an attempt to capture these differences.

Part I

Crime and the Criminal

1

Image and Reality

Any contemporary reference to nineteenth-century crimes of passion inevitably suggests scenes of husbands catching their wives in the act of committing adultery, or of young men being rejected by their mistresses, or of cruel wives poisoning spouses who are irksome or have grown too old. In the collective memory, the idea of the female poisoner, a stock figure in crimes of passion, recalls images of cruel and weak women who possess evil knowledge – the knowledge of drugs and poisons.

These are dusty, antiquated images, which hold a certain fascination but bear no correspondence to reality since young tragic heroes and female poisoners rarely stood in the dock. These incomplete and misleading portrayals are merely reflections of our social and literary fantasies. An examination of the dossiers of legal records covering crimes of passion committed in the *département* of the Seine between 1870 and 1880 sheds new light on this type of crime and on the legal practices of the day. Moreover, by looking closely at the motives involved, these dramas of domestic life can be understood in all their complexity, and the irrational nature of passion can be demystified.

Indeed, passion alone cannot entirely explain such acts; there were many other causes, including alcoholism, poverty, loss of employment and isolation. These were often determining factors just as much as the jealousy or heartache suffered by being abandoned or betrayed by one's lover. Nevertheless, in trying to detect elements of passion in these crimes, one has to contend with the impenetrable nature of the sources. Judges exerted a restricting influence, inhibiting and distorting any attempts to express feelings and passions. From the outset they viewed the romantic attachments of these couples in a negative light; in the eyes of the law, murder and love were incompatible. Their contemptuous and manipulative interpretation of motives was capable of sullying and distorting any statement, since, according to the logic of the legal mind, a man could not claim to love a woman whom he has made to suffer. Judges, in seeking to prove the intrinsically criminal nature of the accused man, tended to emphasize mercenary motives, thereby ignoring the irrational nature of such conflicts; hatred and love were interwoven into these relationships and were particularly subject to misunderstanding since such intense emotions were often expressed according to a cultural and romantic code of conduct far removed from the judges' experience.

The sensation caused by their criminal acts suddenly brought to prominence workers, day-labourers, linen maids – all anonymous men and women – and gave them the opportunity to stand out from the masses and become part of history. The structure of the judicial system made it possible – by means of the preliminary investigation dossiers – to record the story of these men and women who were neglected by historians. At the preliminary investigation, both the judges and the accused set out with different objectives which eventually coincided; the former looked for factors that would indicate premeditated murder, while the latter sought to justify themselves by providing motives for their crime. To this end, the protagonists had to restage the events of their private lives. Through their actual words taken down verbatim, they draw us into the drama of their lives – lives that were punctuated by upheaval, privation and desire. The needs they expressed exposed the substance of their marital conflicts, which revolved around recurrent themes such as money, honour and jealousy. These conflicts revealed how male – female relationships functioned, as well as the complex causes that lay behind crimes of passion.

A Man's World

Women represent a very low proportion of the perpetrators of domestic crime. Out of 824 individuals who were charged in 1871–80,[1] 678 were male, that is to say 82 per cent. These figures can be compared with figures from the *département* of the Seine, where 80 were male and 9 female, with women thus averaging 10 per cent of the total. In crimes where poisoning was involved, however, women outnumbered men: out of 55 cases that took place in France between 1871 and 1880, 16 were committed by men and 39 by women. Despite the significant number of indictments for infanticide and abortion, all these figures call into question the assumption that women were chiefly responsible for domestic crime. Similarly, the wave of *vitriolage*[2] towards the end of the nineteenth century is somewhat misleading. These instances were isolated episodes, representing a form of revenge which, although cruel, was not lethal.

The low figure for women cannot be accounted for by the theory of the biological inferiority of women, which was a theme much favoured by nineteenth-century criminologists. Is it not a contradiction for jealousy, that essentially female vice, to be held responsible for an increase in the murders

16

committed by men? An analysis of crimes of passion provoked mainly by the breaking up of relationships may provide some answers.

Whether it was legally sanctioned or not, separation sparked off suicidal or criminal tendencies more often in men than in women. The vulnerability of men who had been deserted, and their extreme despair and powerlessness, do not, however, suffice to explain the frequency with which they committed acts of revenge. Indeed, a society where women had the status of minors, obliged to bow to their husbands' authority, was in itself an encouragement to commit crimes of passion; the accused defended these acts as their right to take the law into their own hands. With the introduction of the Common Law (1804) and the Penal Code (1811), the state had colluded in these claims by restoring the rights of the head of the family, who enjoyed complete or near-complete power over his wife and children.

According to article 212 of the Common Law, women had to submit to the authority of their husbands; they were not allowed to leave the marital home, go abroad or carry out any transaction without asking permission. More iniquitous still was article 324 of the Penal Code, which gave husbands the right to kill their wives with impunity if caught committing adultery in the marital home!

Whether it was a legal union or not, men were assured of their right to punish the wife or common-law wife who dared to defy their authority by deserting the marital home, either to put an end to a relationship that she found unbearable or to run away with another man. The number of acquittals granted in this type of situation was an implicit recognition of the rights given to men when they took the law into their own hands.

The Marginal Criminal

Perpetrators of crimes of passion came from a well defined milieu, that of the working-class. They ranged from train drivers working for one of the many private railway companies to bakers' assistants and cabinet-makers, more often than not day-labourers; there were also small employers, builders with two or three workers under them, wine merchants or costermongers, all people whose financial resources did not assure them the economic independence of the middle classes.[3]

This selection gives an indication of the complexity of the working-class world. It is not a world that can be reduced to Identikit pictures of workmen employed in big factories or craftsmen who formed a sort of little elite (whose situation deteriorated significantly after the Second Empire). Between these two extremes there were a great many categories which varied according to the type and size of the firm. In all areas of work during the nineteenth century, the working-class condition was marked by complete lack of security. This was due to an absence of social protection, to uncertain employment prospects, exacerbated by frequent periods of seasonal unemployment which affected large sections of the working population. Despite, or because of, their financial difficulties, these men and women led precarious lives. Through the preliminary investigation dossiers, one can trace the courses of their lives, which were marked by an astonishing amount of occupational and geographical mobility, neither necessarily motivated by a desire for social advancement, but rather by a desire to achieve independence.

Indeed, this refusal to put down reassuring roots reflects old working-class traditions. Apprentices and journeymen had long been accustomed to move about, and this was a tendency that grew throughout the nineteenth century with the development of transport and increasing economic change. To move away or simply to change jobs was a common response by workers in conflict with their employers. This behaviour was part of a strategy for working-class resistance to employers. It was certainly a means for the working class to opppose the capitalist order by frustrating the rules of the economic system. Dissatisfied employers complained about the mobility of a workforce that was difficult to discipline and to control. Denis Poulot,[4] a reforming small employer campaigning on behalf of other small businessmen at the beginning of the Third Republic, described the problem of the employer's dependence on workers who stop work when an urgent order comes in or who neglect their work: 'The bad worker changes employers three to five times a year.'[5] The 'bad worker' was characterized by laziness, affectation and drunkenness. It was therefore necessary to deal with this lack of deference which ran counter to social progress.[6]

To leave one's job, to skive off work on Mondays, to lack enthusiasm for work – these were all ways of combating the vicious circle of low wages, hard work and the absence of workers' rights which accounted for carelessness and the number of itinerant workers – especially since living in lodgings and sharing the wages of a (female) companion were conducive to a Bohemian life-style.

A number of life-journeys illustrate the ease with which workers adapted to the different jobs that were determined by chance encounters and by their travels. They also show the casualness with which these men and women left their employers without knowing what the future held for them. At the age of seventeen, for example, Victor Moyaux was working as a cartwright in Touraine; then three years later he went to Paris, where he continued in this trade until starting work as a hatter at home. Two years later he became a collector for a loan institution.[7] Léopold Gassion, a retired soldier, worked first as a town policeman, then as a village policeman, then as a clerk in a bank and in various firms, and lastly at Hôtel des Invalides.[8,9] Victor Parizot worked as a copying clerk for a lawyer, a factory worker, an office employee, an assistant gardener, and a builder in Saône-et-Loire. In 1877 he moved to Paris and found work as a day-labourer, and later he washed coaches.[10]

Finally, the history of Monsieur Lecomte, born 26 July 1823 in the *département* of Calvados, is typical. At the age of fourteen, Lecomte served as a waiter in a café. Four years later he became a postman, but finding the work too hard, as he put it, he left this job in 1846 and became a waiter again, and then a shop assistant. In 1853, at the age of thirty, he opened a tavern, but later gave this up and became a trawlerman in 1856; three years later he joined the Navy. In 1865 he was in Caen, employed in a wash house. In 1866 he went to Paris to work as a concierge, then as assistant to a succession of shopkeepers, before becoming a costermonger during the same year.[11]

With no power over their future, these men lived for the present, savouring their uncertain freedom, and victims of their unhappy destinies. Their lives were interwoven with adventures and experiences. Those who were strongest made the best of it and survived misfortune; others, less resilient, surrendered in the face of adversity. Feeling vulnerable, they weighed up their chances of survival which daily became more precarious. When something unbearable happened, such as an unhappy love affair or a domestic upset, this was sufficient to make them feel devastated and lose the will to live. All the violence stored throughout their lives was then liable to explode, not publicly but in the home, the place most suited for the expression of passions.

According to Norbert Elias, the position and the role of each individual within the social framework determines his or her emotional behaviour. Workers who lived under the constant shadow of financial instability were all too often condemned to a life of destitution, without any hope of social advancement; they did not attempt either to identify with, or to model their behaviour on, their social superiors. For all these reasons, 'their behaviour may be more vulgar but it is more logical, more uniform, less ambiguous and thus more structured. Members of the lower classes are formed in a world apart without aspiring to the prestige enjoyed by those in higher social classes. Their emotional behaviour is far less inhibited.'[12]

Elias's view is perhaps somewhat extreme, since members of the working class themselves were not immune to the process of civilization. Nevertheless, it cannot be denied that violence, while not the prerogative of the working class, was certainly more visible among its members. These men and women were able to give free rein to their emotions; they used violence to express their feelings of pain or to settle a dispute without fear of compromising themselves socially, since more often than not they had nothing to lose. Some lived in great destitution: their lodgings were insanitary; they had no possessions save a little linen, a watch and a few objects such as tools, a knife and a photograph. This material poverty, combined with emotional isolation, was not conducive to planning for the future, and was not likely to make people think about the consequences of their actions.

Domestic Violence

Crimes of passion took place in the privacy of the home, a place of intimacy sheltered from the outside world, where codes of conduct changed as time went by and varied according to different social groups. During the nineteenth century, the gap between domestic and public life widened considerably, and there was a great change in reactions to violence.

However, this tendency to confine one's emotions to the home was closely associated with social status. Indeed, individuals who enjoyed a high standard of living or who wished to improve their social status were forced to alter their behaviour and to adopt certain prevailing values. Thus, for fear of social condemnation, and aware of the threat to their reputations or their inheritance, individuals sought to ignore their instincts and to overcome their emotions in order to protect themselves. This repression to which the middle classes subjected themselves was to reach forms of ascetiscism revealing an intensified desire to protect their social order from outside danger. The bourgeoisie had consciously asserted itself as the ruling class and deliberately set itself apart.

Once they had fought their battles in the world at large, these 'civilized men' then concentrated their efforts on the narrower sphere of domestic life. Although violence was forbidden in the public sphere, it was tolerated within the family and took on various forms in different social groups. The home, far from gaining from this process, became a focus for tensions that generated violence at once manifest and invisible. In their efforts to cope with the instability of capitalism, middle-class society idealized the family as providing a refuge against the perils and immorality of the world. Within this emotional nucleus, the family consciousness was strengthened, roles became well defined, ties increased and grew stronger, so that the life of the community was, of necessity, rejected in favour of a more intimate, domestic life, one that was hidden from sight, no longer exposed to the public gaze.

This change in the structure of the family was accompanied by a withdrawal into domestic life, which had become a new focus for emotional energy, thereby increasing the potential for strained relations between members of the family. But the home was also a place of freedom, where individuals could bypass rules, invent their own code of conduct, their own ways of doing things. While public interactions of an impersonal nature impose self-control, family relationships allow the expression of emotional behaviour which can very easily verge on violence, particularly as they are only partially subject to the strictures of the law. Indeed, it was within the family that the majority of murderers were to be found. In 1833 A. M. Guerry, in his *Essai sur la statistique morale de la France*, remarked that one was more likely to be killed by a relative or a close friend than by a stranger. This assertion, which goes against all generally accepted ideas, was never the subject of further study. But 150 years later, in a work on the history of violence, J.-C. Chesnais exposed the irrationality of collective anxiety which is caused by the sense of insecurity experienced in Western societies today. He showed that this irrational attitude was based on an erroneous perception of criminality.[13] In order to demystify the psychosis of physical aggression, he analysed the complexity of different forms of violence and drew his conclusions from the gradual reduction of the general crime rate since the middle of the nineteenth century, while the population almost doubled. Conversely, crimes associated with money were growing constantly: 'The law has undoubtedly brought to court certain crimes and decriminalized others, but the general tendency is too obvious to be denied.' Clearly, this is a significant indicator of the reduction in the actual severity of violent crimes: the number of convictions gained in court for crimes against the person in the mid-1970s was a quarter of what it was in the 1850s. In particular, Chesnais, basing his comments on recent studies, once again asserted that 'one should be more wary of one's relatives than of strangers'.[14]

The idea of a greater incidence of crime within the family is supported by a study of the statistical records of the criminal justice department[15] for the period 1870–80 for the whole of France. These statistics classified crimes according to how they were carried out, namely by arson, poisoning, voluntary manslaughter or premeditated murder, and categorized them under a number of headings according to their apparent causes. They have been grouped on the basis of the following classifications: (1) 'crime due to greed', which refers to crimes carried out to facilitate or commit a theft, to gain an inheritance, to ensure that the terms of a will are favourable, to pay off a life annuity, to collect insurance money through arson, etc; (2) 'domestic crime', that is, crimes committed within the family, a heading that covers adultery, family feuds, arguments about money between relatives, thwarted love, jealousy, cohabitation and debauchery; (3) 'public crime', referring to acts of violence generated by hatred, revenge against civil servants or others, old quarrels or fights, arguments about money, judicial contestations, wrangles with the neighbours, tavern brawls, fights over gambling, chance meetings and casual arguments, etc. Statistics for France have been calculated on the basis of these figures, and it has been shown that domestic crime represents a good one-third of general crime and is clearly greater than crime motivated by greed.

According to comparable statistics for the period 1876–80, Yvernès reached identical conclusions: 'It is clear from these statistics that government action has little effect on criminal acts, except on those motivated by greed or debauchery, none of which can be observed at close quarters and more often occur within the family.[16]

The first column under each heading in Table 1 shows the overall figure, which consists of cases of arson, poisoning, premeditated murder and voluntary manslaughter. In the second column crimes committed by arson have been excluded, since this study refers only to acts of physical violence.

Finally, crimes of passion have been separated by removing from under the heading 'domestic crime' all crimes that do not concern conflicts within *couples*, such as premeditated murder committed by an uncle against his nephew, etc, or rapes discreetly described as 'Women who rejected the dishonourable propositions of the accused'. Out of 1278 crimes committed in the sphere of 'domestic

21

Table 1 Number of crimes committed in France between 1871 and 1880

	Crimes due to greed		Domestic crime		Public crime	
1871	102	73	204	159	470	317
1872	106	65	216	179	362	212
1873	127	72	185	151	359	207
1874	116	59	137	109	241	148
1875	95	63	160	125	313	159
1876	67	40	165	139	263	163
1877	119	54	143	124	228	157
1878	117	69	149	124	250	131
1879	84	50	110	93	194	90
1880	118	85	98	75	178	75
Total	1051	630	1567	1278	2858	1659
	19%	18%	29%	36%	52%	46%

Table 2 Number of crimes of passion in France between 1871 and 1880, classified according to their apparent causes

	Adultery	Quarrels between husband and wife	Thwarted love, debauchery, cohabitation jealousy	Total
1871	23	50	25	98
1872	31	46	41	118
1873	28	40	29	97
1874	15	28	25	68
1875	11	35	34	80
1876	8	55	36	99
1877	18	33	27	78
1879	9	28	21	58
1880	7	19	13	39
Total	150	334	251	735
	20%	46%	34%	

crime', 735 were classified as 'crimes of passion'. Table 2 shows the large number of crimes that stemmed from domestic arguments which are referred to as crimes arising from 'Quarrels between husband and wife': these amount to 46 per cent, almost half the total. The heading 'Thwarted love, debauchery, cohabitation, jealousy' refers to illicit couples, and it appears that crimes of passion were as widespread among legally married couples as among illicit ones.

Despite the evidence provided by these various figures, criminologists and members of the jury at the end of the nineteenth century minimized crime within the family, often refusing to consider it. They thus gave greater importance to the study of heinous crimes, which there was a tendency to exaggerate, thereby distorting the perception of actual crime. In middle-class families, this form of explosive violence, resulting finally in homicide, was not frequent. If acts of physical violence were committed against a spouse or a child, such events remained hidden from the public view. Where there were serious marital problems, such as adultery or irreconcilable differences, families appealed through lawsuits for a legal separation.[17] More discreet solutions to distance those troublemakers who were held in approbrium because of their deviant behaviour were adopted, such as exile to the countryside, or to a convent or mental asylum.

Fear of loss of social standing was one of the strongest motives that restrained a person's impulses. To avoid being ostracized by society, the bourgeois citizen did not resort to violent solutions. Instead, he chose to compromise in settling personal conflicts. The most compelling reasons for this were fear of social condemnation, the economic interdependence of the bourgeois couple, and the consciousness of the necessity to repress their desires of the moment and to safeguard their future by conquering their impulses. The code of honour of the day required that reparation be made by any means for an insult or a slight. Social and economic changes imposed the need to resort to mediators or to deal with disputes through amicable settlement. Middle-class violence therefore takes place behind closed doors, and although not so visible is nevertheless equally coercive, taking the form of moral constraint, blackmail, disdain, the withdrawal of financial support or even financial domination; and it stops at the point beyond which scandal would be unavoidable.

A Question of Honour

For a long time, criminologists who wanted to study the psychological behaviour of the accused ignored the historic connection between the working-class origin of the guilty and the importance that they attributed to honour. Louis Proal was alone in observing:

It is not so much out of wounded pride as out of love that the kings and queens of tragedy commit crimes of passion; the accused of more humble origin, working-class men and women, are no less easily provoked, no less wounded in their pride by the contempt of the object of their love. It is impossible to imagine the extent to which pride plays a significant part in crimes of passion committed by the common people. They are perhaps quicker to take offence than society people.[18]

The attempt to regain one's honour has never been the sole preserve of the rich. Poverty and low social standing did not deprive people of personal dignity; even the poorest person prized his only possession – 'honour'. A crime of passion was in itself an honourable act, since it was an act of revenge capable of making

23

amends for the departure of one's partner, for adultery, or for a rejected marriage proposal; all these insults implied the loss of social dignity within one's circle.

It was often difficult to distinguish between a question of honour or pride. Honour, that moral possession which had to be safeguarded to protect one's position in society, developed both in the domestic and the public social context. This attitude was concerned with how one was regarded by others, which was even more important when it concerned a group linked by social and economic ties of mutual dependency. In an urban milieu where customs were different, the same right to pry into the individual's private life no longer applied. Marital conflict, unhappy love affairs and infidelity then became more private, and stemmed from pride involving only one's self-esteem.

The significance of crimes of passion at the end of the nineteenth century is related, in a certain sense, to these feelings of honour and pride. It was the notion of personal revenge embodied in the crime of passion that transformed the feeling of wounded pride into one of dishonour. Within the precincts of the court of justice, the accused and the judges did not dwell on such nuances; it was honour that the law claimed to be defending, and it had been their own honour that the accused had been trying to defend through revenge, even if their statements alluded to this only implicitly.

This was so in the case of Catherine Sthul, a rather loose-living seamstress who was in love with Monsieur Maray, a clerk whom she met in 1869. After living with her for six months, he left this hot-headed young woman. She pursued him violently and relentlessly for three years and was even charged twice for treating him roughly. As this letter shows, she felt herself dishonoured and betrayed, and this feeling of injustice reinforced in her a need for redress through revenge.

My dear Maray,

The fatal moment has arrived, therefore I am writing to tell you my last wish; you are free to do the same. One death in exchange for another, so I must die for you, but before doing so I want you to die by my hand. You wanted to be rid of me because you had other lovers, but you may well benefit from these others, for I swear that you are mine and that you belong to me. I must have your life and you mine.

At the beginning of our relationship I warned you that if you left me for someone else I would harm you. And now that day has come. If you had left me to get married or to make a career for yourself, I would have forgiven you. You have dishonoured me, as well as my family, and you have squandered my fortune. You are responsible for the death of my cousin, but I am happier than ever since I have a mistress who will make me rich, but money means nothing to me; what counts is the honour of dying on the scaffold to show that I have the courage to avenge myself. What a cowardly man you are to deceive a poor orphan who left her village and was alone in Paris! You swore to spend the rest of your life with me, and now you are abandoning me, you have other women but you will not play the pimp for

24

long. God's justice will always be on my side and you will see that God will never
forgive you, nor me.

You have squandered my money and now you think you are rid of me. Never!
Never![19]

Sexual honour, symbolized by female purity, has always been the highest stake
in power relations in our society. Men consider themselves responsible for the
behaviour of their wives because this is where the essence of their moral honour
lies. The greatest insult a man can receive is not to himself but to his mother, his
sister or his wife. Although this sensibility is no longer as starkly evident in male
relationships, it still provokes some reactions from them. Monsieur Marambat[20]
would no doubt have tolerated his daughter's loss of virginity; but to discover
that she was expecting a child, public evidence of her loose-living, was a
dishonour to his manliness and especially to his status as a father. His daughter's
loss of honour signified the failure of her upbringing, and the judge did not fail
to point out the father's responsibility. To avoid shame and loss of social
standing, as well as to assure his daughter's future, the only possible alternative
was to force the guilty party to marry his daughter, or kill him.

Monsieur Marambat, who works in a jeweller's shop in the rue Saint-Jacques, is
well respected in his neighbourhood. He was widowed in August 1873 and was
left with an only child, Jeanne-Justine, who was eighteen years old. While
working in a draper's shop at the Panthéon, which was also situated in the rue
Saint-Jacques, the young girl met Monsieur Henri Robert, who was twenty-four
years old and had just started work there. Within a few months she was courting
him. In October they began an affair, which continued after Robert left the
Panthéon to start work at one of the shops near the Louvre the following
February. Jeanne Marambat went to see him at his home two or three times a
week. These visits took place after the shop was closed, and Jeanne's father was
unaware of them. Since he did not return home until eleven o'clock at night he
could not keep a careful check on his daughter's behaviour. The young girl even
used some excuses which enabled her to spend the night with her lover on three
occasions.

Last May she discovered that she was pregnant and informed Robert;
according to Jeanne, he told her not to worry about her pregnancy since he was
going to marry her. The couple disappeared at the end of the summer and must
have broken off their relationship at that time. On their return, Jeanne
Marambat, distressed by her condition, confided in a neighbour and begged her
to tell her father, since she did not dare tell him herself. The following day,
September 29th, the accused summoned his daughter who confessed to her
relationship with Robert, and added that he was the only man who had received
her favours and was definitely the father of her child. Marambat immediately
went to the Louvre shop to obtain an explanation from his daughter's lover. The

latter arranged to meet Monsieur Marambat the following day, September 30th, between nine and ten o'clock at night, at the café des Ecoles. They both arrived punctually and went upstairs to a room on the first floor. The accused spoke to Robert about his daughter's condition and asked whether he was prepared to marry her in order to make amends for the insult to her honour. The young man replied that he had been ignorant of Jeanne's pregnancy and that, at any rate, there was no proof that he was responsible, since she had had affairs with other men after him. He implied to the father that he should have kept a more careful watch over his daughter. At this point the accused asked Robert to go out into the street, to prevent this discussion, whose tone had also become wounding, from being heard by strangers. The young man went and sat at the shop front of an adjacent café while Marambat, who remained standing, repeated his reproaches and warnings and asked him categorically whether he was willing to marry his daughter. 'Never!' answered Robert.

The accused immediately pulled out a knife with a very sharp blade, which he had kept hidden inside his cardigan, and plunged it right into Robert's chest. They fell down together on the pavement. Monsieur Poirier, the owner of the café, came running out and pulled the knife out of the wound. Robert was taken to hospital. He had a wound across his chest which had ruptured a pleura without directly affecting the lungs and had caused subcutaneous emphysema. This wound, which might have killed him, healed quickly.[21]

When he was questioned, Marambat stated that it was his duty to restore his daughter's honour: 'How old are you? Where were you born?' 'Forty-nine. I was born in Bordeaux.' 'Where do you live?' 'Rue Saint-Jacques.' The presiding judge briefly summed up the events previously related. When he reached the account of the relationship between the two lovers, he asked the accused whether he considered that he had been sufficiently vigilant with regard to his daughter and whether his conscience was clear on this matter.

'I think I acted like a good father. I trusted her.'

'And yet your daughter often spent the night out and the following day told you that she had spent the evening at the house of her friend, Mademoiselle Héloïse Langlois, and that they had been out dancing, or to see a show. It seems that this was of little concern to you. Did you never suspect anything?'

'Why should I? I trusted my daughter so much.'

'The members of the jury will bear that in mind. When were you informed of the relationship which Jeanne was having with the young man, Henri Robert?'

'I learnt on the same day, September 28th, that Jeanne had been his mistress and that she was pregnant; a kindly neighbour brought me this terrible news on behalf of my daughter.'

'And then?'

'And then, your Honour, I was like a lost man. All I could think of was

26

Jeanne's dishonour. I resolved to find Robert and to enjoin him to save my daughter by marrying her.'

Does a father have the right to defend his daughter's honour? This was the question asked by Marambat's lawyer. The acquittal granted by the jurors can be interpreted as society's answer to this act of personal justice. It was even more readily accepted because Marambat did not have recourse to the law to settle this conflict, since civil law made no provision for paternity to be proved. The only option available to the insulted father was to settle this problem himself.

While honour is not dependent on social status, it does, however, greatly influence it by determining choice of behaviour. The middle classes and the aristocracy prefer less sensational solutions than criminal violence; in the nineteenth century duels were merely occasional memories of bygone ancestral practices. Suicide, the expression of the death wish, was used as a substitute for revenge to save lost honour. By choosing to die instead of killing his rival, Werther's suicide marked a change in social practices and provided a model for behaviour.

On the other hand, although members of the lower classes were more likely to turn to violence, this violence belonged to a certain code of conduct which one should be careful not to attribute to barbarism or cultural backwardness. It is too easy to equate 'working class' with 'dangerous class', but this is not a useful description. This violence belonged to a way of thinking that appealed to the common sense of the people, and which indulged those who wanted to re-establish the order of things by using physical force.

Violence, synonym of force and power, is part of the male makeup. Suffering an affront to one's honour without hitting back is tantamount to admitting to a lack of virility; and the cult of virility is very strong in working-class society. Witness the challenge issued by Auguste Poujet to his rival Jean Mattey to come out of his house to settle a conflict: 'Come on then, you're not worthy of having a wife if you're incapable of defending her'[22] (1876). Similarly, Pierre-Auguste Barreau, in a jealous fury because his mistress (a married woman) had broken off their affair, went to her home and shot her, wounding her in the shoulder; he then tried to shoot himself, but the woman's husband managed to disarm him. It was at this point that the lover-turned-criminal cried out: 'If you are a man kill me; I have done you enough harm'[23] (1876).

Virility signifies physical strength and courage, as well as an ability to take one's drink. Alcohol is another factor responsible for violence. A great many arguments have started in a state of inebriation which, by encouraging susceptibility to emotion, lessens inhibitions and encourages an outbreak of criminal behaviour. At the end of the nineteenth century, the establishment condemned the havoc wrought by alcoholism, which was perceived as a significant threat to modern society. To combat this scourge statistics were demanded, and these proved alarming. The consumption of spirits and absinthe had increased considerably: from 100 million litres in 1840 to 300 million litres in 1863. In Paris, the average man who drank 8 litres of spirits in 1840, was by 1863, consuming 30 litres: 'Alcohol was once restricted to the pharmacist's dispensary; nowadays an enormous quantity of equipment is available for giant distilleries, for the manufacture of absinthe and spirits.'[24]

Alcoholism was rife especially among the common people, of course, who because of their life-style were more likely to seek a means to alter their state of consciousness. The tavern and the wine merchant's stall were more familiar to such workmen than the recently opened and more middle-class cafés. They played a fundamental part in working-class social life, for there was no other place they could go to enjoy themselves, make friends, and escape from solitude into a warm, carefree atmosphere. Furthermore, in the context of work it was very difficult to avoid frequenting the tavern. To conclude a contract, to celebrate pay-day or the arrival of a new member of the workforce, or simply to refresh oneself after a hard day's work, one went out for a drink with friends and proved one's manliness. Evenings were spent in the tavern, chatting with one's wife or lover, to escape lodgings that were too cold and inhospitable. There were many opportunities for drinking, and not only wine, but strong alcohol, which allowed one to forget the reality of everyday life, warmed the body and the heart, and altered one's behaviour. Drinkers of wine and absinthe gradually lost control of themselves and could show aggression towards other people for no reason. The violence caused by excessive alcohol brought a number of people to court for murder or manslaughter, according to their own version of events.

Violence, whether verbal or physical, was more likely to be found in a working-class environment, where it was also more visible. Blows and threats were exchanged in public, in the street or in the tavern. Furthermore, custom and living conditions lent themselves readily to intimate relationships between members of a family, since working-class housing made it impossible to shut oneself up away, sheltered from the outside world behind thick curtains.

Working-class accommodation, which was a casualty of large-scale town planning, afforded little comfort or intimacy. Forced into the suburbs, ordinary people had to make do with one or two insanitary rooms for which they paid an exorbitant rent. Accommodation problems were so serious that emergency measures were instituted during the Paris Commune: bills still owed by tenants were cancelled and empty properties requisitioned. In addition to high rents, there was a lack of accommodation. Faced with this shortage, people crowded into lodgings in wretched conditions. Dirt and cramped space forced the tenants out into the street. Whether they liked it or not, the working-class household constantly found themselves exposed to the view of the outside world. It was impossible to keep one's domestic life private, out of sight and earshot of the neighbours, whe knew everything about the most trivial events and the most intimate behaviour. In living conditions such as these, the intimacies of married life soon became open secrets. One can well believe the woman who claimed that 'she could hear everything that went on at Ponsard's place from her bed'.

There is further evidence to confirm the lack of privacy: 'On the day of the crime when the accused killed her, I didn't hear a thing. And yet from my bedroom it was even possible to hear the accused reading a newspaper.' A few words or the slightest noise were enough to be heard: 'The dividing wall was not thick and so I knew what was going on in Madame Langot's bedroom. When Helfrich went there, you could hear the children calling out while they were playing dominoes or else the newspaper being read out loud. Then, after Madame Langot had said goodbye to Helfrich rather formally, he would go home.'

Neighbours were often present at the scene of the crime: 'Our bedrooms are separated by a partition made of wooden planks; you can hear everything that's going on in both rooms. They were constantly arguing, but in Flemish. On the day of the crime, I had been working all night [she was a seamstress] and heard Madame Dée cry out: "Help! Help! He's killing me!" After escaping through the window, she knocked at my door but I did not dare let her in as I was shaking with fear.'

In these living quarters which were open to the view of the outside world, arguments and death threats reverberated and no one failed to hear them; it was even likely that people did not seek to conceal their behaviour, since any desire for privacy would be frustrated by the reality of their living conditions. In working-class districts the street had always been a place where people lived, a place animated by a varied and intimate daily life. For everyone who traversed it, the street was a place to meet in, a place for conversation. There were also public places such as the tavern and the small restaurant, which were virtually extensions of lodgings, and the places where working-class sociability developed.

Because of the cramped and uncomfortable conditions of accommodation, many activities took place outside the rooms, such as cooking, which was prepared with the help of a small stove on the outside landing. The comings and goings on the stairway to bring up fresh supplies of water, to fetch coal, to borrow something from a neighbour or to empty the chamber pot into the bucket in the corridor – all provided opportunities to meet other tenants and to be seen by them. It was impossible to live in isolation, and domestic life was inevitably shared with one's neighbours.

The other key factor in this type of sociability was the concierge's office, which was a valuable source of information. It was a meeting-place, a room one passed by of necessity, through which each individual's life was filtered. The concierge was an almost mythical character, often viewed as a kind of Cerberus figure. His or her role was both as protector of the tenants and as mediator. They were responsible for maintaining order, and therefore had to evict tenants who were a nuisance or were too noisy. While they did have some powers, their social status placed them on the same level as the tenants, an apparent equality that encouraged the exchange of confidences or of favours. When they gave evidence, certain details confirmed this mutual support: 'I sent the concierge's daughter with a message telling her mother she could put her pot on the stove since it was already lit.'[25] Meals were shared: 'That evening, he was waiting for me; I went out again, then I went to eat at the concierge's and he went to eat at the wine merchant's. On returning home I was told to be careful because he was waiting for me.'[26]

Concierges were confidants and advisers and often found themselves accomplices to illicit love-affairs since they protected the guilty lovers from the intrusions of their spouses who wanted to confirm adultery. In the Leroy–Dubourg affair, the husband tried to bribe the concierge by offering him 20 francs to let him in; despite this large sum, the concierge refused.[27] In the Pourcher affair, the wife unsuccessfully attempted to enter the building where her husband's mistress lived.[28] Concierges could not help but be involved in the private lives of the tenants, and at times were called upon to intervene in moments of crisis. Women would shelter in the concierge's office to escape from their husbands' violent behaviour. 'Madame Santin had decided to leave the marital home, and her husband was trying to stop her; the door was open and you could hear noises coming from their rooms; the concierge helped Madame Santin to get away . . . ' The following day she took refuge with him again.[29]

In marital disputes, the concierge sometimes acted as a mediator. Thus, Madame Lagache asked the concierge to tell her lover Monsieur Pierrelar that she wished to break off her relationship with him, as evidenced in the statement of Monsieur Juy, the concierge at the rue du Faubourg-du-Temple: 'On the day of November 18th, the widow Lagache told me that she wanted to be free of Pierrelar. She even asked me to go up to her rooms and tell him this, but I refused. I told her to fetch the police. The following day I saw Pierrelar and so I told him then. He replied: "Very well".'[30]

Invested, in a certain sense, with the role of keeping the peace, the concierge was often called upon to help the victims, and generally speaking he or she did so without hesitation: 'I saw that Madame Hemerling and the uncle of the accused here present were preventing him from entering his home. I told the accused to come down immediately but he did not comply with my order. I was forced to obtain assistance from two policemen.' The presiding judge added: 'He underestimated your authority.' A concierge who did not intervene would be falling short of his duty, as is demonstrated by the remarks made to the concierge in the Lebersorg affair:

THE CONCIERGE: In the morning a neighbour came and told me that she could hear groans from the Lebersorg home. I had in fact heard the sound of a pistol. I didn't want to go and see what was going on. That evening the accused knocked at my door at about eleven o'clock; he said his wife was wounded and that he wanted to take her to hospital.

THE JUDGE: Surely you must have been curious when you heard the noise, and the sound of the pistol and the neighbours' comments? Truly, this house has a most discreet concierge.[31]

During the preliminary investigation and during the trial, judges listened with interest to the statements concerning the behaviour and morality of the protagonists of the drama. This was valuable evidence, upon which rested, to a great extent, the basis of the indictment. The neighbours who testified were well informed about everyone's daily life. They recounted what they saw and heard: domestic quarrels, violence, arguments, and death threats made by the accused in front of anyone who cared to listen.

This information shows the degree of meddling and the lack of privacy that affected the lives of the working classes and reveals the nature of marital conflicts; it does not, however, tell us anything about who the criminal was, his age, his previous history, his marital status or his family background.

The Civil Status of Criminals

Out of 89 individuals who were brought before the Parisian courts in 1871–80, only 12 were born in Paris.[32] These figures are representative of the composition of the Parisian population during the second half of the nineteenth century. Ever since the beginning of the century, Paris had received an enormous influx of people. The rural exodus, which had begun in the eighteenth century, increased sharply during this period, reaching its highest point between 1871 and 1881,[33] and surpassing all the peaks of the nineteenth and twentieth centuries. Due to the growth of the railways, immigration increased and also changed. With this great rise in population, the city was transformed and grew; it was in part gentrified and in part proletarianized.

The preliminary investigation dossiers tell us something about how these provincials adjusted to life in Paris and how they integrated with the environment. The majority were workers, already used to city life. Unfortunately, there is not much detailed information concerning their reasons for leaving the countryside when this move was not recent. Attracted by the bright lights of a rapidly changing capital where everything seemed possible, they came in search of an easier life. They also wanted to make money and to imbibe the excitement of Paris. With Haussmann, Paris had been modernized and sanitation improved; the filth, the gloom and the danger were pushed out to the east into the suburbs. In the centre of Paris, insanitary lodgings made way for impressive and respectable buildings, streets were widened, and prosperity became evident. The middle classes who had deserted these neighbourhoods returned to them and displayed their wealth. Fascinated yet at the same time terrified, the workers who had come to try their luck in the capital had no alternative but to move into one of the countless furnished lodgings in the working-class areas in the east and in the north of Paris. They barely knew anyone, but what did it matter? They would soon make acquaintances in the workshop or the tavern. They were isolated but surrounded by people who shared their way of life, people with whom they could identify and with whom they could become friends. Some had come in search of a better life, others had come to merge with Paris, looking for anonymity, so as to be forgotten, or to forget a bankruptcy or a scandal.

Being uprooted and isolated made these men and women more vulnerable; their only emotional bond was with the person with whom they shared their daily lives, since geographical distance made family separations more pronounced, if not final. Both during the preliminary investigation and during the trial, it was unusual for families to testify. It is not clear whether this absence, this silence, should be interpreted as a lack of interest on the part of judges, as a disregard for the accused's past, or as an indicator of the break with the accused's background. It is worth remembering that the majority of these individuals were forced to leave their parents at a very early age in order to learn a trade and to work. Family ties were weakened by their having to leave home so young. As for economic ties, parents did not have the means to create any. The fabric of the family had difficulty withstanding all these ordeals. When the break was not absolute, relationships were maintained by intermittent letters. Whether or not this separation, this uprooting, was by choice, it was none the less painful. Left to their own devices, these men and women had many problems to contend with, and their exhilarating new-found freedom did not offer them a prop in the event of social or emotional upsets.

In their state of distress, some of the accused blamed their misfortune on the harmful and pernicious influence of the big city. For them, Paris represented a city of temptation and corruption; this was a typical attitude of people who had been forced to leave their home towns or villages after a bankruptcy and who then cursed the adverse effects of the capital city on their private lives.

This was the case for Alphonse Dupont, who received the death sentence on 26 August 1877. In 1871 he had married Maria Montabrut at Soulaires in Eure-et-Loir. Alphonse's father, a widower, had himself married Maria's mother in 1864, which meant that the newlyweds had been brought up together as brother and sister. Maria's mother was not happy about the marriage: 'He was nasty and treated her badly.' But Maria disregarded the ill treatment because she was in love with Alphonse. The accused started working at the grocer's and printed cotton goods shop which his father ran at Soulaires. Several years later he was bankrupt, and on 30 August 1876 was sentenced to one month's imprisonment. Afterwards the couple decided to leave Soulaires and to settle in Paris. On 15 November 1877 Maria found employment in the bazaar of the central market, the *halles centrales*, and was paid 35 francs a month. Alphonse did not work and was supported by his wife; from time to time he would visit her at her workplace and ask for money. Maria had tried to leave her husband on a number of occasions, but each time he had promised to mend his ways and to treat her more kindly. In May, Maria fell ill and was looked after by her parents at Soulaires. In her absence, Alphonse sold part of the furniture, and pawned the bedding. Maria's patience was exhausted; the sale of the furniture was tantamount to a denial of their life as a couple and the beginning of the breakdown of their marriage. On her return Maria decided to leave her husband once and for all, and she moved in with the other employees of the bazaar at the lodgings of Monsieur and Madame Spira, her employers.

Alphonse threatened to 'do her in if she did not come back and live with him'. Maria confided in another shop girl, adding that she 'did not attach any importance to her husband's talk'. On 1 June he came to the shop and they spoke together for a long time. An employee at a nearby counter heard Madame Dupont say to her husband: 'You've caused me trouble for too long, I've had enough.' A short while later, Alphonse cried out: 'Is that right, you won't? So you won't, then?' while taking a knife to her throat. She cried out and tried to run away, but he followed her, pushed her down and struck her again.

This is the letter which Alphonse wrote to his parents just before committing his crime:

Paris, June 1st 1877, an extraordinary day

My dear parents,

I hasten to write to beg you to come as soon as you receive this letter. Let me tell you why: it is now six o'clock in the evening. Maria has got me worked up about everything, she won't see me whatever I suggest, and she tells me it's for good. This is what has led me to the crime which I am about to commit today. For my part, I accept my faults, but I am not as black as I'm painted. I am so disheartened that, tonight at about eight or nine o'clock I intend to kill Maria, and to surrender myself to the gallows. It's unfortunately a shame for Maria because I know full well that people have put ideas into her head, but she is so full of herself that, for me to leave her in Paris is to lose her one way or the other, for here everything is bewitchment, clothes, jewellery, theatres and so on.

I cannot say any more on this subject as I tremble at the thought of what I am about to do.

Try and bring up our little orphan as best you can. The Good Lord will reward you, for I am sure to be locked up for the rest of my days. I shan't have time to kill myself before I am prevented from doing so by the police.

And lastly, my dear parents, forgive me for everything. Before carrying out what I have written to you I have cried many times and the tears still flow from my eyes as I write to you. This is why I do not wish to destroy myself alone and to let her play the madam. My one regret is that I ever came to Paris. Please kiss little Aristide for me, for I know that I must leave – either to go to prison for life or to be beheaded. But the scaffold does not frighten an honest man. She refused to kiss me or even to greet me, for Hyppolite had offered me her room to sleep in but she wouldn't let me. Ever since then I haven't been able to speak to her, for she refuses me.

This is why I was so overcome with disgust, sadness and discouragement that I have reached this point. And, like yesterday, I shall go to see her to tell her that I am going back to our home, and she will tell me she wants nothing to do with me and that I must not come and speak with her, that it is over for ever. This is where my suffering increases . . . [34]

Jacques Billet's story is slightly different, but, like Alphonse Dupont, he went to Paris in 1879 because his butcher's business in Abbeville, his native town, was going badly.

The Billet couple settled in the rue de Flandre and Jacques started work as a butcher at La Villette. They both started to drink and quarrelled frequently. Marie, his wife, reprimanded him for working irregular hours; according to witnesses, she would insult him, calling him a pig, a whorer, a drunkard and an idler, and even went so far as to strike him. When they were not arguing, the couple appeared to get on well. On 12 May 1879, Marie woke her husband towards three in the morning; a violent argument broke out because Jacques refused to get up and go to work, according to Marie, whereas he claimed that she prevented him from getting up. During the altercation Jacques Billet seized his meat cleaver which was on the chest of drawers and struck his wife several blows on the head. She died within a few hours as a result of her wounds. Jacques was later to explain to the judge that he killed her so as not to be killed by her, yet there was no sign of any blows that had been dealt to the body of the accused. Then he declared: 'Right up until the moment we arrived in Paris, the harmony of our domestic life was never disturbed, apart from slight disagreements such as are experienced even by the happiest of households.'

The letter sent by the teacher to the examining magistrate confirmed Jacques's account of their life together as a couple: 'They had childlike personalities and they joked about and behaved like children, which seemed to indicate that there was mutual affection.' The tension apparently started in Paris; Marie confided to her sister that for some time 'her husband had shown her less affection and that she wouldn't be able to stay with him.' Jacques found his job as an employee hard to bear, and in order to forget he drank 'no more than four litres a day', as he was later to tell the judge. Having been completely intoxicated, the doctors deemed him to be irresponsible. The counsel for the prosecution thought that 'he was less able to resist a guilty thought and an emotional impulse'; after being provoked by the victim, 'he struck without apparent premeditation'. The examining magistrate shared this opinion; it was he who explained to the accused the reasons for his crime: 'After several jealous scenes, your wife mistreated you; instead of answering, you had the good sense to back off, in tears, but the bitterness which was gradually building up in your heart ended up by overflowing, and you killed her.'

The mayor of Abbeville wrote a letter attesting that Jacques Billet was of good character, and was even considerate towards his wife. The prosecution proceeded to hold the victim responsible for the criminal act and to present her as a shrewish, dissolute woman. Billet merely defended himself; the jury acquitted him, finding him innocent.[35]

Male, working-class and from the provinces, perpetrators of crimes of passion tended to be middle-aged. Contrary to popular belief, these were not youthful crimes. Over two-thirds of the criminals were in the 25–40 age group.[36] Furthermore, the concept of 'youth' must be understood as relative in so far as it was applied to workers who entered the labour market at the age of 12 or 13. The so-called youth factor does not affect this type of crime in the slightest, with the exception perhaps of crimes committed after a marriage refusal – the average age here is between 20 and 25.

Because of their age, these men had already experienced sexual relationships, whether lawful or not. Out of 89 accused individuals, 53 were or had been married. At the time of the crime, 47 couples were living together. The men and women involved were often not officially separated; this was considered pointless when the couple did not own anything jointly. In some respects, poverty encouraged freedom in marriage; however, one should be wary of regarding cohabitation as a working-class practice.[37]

The accounts – often incomplete – that have been left by working-class men and women provide information on their behaviour in marriage and cohabitation, and enable us, partially, to piece together the jigsaw puzzle of social attitudes.

In spite of the desire on the part of moralists and politicians to denounce the dissoluteness of working-class morals, there is no evidence that the situation that prevailed was restricted to the labouring classes and as such was an indicator of their sexual liberation or of conscious resistance to middle-class morals. While it was the case that unmarried women who cohabited belonged mainly to the lower classes, the male cohabitee came from all sections of society.[38]

In many cases, this way of life was a reflection of a failed marriage rather than a determination to assert free love, as can be seen from the crimes motivated by a marriage refusal and the large number of couples separated without having made a formal request for legal separation. In the working-class way of life, cohabitation and illegitimacy were not in contradiction.

Marriage had a different meaning according to the social group one belonged to. For the bourgeoisie, it involved a proper matrimonial strategy with an essentially economic stake. Once the contract has been signed, only very serious reasons, such as the risk of seeing one's inheritance endangered by the misbehaviour of one partner or the other, could lead to a proper separation. Workers with no capital to yield a profit or to hand down had different concerns. For those who lived in rented accommodation, and did not even own any furniture, marriage was perceived not as an act that had long-term economic consequences and objectives, not as a financial proposition, but as a pact between two individuals 'for better or for worse'. To seal such a contract, it was not thought necessary to have to turn to the institution of marriage, which was, besides, too expensive; one 'set up house' or 'had an affair' without too much soul-searching, since the commitment was not irrevocable.

Some couples described themselves as married and their associates accepted them without criticizing or condemning them; the morality of a man or a woman was to be judged according to different criteria!

In the working-class milieu, the choice of partner was determined, above all, by physical and emotional attraction; this is testified to in the following statement made in connection with the Gendarme case by Esther Clerc, aged twenty-eight, who worked as a cook for Monsieur Lesage, a lawyer in the Court of Appeal:

In June 1876, some of the women I was friendly with in the neighbourhood said that if I wanted to get married they knew a very respectable young man, a hard worker who would suit me – this was Gendarme. I agreed to meet him and as I didn't fall for him immediately, they persuaded me to let him come back again, either to my employers' or to another place until I got to know him better. So I became his future fiancée and our relations were thus perfectly proper from July to September 15th. Since I hadn't grown fond of him, I was afraid that we wouldn't get on well together, and so I broke off our engagement for good. I made this decision on September 15th so that he shouldn't give me presents as we approached New Year's Day. During our relationship, Gendarme sometimes took me to the theatre in the company of my parents, and I had dinner once or twice with him. The only presents he gave me were a scarf and a woollen sweater. I never knew what his financial situation was, I was always waiting for affection to develop before asking him that question. As the wedding plans never became serious, I didn't go into the question of his means.[39]

As in the case of the propertied classes, one does however have to consider the financial situation of the future husband or wife. This factor can assume great significance later on. In the working-class household, the wages of both partners influence the couple's relations; if one of them fails to maintain his or her commitment, then problems soon start to appear. As will be seen in cases of break-ups, the economic factor, far from being unimportant, is very often responsible for such behaviour.

For the bourgeoisie, cohabitation was equivalent to social disorder. This class did not easily tolerate the freedom of morals that workers flaunted in urban circles – a freedom, moreover, that was even less acceptable since it tried to present itself as devoted to certain puritanical values by attempting to check this practice through institutions such as Saint-François-Régis.

Zola's article on the female urban worker shows clearly how this bourgeois theme of immorality as a source of destitution held sway, or, according to the socialist variant, how destitution was responsible for immorality:

Let us now look at the female urban worker. Here, everything is different. We are still dealing with a class of illiterates, but already we can see an early manifestation of the omnipotence of women. The female worker can be born to a married couple or from a chance liaison. In the whirlwind world of Parisian workers, there are a great number of illegitimate girls. Besides, whether or not the father and mother are married or simply live together under the same roof does not make any difference to the future of the young girl. You can count on the fingers of one hand the number of respectable families who bring up their children properly. Nearly always, the little girl grows up without supervision.

Then comes the workshop and, henceforth, if her temperament is even slightly disposed, she is ready for vice. The workshop is even worse than school. When we finally decide to take care of the morality of the working classes, it will be crucial to focus on workshop apprenticeship, which leads so many of our young female workers to their ruin. One can say that everything contributes to their being led astray: the bad influence of the whole family, the freedom they have grown up with, the lack of any clear principles, the hunger for luxury which dazzles them, and of course the bad company they mix in at school and in the workshop. It's a miracle if they stay on the straight and narrow path, for the opposite is but the logical consequence of the wild way in which they have been brought up. In spite of this, some of them have respectable marriages, but these are very unusual. Others, when the time comes, give themselves to the first man they meet. I should add that this man is usually a worker himself, for the female worker feels more relaxed with a member of her own class. However, her second lover nearly always belongs to a higher class.

Then lovers follow each other haphazardly. I am not referring to girls who live from their vice, but to the real female workers. Many of them prefer to remain free and take lovers who help them. Others live for years at a time with a man, without ever thinking of marrying him. Still others marry their lovers or give themselves to men who love them only after getting married.[40]

Illicit love-affairs, immoral love-affairs – the freedom of these girls from the suburbs was intolerable, even a threat, to all those who were trying to clean up these 'dangerous' areas for fear of their contaminating the city centre. Female workers, possible prostitutes, from whom one had to guard oneself for fear of venereal disease (the real proletarian weapon against the bourgeoisie), represented the dread of a whole social class. So the lives of these women were deliberately blackened, with all the sordid details included; they were depicted as women who were lost to vice, weak and sickly, ending their sad lives in chronic poverty, a just punishment for those who had lived a lewd life.

2

The Cry of Rebellion

Within the section of the population from which a large number of criminals are drawn, it is the most unstable individuals, both emotionally and financially, who commit an irreparable act. For, at the time of the crime, the majority find themselves in a critical situation, with no way out. Utterly hopeless, some commit suicide; others, after playing with the idea, turn their violence on the outside world and commit the suicidal act of revenge which precipitates them towards the point of no return. Only those who no longer have anything to lose can allow themselves such a spectacular deed which propels them into illegality. For a few moments, they try to defy the social order by avenging themselves on others for social injustices.

Some of the accused claimed that they preferred penal servitude to the miserable lives they were leading. These men had developed a thick skin because they had been bowed too often by adversity; they wanted to break the endless chain of failure and misfortune which bound them like a curse. In an explosion of revolt and confused hatred, they exposed themselves to death through death. This meaningless act raised them out of anonymity by allowing them at last to be heard.

Wounded pride and love betrayed, which the accused offered as motives, concealed great heartache and deep wounds. Caught in a trap of their own making, unable to carry on struggling and at the end of their tether, they made others pay for the injustice of their fate. The criminals themselves were not conscious of this aspect of their crime as an act of rebellion; it was not society that they were accusing, but their victims, who alone were felt to be responsible for their downfall. For it was in society's name that these criminals set themselves up as dispensers of justice to carry out a sacrificial and glorious murder. By acquitting some of the accused, the judicial process guaranteed the legitimacy of the right to take the law into one's hands and neglected the social problems underlying these personal conflicts. In this way, the crime of passion was rooted

38

in the context of domestic life and was not subject to sociological analysis. It was thus rendered neutral and mundane and was no longer to be feared.

Louis Proal was the only nineteenth-century lawyer to examine this aspect, although he did not do so in any great detail: 'In "crimes of passion", one kills and one commits suicide, not only because one's heart is broken but also because one's purse is empty.' Emotional starvation and economic poverty were in fact identified with the majority of crimes of passion. Emotional tension was often fed by failure and financial problems. The loss of a job sometimes preceded a break-up or a domestic quarrel. Before reaching crisis point when the murder was committed, the criminal was subject to a phase of withdrawal from society, a sort of overall feeling of confusion, the effects of which were intensified by a diversity of causes. Because misfortunes never happened in isolation, one final emotional upset was enough to hasten the destructive process which led towards an inescapable fate.

Fathers as Murderers

The Moyaux affair charts the course of a desperate man, fallen and outlawed by society, who focused his more or less justifiable hatred on his wife. His first victim, however, was his daughter. This story is interesting for two reasons. On the one hand, it contains the various elements of conflict that contributed to the planning of the murder, features that occurred in the vast majority of criminal cases; and on the other hand, it reveals much about the strategems that the criminal used to construct his image, the image of a dispenser of justice whose honour has been ridiculed. This is a doubly terrifying approach, since the violent act committed against loved ones did not bring the expected relief. This violence was initially directed against the murderer himself: the backwards and forwards motion of suffering was specific to the mechanics of revenge. Misfortune dominated these sad crimes of passion, misfortune that was irremediable and irreversible.

On the night of Friday, 2 February 1877, Victor Moyaux went on foot from Montmartre to Bagneux carrying his baby daughter in his arms. When he reached a dilapidated house, he went to a well nearby which was thirty metres in depth and threw Marie-Jeanne, who was still asleep, down into the abyss. The child did not die at once, for the impact was broken by the body of a dead dog. Then began the child's long ordeal. Victor Moyaux stayed by the well and listened to the unceasing wailing. At dawn he reluctantly returned to Paris, abandoning his dying child. Several hours later, two inhabitants of Bagneux, who were on their way to work, heard the child's groans. She was carried off to hospital but died the following day.

As soon as the police identified the murderer, everyone who knew Victor

39

Moyaux was astonished. Marie-Jeanne's two wet nurses were incredulous: how could this man, who 'adored his daughter', have been capable of committing such an act? There was the same reaction from one of Victor's friends, who testified that this man 'only lived for his daughter'. It never even occurred to Marie-Jeanne's mother, the first person to go to the morgue to identify the corpse, that the perpetrator of this crime could be her husband. When she was later questioned, she admitted: 'I could not believe that it was my husband who had killed her. I thought he was away on a trip. He loved his little girl so much that I didn't dream of accusing him.' So what, then, was the motive for this crime?

Victor Moyaux, brought up by his widowed mother, learnt the trade of cartwright at a very early age in Touraine. In 1867 he went to Paris to work for Monsieur Minard, whose daughter, Adrienne, he married in 1868. He was twenty-one at the time. They had three children, but only Marie-Jeanne survived. Adrienne, who at that time was making caps, taught this skill to her husband, and both of them were employed by a hat-maker for three years. Then in July 1872 they began working for customers from home. Unfortunately, this work did not prove to be sufficiently profitable. In February of the following year Victor started work as a clerk in a hire purchase company run by Monsieur Crespin.[1] In 1876 he was obliged to leave the firm after refusing to pay off a fine which had been imposed on him as a penalty; he justified himself by saying he 'did not wish to be exploited any more'.

Disgusted by his employer's attitude, Victor decided to take his revenge by forging credit vouchers in the name of the Crespin firm. Referring to these forgeries on the day of the trial, the counsel for the prosecution exclaimed: 'Fraud was Moyaux's first crime, and it was fraud that led him to murder.'

Victor's version was quite different: 'It was my wife's loose living that was the cause of my misfortune.' After Victor's dismissal, Adrienne started work as a charwoman for Monsieur Sentenerre, a coffee merchant and neighbour of the Moyaux family. She later became his mistress. Victor, who had learnt of his wife's infidelity through public gossip, decided to force her out of their home. A further source of discontent had compounded the situation: Adrienne had refused to take part in her husband's activities as a forger, even threatening to denounce him to the police, whereupon he had told her he 'would blow her brains out'.

Monsieur Sentenerre had to travel to America for work; in order to be in a position to accompany him, Adrienne obtained her husband's permission to leave France. This permission was signed by Victor in front of the police commissioner, a decision for which the judge criticized him. Adrienne claimed that she had been forced to leave: 'He was the one who wanted me to leave, to go anywhere, it didn't matter where, so long as I left.' 'You slut, you filthy liar,' replied Victor, 'if I had known with whom she was going to Philadelphia, I would have finished off the pair of them. She told me that she had found a job in America, but she didn't tell me that she was going there with her lover.' Asked to testify, Monsieur Sentenerre, a determined young man who wore a diamond on his finger, and had cultivated the affectation of calling the accused 'Monsieur Moyaux', denied any adulterous relationship.

At this stage, there were already a number of points of similarity between the Moyaux case and other cases. On the one hand, there was separation, or rather desertion, a common feature of crimes of passion, and on the other hand, there was the man's background. Like many others, he had left his native province to go and settle in Paris. The deaths of his children were possibly his first great sorrows after the death of his mother. The loss of a child, however natural an occurrence in the life of a couple during the nineteenth century, was not a matter of indifference – far from it. Later, Victor Moyaux found himself without employment. As a result of this indignity the couple's instability began, and the shadow of their emotional imbalance loomed large. The adultery and then the departure of his wife hastened Victor's descent into illegality. It is worth noting that the break occurred when Victor became a financial burden on his wife.

The failure of both emotional and working life, and desertion by the partner who had become the only economic support, often accentuated the vicious circle of extreme poverty and decline. Being abandoned emphasized the impotence of these men in coping with the difficulties of life, and revealed their vulnerability, while creating feelings of destructiveness and revenge. During her mother's absence, Marie-Jeanne was placed in the care of a wet nurse in Sens. Victor, who had just come into a small inheritance, was still out of work. On her return to France, Adrienne wished to see her daughter; she had discovered the wet nurse's address and had gone there, but Victor arrived before her to prevent her from taking back the child. Once again, his wife threatened to denounce him for forging credit vouchers. Much angered, Victor went to Paris to buy a revolver and returned to Sens. 'What did you want to do to this poor woman?' the judge asked Victor, who answered in a subdued voice: 'I wanted to do her in.' 'Fortunately, you didn't find her, but you took your daughter back and left her in Montmartre with a woman called Daviot.'

From then on, Victor Moyaux's life became a long succession of aberrations and anguish which always led him back to Marie-Jeanne. The idea that his wife might take his daughter back was unbearable; he apparently even told the wet nurse: 'I would rather see her dead than know that she is with my wife.'

Taking advantage of the fact that the child was safe from her mother's pursuit, Victor, who was afraid of being informed against, left Paris on 6 September and went to Belgium. Because of suspicious behaviour, he was stopped in Brussels by the police for vagrancy and released a few days later. While he was being held, Victor, unaware of the reason for his arrest, imagined that his wife had denounced him. In despair, he tried to kill himself. After being released he went to Mons, 'where he met Louise Decrucq, a girl of ill repute who willingly agreed to go with him to Paris'.

On 19 November the couple set up house together with Marie-Jeanne. Victor decided to use the forged credit vouchers. On 6 January 1877, Louise Decrucq left her lover for reasons unknown to us and went back to Belgium. Victor then took his daughter to a wet nurse in Bagneux. When she found out where her daughter was, Adrienne, accompanied by Sentenerre, went to the wet nurse's house. On 9 January they met Victor at the tramway stop at Bagneux; he rushed forward violently to strike his wife, but was prevented from doing so when some passers-by intervened. Since Marie-Jeanne's hiding place had been discovered, he took his daughter away. Then he returned to Belgium and asked Louise to look after his child, but she refused to go with him. On his return to Paris, penniless, not knowing what to do, he entrusted Marie-Jeanne to the wet nurse in Sens and stayed there for a few days. On 2 February he went to Paris with his daughter, and they dined with Monsieur Barreau: 'He was sad and worried. I said to him: "Come on, cheer up, you've only got one child to feed, it's nothing." He replied: "What do you expect? I'm confused, I've lost all my money wandering about, I'm finished."' After dinner they went to the café to play billiards, then around midnight he left Montmartre with Marie-Jeanne and went in the direction of Bagneux to commit the dreadful act which the presiding judge found so inexplicable.

During the hearing, Victor Moyaux refused to answer any questions; he knew that he was doomed and could no longer bear to hear his daughter mentioned. Despite the accused man's silence, the judge continued to interrogate him in a relentless monologue. And for what reason? The facts were established, Moyaux admitted to his crime and accepted the punishment. Everything seemed to be in order. And yet, the judicial process could not function without Moyaux participating. He was compelled to clarify his motives for the murder. Not only did he have to admit to the crime, he also had to make a full confession, otherwise the punishment would be absurd and inconsistent. Victor Moyaux was obstinate: why should he justify himself, since he was the one responsible for his conviction? Besides, since his imprisonment, he had tried to kill himself twice.

At last the judge got the better of his silence: 'He rose, his countenance pale. "What did you expect me to do?" he said in a broken voice. "It never occurred to me that I might survive my child. I had no money." He was later to repeat: "I was tired of life, and didn't want my child to end up with her mother after my death. I no longer wanted to live."'

Victor Moyaux was not always so secretive; indeed, shortly after his arrest, he defended himself in a letter addressed to the *Petit Journal* for publication:

I read about the Bagneux crime in your esteemed paper. There was much truth, but also many lies in it; you can only write what is reported to you. Here then, are some details relating to this terrible affair. After my wife left me and abandoned her child, she said she was going to America and that on her return she would behave properly. I never had any news until three months after I had taken my daughter away from Bagneux to Sens where it was less expensive for me to keep her. I had barely arrived when she turned up to take the child; she was accompanied by Sentenerre, the individual who took her away or rather with whom she left of her own free will . . . She swore to the wet nurse that they would remove the child whatever happened. I swore that they wouldn't have her, so I took the child away . . .

[Referring to his wife and his sister-in-law:] They were kept women, not charwomen. Therefore every month I always paid the wet nurse, and even the other debts incurred by this *femme fatale*. I would have been happy to leave the child with the wet nurse, but I was afraid she might end up with this woman of ill repute and that crook Sentennere. I didn't want my child to have any father other than myself and I had sworn that when I died she would also die. But on the day of the encounter at Bagneux, fate decreed that I didn't have my revolver, otherwise I would have killed the mother and that Sentenerre, who claimed to be the child's father, even before the separation, and the child might have been saved, but since she would have remained an orphan, it was best for her to die . . . And so it is all my wife's fault! I come from a family that could not be more honest and worthy of respect; but even a lamb can be turned into an executioner. If I had known that my daughter would suffer so much, I would have preferred to shoot her in the head . . .

These are sufficient details, the only guilty party is myself, everything that I write confirms this and nobody can prove the opposite, not even that woman who is to blame just as much as I am. I would put the whole blame on her, but then I would be told: 'you killed your child.' But it is her fault entirely. A warning to couples: love each other well, love your children well or if you part, then show more courage than I have done. I can't write any more as I'm trembling.

Like all criminals-to-be, Moyaux felt overwhelmed by urgent suffering. His letters and certain passages from his private diary are very revealing of the pain that remained with him from then onwards. The snare tightened about him: abandoned by his new mistress and penniless, he lived in fear of being denounced and separated from his daughter. Death then seemed to be the only way to put an end to this unbearable life. But first Victor wanted to avenge himself on the woman who, in his eyes, was the sole person responsible for his misfortune. He felt he was the victim of another victim, a classic leitmotif in crimes of passion. In their desire to blame women, the accused generally claim to respect current values in order to attract possible goodwill from members of the jury and from the judges. Victor had no trouble proving that his wife was unconventional, a bad wife, an immoral woman and a bad mother.

Not only did Moyaux write to the press, in an attempt to publicize the drama of his life and to be heard by everyone, especially his wife, but he also recorded his thoughts and his slightest acts and movements in a private diary. After Marie-Jeanne's death, Moyaux wandered about Paris with one idea in his head: to kill the woman he held responsible for the death of his daughter. At his arrest, this diary, which was meant for his wife, was found on his person:

Madame Moyaux,

You have seen the terrible deed for which you are responsible. It was the threatening letter you wrote to me at Sens which pushed me to do this. You wrote these words to me: 'Victor, if tomorrow at two o'clock Jeanne is not at Bagneux [since his return Adrienne had been living at Bagneux], I will denounce you to the police for your behaviour.' You see that I was not afraid of you, for I did nothing. It was thus to remove any suspicion of complicity from yourself that you denounced me to the public prosecutor as you had threatened, for you knew what would happen! I believed your threats, that is what pushed me to make use of them . . . Your plan was to have me imprisoned and to take the child back. It didn't turn out like that. That is why I always said: 'I'd rather see her die than see her back with you.' You're the one to blame for all these misfortunes . . . Had I known that you were trying to take the child away as you did, I would have destroyed you! When my little Jeanne was hurled down the well I wanted to follow her, but it occurred to me that I still had time to avenge myself on you. Watch out, or else! If I don't try my gun out on you, it will be because I don't get the chance, but I will try my best.

If I wrote to the *Petit Journal*, it was to catch you in the trap, for I will use all the means at my disposal to put an end to your life.

It would be just as well that you did not read this letter. As for me, I don't care about life, although I am not completely penniless as the papers are saying. I can give you an idea by telling you where I spend my time.

The account of those days spent tracking his wife was a challenge to the social order and shows how it was possible to escape the police, something that perpetrators of crimes of passion usually did not try to do. After committing their crime, they would allow themselves to be arrested, or else would turn themselves over to the police.

For over a week, Victor wandered around Paris. Each day, he waited for night to fall to try and surprise his wife and kill her. To keep himself occupied, he walked through the streets.

In the morning I always have breakfast at ten o'clock so that I am alone in the restaurant, and I spend my afternoons in the café . . . Sometimes, in the evening, I go to Bataclan, to the Louvre, to the Luxembourg, or to the Bois de Boulogne. Yesterday, February 11th, I had dinner in the Route d'Orléans with Monsieur Pujol, a former wine merchant at Bagneux, and we discussed the crime: 'I know him well,' he said 'the father of this child, he's a very good boy, a man just like you.' His words left me feeling very moved, for I really thought he knew it was me. I was in the middle of reading the newspaper, but I couldn't see anymore. But then, everything turned out all right and he said to me: 'I would have preferred to kill the mother.' He didn't know that I had my ten-shot revolver and that I was on my way to Bagneux with that very intention.

Every morning, Moyaux kept a record in his diary of his attempts to murder his wife.

I was unsuccessful again this time; you were getting ready for bed. It's the fourth time I have made an attempt at Bagneux, I'll try again tonight. This morning I got a shave in the rue Saint-Dominique, where I also ate, then I went to the Champ-de-Mars.

As I hadn't spent much time in the café, I wandered around Paris, and didn't try to hide. I even saw a few friends who didn't recognize me. Although it is true that I avoided speaking, we did stare at each other. Several of Crespin's employees whom I often bump into as well did not recognize me. Nobody has recognized me yet. It is true that I have disguised myself well . . .

Today is February 13th. Yesterday I headed for Bagneux, but everything was shut. I am going to leave earlier this evening; I don't care if I'm caught, but I want to kill the woman who lost me my job. If I'm arrested before I carry out my plan, then it may go badly for whoever arrests me because I'll defend myself all I can . . .

I'm leaving right now on foot; it is six o'clock. Yesterday I was not any happier than usual . . . It was too dark, I thought I recognized you, but I was too far away, hidden in the lavatory. I am eating breakfast in the rue de la Ferronnerie. It is two o'clock. No luck yesterday, either! You didn't go out, but I felt certain that you were in. You even spoke about your trip to Philadelphia. I'm going to Bagneux tonight.

February 16th: I went to Bagneux last night; I hid near the reservoir and slept there: you hadn't gone out yet . . . I don't dare show myself anymore, as I'm afraid of being arrested. Yesterday I was followed.

The net was drawing closer around Victor. He wrote for the last time in his diary:

How well you have locked yourself up tonight! It's not easy for me to catch you! Only your father is with you, but I don't hate him enough to kill him, even though I may be forced to it, if he comes in or goes out, when I'm trying to get at you. One more, one less, once you've started! But it's all your fault.

Today, I went for a shave at the rue de Vaugirard and a policeman was there. I am going to Bagneux again tonight, although I was undecided because I had been followed, but they've lost my trail. Luckily I know Paris like the back of my hand. I have decided to shoot.

Victor Moyaux carried out his plan that very evening. Adrienne managed to escape, and only her father, Minard, was wounded in the shoulder as he tried to protect his daughter.

*   *   *

The Moyaux affair shows, conclusively, the criminal development of a very ordinary man, a man with no previous history of trouble with the law until the day he left his job, which was the symbol of his rise in society. This was the first

45

mistake, followed by counterfeiting credit vouchers. Victor did not have the forger's nerve; he was far too afraid of coming up against the law. At the same time, he felt betrayed by his wife. Her departure was perhaps the final disaster which shattered his last hopes. But the role which he cast Adrienne in throughout his descent into crime concealed the real causes of his social withdrawal. The fact that he made public his accusations towards his wife testified to his will to accuse society and to make his wife responsible for his troubles. He wanted to break his silence in order to proclaim his anger, and the publicity that his diary received gave his act a special dimension.

Victor Moyaux demonstrated great skill by distorting his criminal behaviour so as to mobilize public opinion in his favour with the help of the press. His murder attempt, far from prejudicing his case, made it more understandable, in the eyes of the public, that he had not tried to kill himself after murdering his daughter. Because of his murder attempt, not only did he appear less of a coward, but his suffering and desire for revenge at last became a reality. His tactics were crowned with success; because of his wife's misconduct, which was considered shameful by everyone, Victor Moyaux escaped the death penalty, and on 15 May 1877 received only a life sentence of hard labour.[2]

The Unemployed as Murderers

Hard pressed by daily problems, men who were out of work felt unjustly treated. Their oppression became unbearable when they had to suffer marital rebuffs. Deeply wounded, they wanted to put an end to all these humiliations. But as they were unable to devise a plan that could satisfy their desire for redress, they shifted their feelings of hatred and of injustice suffered, and focused them on a more accessible object. This obsession was more easily fuelled when the victim's bad behaviour offered them something on which to fix their demands. The unfaithful or unruly wife easily became the ideal victim of revenge.

This process can be seen clearly in the Barbot affair. Unlike Moyaux, the accused had suffered the public humiliation of being sacked for theft. As he was shamed and desperate, he took revenge on his wife. On 20 June 1868, Louis Barbot, an accountant, who was born on 10 July 1829 at Saint-Pierre in Martinique, was married in Paris to Pauline Fouley, his junior by some twenty years. They both found work as employees in the shops of the Compagnie française, run by Monsieur Pelletier:

Barbot, who was at first an assistant accountant, had become chief despatching clerk and worked as a cashier and was therefore responsible for taking cash sales. Towards the end of 1875, Monsieur Richard noticed that he was spending a disproportionate amount of his salary, and had suspicions about Barbot's honesty. Nevertheless, for all his vigilance he could not catch him out, until in July 1876 he joined forces with Monsieur Pelletier to put him to the test. On two occasions he placed the small sums of 8.15 francs and 6.80 francs in Barbot's till, and the accused did not record these amounts. To be certain of not making any mistake, Monsieur Richard had recourse to a different kind of check. For retail sales Barbot used a counterfoil book, and pulled out the receipts which he would give to the customer. Monsieur Richard noticed that several blank receipts had not been removed, even though the counterfoils were missing, and obtained proof that this was how the accused had used it to embezzle funds, by asking some accommodating friends to go into the shop and make some purchases.

The accused was caught red-handed in this way, and was unable to deny his guilt; he admitted to it in a written declaration which he handed to Monsieur Pelletier, merely adding that it was impossible for him to give the exact amount embezzled, which his employers were also unable to guess, even approximately. Nevertheless, Monsieur Pelletier, out of respect for his wife's family, did not want to hand him over to the police and he merely dismissed him at once from his shop.

Barbot was dismissed in July 1876 and replaced by a young man of twenty-one, Basile Goujaud. From this period onwards he started to drink a little too much and worked intermittently. The summing-up for the prosecution noted that 'this event had a serious effect on the inner peace of the Barbot household'. Louis Barbot started to have doubts about his wife's fidelity and convinced himself that she was deceiving him with Basile Goujaud. In a Machiavellian scheme, he forced his wife to write letters of confession, dictated by him, and he sent these to various people, such as Basile Goujaud's fiancé and Monsieur Pelletier. The following is the letter which was addressed to Pelletier:

Sir,

You have watched me grow up, you have always shown your concern for me, and thanks to my father's care and long years of service, you bound me almost permanently to your house. Forgive me, sir, for I am indeed guilty. Far from recognizing your goodness, I betrayed your trust in the most shameful manner by harbouring my licentious behaviour under your roof for over a year.

I am a mother unworthy of loving my husband so much. He has always been the best of husbands to me and to my children. How could I have polluted your very house and turned it into a brothel, forgetting the holiest of promises made at the foot of the altar, while all the time I defied the most severe strictures which my past had certainly justified?

I am unspeakably vile and I beg you on my knees, Sir, to pardon me. But I still have enough decency to understand that I must keep out your sight and that for the atonement that I owe you, I must no longer be considered as one of your employees.

I wouldn't tell you that for over a year, and almost daily, I have had shameful and adulterous meetings in the archives of the Compagnie with Monsieur Basile Goujaud, if he—more cowardly still than myself—had not, allowed his repentant mistress, whom he knows must leave your house so as not to continue having sacrilegious relations—had not, as I said, allowed his mistress to give up her position while he remains undisturbed and honoured in his job.

He knows this; eight days ago I told him that I wanted to stop my affair with him, and he was warned in advance that if we broke it off I would not remain at the Compagnie.

I thus accept equal responsibility for being an accomplice to this, and since Monsieur Goujaud does not offer you the same redress as I do, I dare hope that, out of respect for my father to whom I have confessed and who should not suffer the sight of my seducer for much longer, you will not keep a man who has, just as much as me, betrayed your trust and dishonoured your house. . . . I am writing this spontaneous confession of my own free will. I dare to hope, sir, that you will deal with this matter, whatever your decision may be, with your customary discretion.

Pauline Barbot[3]

The intention was obvious: Louis Barbot wished to discredit his successor. But his scheme failed. Nobody believed these confessions. This was another failure for this man who was firmly convinced of his wife's adultery; as a last resort, he avenged himself on her by killing her with two shots of his revolver on 2 July 1877, exactly one year after being dismissed.

The long statement addressed to the examining magistrate testified to the delirium suffered by the accused; unconvincing and obsessive accusations which nevertheless evince forcefully the classic process of self-justification adopted by perpetrators of crimes of passion.

The influence of social and economic factors on a person's emotional life is obvious in many conflicts. J.-B. Santin's crime, committed the day he was dismissed, demonstrates this. For it is not unusual for a chain of events to provoke an immediate criminal reaction. Vexations and desertion were experienced even more keenly since they exacerbated less than ideal social circumstances. The slightest squabble or provocation provided the stimulus for the criminal-to-be to avenge himself on social injustice and the indifference of others to his lot. This was the case of Jean-Baptiste Dubien, aged twenty-two. In February 1878 he came to Paris to work as a waiter, at Monsieur Dubas's restaurant, in the rue de Grenelle. Jean-Baptiste rented a room in the same street, at number 94. It was in this building, and more precisely, on the stairs, that Jean-Baptiste met Joséphine, who worked as a maid in the service of the Demesnay couple.

In the course of these encounters Jean-Baptiste fell in love with the little maid and asked for her hand in marriage. But he was rejected, albeit very tactfully, for the young girl felt very sorry for the poor crippled boy who was small and lame: 'I was loath to hurt him and I thought him worthy of an affectionate respect, but he didn't understand. I had to repeat my refusal and even had to reject him in public rather forcefully.'

At the end of July 1878, Jean-Baptiste's employers became dissatisfied with him and dismissed him. He remained at the rue de Grenelle without looking for work and pursued Joséphine unremittingly, but she obstinately refused to marry him. Increasingly lugubrious and unable to cope with so much rejection, he wrote to Joséphine, saying that by refusing to marry him she was causing them both unhappiness. The following day, 5 August, while she was doing the washing in the courtyard, they got into an argument. An hour later, she went upstairs and was followed there by Jean-Baptiste, who asked her: 'Is it yes or no?' The little maid replied: 'No'. At that, he drew a revolver out of his pocket, crying out: 'Your fate will be mine', shot her and then himself.

The wounds received by the two young people were not serious. On the day of the trial Jean-Baptiste cried profusely and repented at having committed this crime. The members of the jury sentenced him to two years' imprisonment.[+]

'Down with the Versaillais, long live the Communards!'

Was the combination of these different events the result of unfortunate coincidences? Only in appearance, for a more detailed analysis soon reveals the extent to which financial and emotional problems were responsible. However, on both sides there was a desire to pass over these social failures in silence so as to turn the crime of passion into an act that was purely and simply sentimental. Jealousy, betrayal, desertion – these were motives that showed an irrational character, which could justify these insane, indeed even monstrous, acts. Yet it is difficult to deny the importance of these factors in the social origin of crime; and it is even more difficult to stifle that unspeakable cry of revolt which echoed through the majority of these crimes committed by men who were more vulnerable than the rest, men who, like Breffeil, experienced the failure of the Commune. The bearer of hope and of revenge, the Commune offered society's outcasts the opportunity to enjoy the progress of capitalism, to express their claims and to dream of better days. Its defeat was part of the life-journey of each individual, even more cruelly felt because it sometimes meant an irreversible failure.

Thomas Breffeil, a blacksmith who was the son of a worthy and gallant policeman, had the honour of being sergeant major in a light infantry battalion. This ordinary man might easily have led an unremarkable life, without one day seeing himself make the front page of the newspapers; but for some inexplicable reason he was demoted. More serious still was the fact that he had taken part in the Commune as an irregular soldier for the Republic. He was arrested on 22 May 1871, and sent to a prison ship for eight months.

When Breffeil returned to Paris at the beginning of 1872, he was no longer the same man. Since he had been professionally downgraded, he worked only at irregular intervals and gave the impression of being a bad worker. He quickly turned into an alcoholic; according to the bill of indictment, 'he sold his household for drink'. His marital circumstances deteriorated; he suspected his wife, who kept her distance, and projected his feelings of failure on to her.

At the end of February 1872, arming himself with a sharp awl, he went to the market at Château-d'Eau where his wife worked, with the intention of threatening to kill her. Not finding her there, he wrote her a letter and dealt himself several blows with the instrument. He was taken to hospital by the police, and he cried out in great exaltation: 'Down with the Versaillais, long live the Communards!'.

This suicide bid marked the start of a process which gradually turned into criminal behaviour. Faced with his wife's independence, and her refusal to bow to his will, he convinced himself that she was deceiving him, and concentrated all his energy on badgering her and keeping watch over her. But he was conscious that he was losing her, that he no longer had 'a hold over her'. In this climate of hostility, he made his first murder attempt at Le Havre, where his wife had gone to take refuge. Breffeil managed to track her down. For eight or nine days he was constantly drunk and threatened her because of her alleged infidelities. One night he dealt her a blow with a knife, which she was able to fend off with her left hand. Breffeil claimed that he wounded his wife while trying to kill himself.

In prison he tried to kill himself again, and wrote to his wife: 'Faithless wife, you have been strong. Great strength is one thing, but those unfortunte men of Versailles owe me respect for all that is happening. I can no longer suffer on this earth. I am going to get rid of you today. The honest man dies according to open principles.' On the envelope was written: 'Come and watch me die.'

Because of his alcoholism, he was not deemed to be responsible for his behaviour. The Le Havre court pronounced a verdict of insufficient evidence. When he was released, he could not find a job; idleness, rancour and alcoholism fed his delirium and his rebellion.

On 14 April 1872, Madame Breffeil made a request for legal separation which ended twenty-one years of married life. She took her belongings and went to live with her daughter at the rue du Faubourg-Saint-Denis, and started to work as a stallholder again at the central market. Henceforth events started to speed up. It was no longer his wife who 'wanted to destroy him', but society. Two months before the final act, he kept an even closer watch over her, to the point of obsession. His wife could no longer make a move without seeing him. She had him arrested on several occasions, but as soon as he was released, he continued to pursue her and became threatening: 'I want to kill her, I'm a revolutionary, she's deceiving me' – this is how he spoke in public.

On 4 June at about a quarter to seven, Madame Breffeil went out, and walked up the rue Saint-Denis. Suddenly her husband dashed out of an alleyway where he had been hiding, ran towards her and struck her on the head with two blows of the awl, which he usually carried. She staggered and collapsed. He carried on hitting her, and then brandishing the awl he struck himself. As the blows were not fatal, they soon recovered from their wounds. In prison, he wrote to the public prosecutor. This document, confused through lack of syntax, shows how the criminal's course evolved because of his misinterpretation of real events. Unlike other accused men, he did not try to justify his act by claiming to be the victim of a bad wife. He did, of course, complain about his wife's infidelities which tormented him, but he did not accuse her explicitly of having pushed him to the limit. Whatever the approach, the purpose of this type of written account is two-fold – defensive and conciliatory. The accused organizes the story of his conflict, and the direction his emotions take, with the aim of preserving his self-image in the context of the crime. To this end he cuts up and interprets reality according to the needs peculiar to the psychic behaviour of the criminal. These stories testify to the difficulty that such individuals, whose lives were marked by the break-down of relationships and by traumas, experienced in reconstructing consistently and coherently their own past. The story of their lives became a means of organizing the memory of their marital conflict and emphasized their emotional suffering, thereby overshadowing the narrator's past history. These silences can be interpreted beneath the surface and form the main theme of the events that punctuate them.

Breffeil refused to accept a link between his crime and his social conditions, yet his frequent allusions to the Commune were not gratuitous – they provided a point of reference by situating crimes of passion beyond the domestic sphere. His rebellious and provocative behaviour towards society was unquestionable. This paltry drama of jealousy, whose protagonist was singularly lacking in breadth of character, represented an act of rebellion against the law and gave the character who committed the act the illusion of being free to determine his future:

To the Public Prosecutor:

Sir, please forgive me if I take the liberty of writing to you to tell you about my situation. During the Siege I joined the guerrillas and served as a non-commissioned officer. After the Siege, unable to find work, I gave my wife some advice and told her that since I couldn't find any work we were going to set ourselves up as wine merchants, and run a small shop. Unfortunately, on the first day I was picked up – with my wife, my sixteen-year-old daughter and my twelve-year-old son. My children and my wife were released a few days later, and I was taken to a prison ship where I remained for eight months and twelve days. During my absence, my brother, who works as a doctor in lower Charente, at Ciré, gave my family the money they needed to live on, and all the time I was on the prison ship my wife was being unfaithful; she would go to Meaux-en-Brie and make merry with someone called Guérin who was a wine merchant from Meaux-à-Vilnoy, a small village near Meaux, and I knew nothing about their carryings-on.

When I arrived back from the prison ship my daughter was no longer at home; there was only the boy, and my daughter had left with a young man; ever since my wife had been making merry on the side my daughter had been doing the same herself. I asked my wife where my daughter was, she replied that she had obtained a situation. I asked for her address so that I could go and see her. She replied that she couldn't remember it. I realized that my wife wasn't the same any longer, her character had changed. She was working in the market and instead of leaving to come and be with me, she only came home two hours or two-and-a-half hours later. I wasn't pleased and I told her so; she replied that she wanted to be her own master. I made it clear that if she continued to come home when it pleased her she needn't return. She persisted, and because of her I acted impulsively, selling our house, and a few days later I wrote her a letter saying I was going to do myself in, and then, straightaway – this was about thirty months ago – I struck myself five times in the chest. I was taken to hospital, and she came to visit me and we 'made up' and we went home together.

The following week, my wife left without saying anything and only returned after four days, when she arrived with my son. It was Sunday morning and I was still in bed. She changed and went out and only came back at about nine o'clock in the evening when I was sitting eating. She grabbed a bottle and went to get some wine. Meanwhile I asked my son where they had spent the day; he said that he had come to the house but that no one had been there. And where was your mother? She went out alone and slept on the grass, the child ventured to answer. She came back, they had something to eat and then we went to bed.

A moment later, I asked myself what's the point of being unhappy for the rest of my days. I got out of bed, I took my knife and, trying to strike me, she moved her hand towards me and she received the blow. I gave myself up to the police and gave an account of what had happened, seeing as how I had been prosecuted and had spent forty-eight hours in custody. I was released and given a free passport. I set off for Rochefort, but I had to eat; I arrived at Beaumont-Le-Roger where I spent a month working for Monsieur Lebouc, the mechanic, and I went back to Paris.

Breffeil's memories are confused, for this episode took place during his stay at Le Havre. He finally found his wife, but she refused to comply with his demands:

One fine day she informed me that we were legally separated. No, I would never agree to it. I continued to go and visit her at the market, but she turned me away so brazenly that I had to draw back, seeing that she continued to spurn me, I said to myself: she must be having an affair, some man must have courted her, and it must have gone to her head for her to reject me like this. I decided to lie in wait for her night and day. Then, one day, about three months ago, I kept watch from seven o'clock in the evening until eight o'clock the next morning but I didn't see my wife. Hmm, I said to myself, I'll go and have a look in the market, which is where I found her. So, I said to her: you didn't sleep at home, she asked who told me that, so I told her that I had spent the night keeping watch and that she hadn't left by the roof to go to the market. I let her know that I would have her officially classified as a prostitute. She insulted me and had me arrested.

When I wasn't working I went to see what she was up to, I used to work for the two Lecoq brothers at the rue Saint-Denis, at number 226, as a day-labourer, because I couldn't find any other work. I should tell you that before working for the Lecoq brothers, I had come from the country where I had gone to look for some work. While at Meaux-en-Brie, I went to see Madame Alphonsine Guichard, a fishmonger at Vilnoy, who told me that, ever since the time I had been on the prison ship, my wife had been enjoying herself with a man called Guérin, a wine merchant from Meaux and that she had been carousing at Monsieur Bacheret's restaurant in Vilnoy, so I asked her for the address of this gentleman, she gave it to me, and off I went to Meaux . . . I introduced myself, I said I was Monsieur Breffeil, you've been carrying on with my wife. He replied did I know anyone in the town, I replied no, but that I knew, as I said earlier, Madame Alphonsine Guichard, who had put me in the picture; so I said to him: very well, since it's like this you're not going to tell me that you've not been carrying on with her? I looked in my pocket and I showed him the paper with his address written on it and that of the wine merchant which Madame Guichard had given me, written in his hand, and I said, here you wretched man, these are written in your own hand, you can't deny it, he confessed the affair but he was impatient for me to leave. . . . I went and told Madame Guichard all about the affair and I said to her: I never would have believed my wife capable of this. I had some suspicions but now I am convinced. I went to work in the country where I remained for about a month without finding work in Paris. My wife decided to leave her job (she was then employed at a fishmonger's at the market in Château-d'Eau) to go to Le Havre with someone called Dufraité. She had forbidden my daughter and her son-in-law, as well as the women in the market, to tell me where she had gone.

At last, Breffeil managed to get some information from a housekeeper and left immediately for Le Havre. He found his wife in the marketplace and managed to persuade her to return home. Then he made his first murder attempt. When he returned to Paris, he started watching over his wife carefully:

The Sunday before the unfortunate event happened to me, I went to lie in wait for her, she had me arrested and I was released immediately afterwards. On the Monday, I went back to lie in wait for her, she left her stall at five o'clock. I followed her to just below the Saint-Martin entrance when she noticed me, she had me arrested again and released. So I thought instead of me having a hold over her, it's her who has a hold over me. On the Tuesday, I returned, she had left. On the Wednesday, she noticed me, she left by the back way out of the market, and on the Thursday I was at the wine merchant's, waiting for the workshop to open at seven o'clock, she passed by and I was bursting with anger. I ran up to her and hit her out of anger but I don't know how, I asked her to ask for my forgiveness, she got down on her knees and I immediately dealt her four blows in the chest in spite of this I love and I will always love her. I beg of you, Sir, as Public Prosecutor to take into consideration an honest family. I remain, yours sincerely.[5]

3

The Path to Crime

Commonplace Othellos

Conflict, which lies at the root of crimes of passion, is a part of everyday married life. Many couples have had to face the same tensions, and the same violence, without the finale of a bloodbath. The decision to actually carry out the crime is what essentially distinguishes the criminal from other individuals; for this in itself is the expression of a difference. Before reaching the moment of transition to the crime, the criminal-to-be prepares himself by auto-suggestion, thereby setting up within the couple a specific relationship of criminal and victim, which develops by stages until the criminal process is set in motion. Disappointed, betrayed and rejected, the criminal-to-be finds himself plunged into a state of acute suffering which lasts until the crime is committed. This emotional and moral anguish, which is expressed and externalized without any self-restraint by some individuals, endows crimes of passion with a more human dimension, thereby sensitizing public opinion.

The suffering of individuals driven by jealousy prompts a sudden re-evaluation of the persons they have lost. This is an instinctive reaction, which is not without ambiguity and contradiction, and which often baffled nineteenth-century judges. How was it possible that a man could ill-treat his companion, be indifferent to her fate, and then claim to love her passionately? Infidelity, and especially the threat of being deserted, considerably reinforced this process of re-evaluation. One's entire energy was then concentrated by the desire to keep, or win back, the partner who, momentarily, enjoyed a certain immunity because he or she had been idealized, sometimes to the point of worship. On 3 August 1875, the County Court of the *département* of the Seine granted Elisabeth Savary a legal separation from her husband, who was known to be violent and lazy. Enraged by this decision, he tried to persuade his wife to live with him again, threatened her, and then bought a gun. Several days later, he was arrested for carrying an illegal weapon and imprisoned at Mazas, from where he wrote this letter to his wife:

Elisabeth,

I have tried everything to forget you, but nothing works. Today I am resigned to die or to live with you; one of us must die. I never would have thought it possible to love you so much. Time has not healed anything; on the contrary, my affection for you has grown. I beg of you, dear wife, let us forget the past and live together again; otherwise, either death or hard labour await us. I will never be able to resign myself to living without you. Think about it carefully; these words are written calmly, with a cool head. Thus, it is my intention and my firm desire to put an end to this state of affairs. I will never mention the past. Please show me enough friendship to answer one way or the other, so that I know what to expect.

I beg of you, agree to see me and prevent great unhappiness.

Your ever-loving husband,

Médard Savary[1]

Once the loved one becomes inaccessible, he or she becomes very precious, life becomes meaningless without reciprocated affection, and at this stage in the conflict suicidal tendencies may appear. However, if such tendencies are not realized immediately, this process dissolves to make way for withdrawal and a desire for revenge. Gradually, life becomes too unbearable, too painful because of the existence, or the actual presence, of the one who is loved and at the same time hated, in the time-honoured ambivalent way. To this spiritual suffering are sometimes added material problems which are reflected by the hastening of the emotional and social downfall. Individuals feel that their lives are wasted, destroyed on account of their partners. They project and focus their aggressiveness on the persons they consider responsible for their painful existence: their future victims, who no longer enjoy their protection. In some cases they reproach their partners for having spent their money, and before long money becomes the focal point of the conflict.

Blinded by suffering, the individual develops a distorted perception of reality. By now, the partner is the personification of evil power, immorality, and the threat of a danger against which he must struggle in order to preserve his dignity. It is in the name of justice that he will claim the right to remedy this harmful and undeserved situation. Such people will never explicitly express their desire for revenge. Often this process starts with a period of withdrawal. Indifferent to their own fate, individuals abandon their moral standards and live in a state of despair conducive to developing the idea of murder. This enables them to re-evaluate themselves, for the decision to act signifies the affirmation of self by the negation of the other person. 'It could not last any longer; he or she was preventing me from living, one of us had to go', is how the accused express themselves. This preparation and self-justification make it possible, by altering the individual's ethics, to overcome all moral and psychological resistance in order to carry out the act. The criminal acts with the conviction of the inevitability and inescapable necessity of his destiny. Here ceases any similarity to the person with suicidal tendencies who, instead of attacking, prefers to retreat and direct the violence against himself, while the inner struggle of the criminal-to-be is an attempt to persuade himself to act in his own defence.

This development of the criminal idea, as perceived by the individuals themselves, has three characteristic stages, which have been ably analysed by Etienne de Greeff.[2] The first stage is that of ineffectual acquiescence: the desire to get rid of their partner is still only an idea in their mind, without a desire to take action; they imagine a serious illness or an accident which would force the hand of fate. For the majority of individuals, this is as far as they go in the direction of crime. The second stage is characterized by the articulation of their acquiescence: the criminal scheme takes shape with the intention of their taking part in it. This period varies according to the individual and can last between several days and several years. Nevertheless, the scheme is not yet sufficiently developed to be carried out; the individual struggles with himself and experiences periods of hesitation and even thinks of giving up. During this stage the criminal-to-be publicly manifests and expresses his intentions by verbal and even physical threats. Frequent death threats are terrifying in their violence and the images that they suggest. Expressed impulsively, they nevertheless have a very theatrical dimension, indicative of the inner conflict experienced by the individual; this appears to such a degree that one cannot help wondering whether the criminal-to-be is not trying to ward off ill fortune by behaving in this manner. Here are several examples of threats, couched in language that bears witness to a different social and cultural milieu from that of today:

'If I ever catch you with another woman, I'll run you through.' She said she 'would bleed him like a chicken'; she would wait in an alley 'to do him mischief'. 'I'll do you in, I'll lay you out'; 'I'll disembowel her, she won't even live twenty-four hours'; 'just wait till tomorrow night, I'll kick your belly in, your guts will spill out'.[3]

Although these threats were frightening, it is surprising that they had so little effect on future victims or witnesses. The police themselves did not take the threats seriously and therefore refused to intervene. In his statement, Monsieur Despres explained how he was dismissed: 'On the Monday I had learnt that Tiétard was threatening my wife with a gun. I had gone to tell the police commissioner so that he would have him disarmed. In the police commissioner's office I was told: "Oh, just let him be, it doesn't mean anything. They point a gun but never use it"'.[4]

In certain types of conflict, the criminal's friends and acquaintances would be sympathetic towards his demands. This approval would reinforce his self-justification and encourage him to act. Strengthened by this support, the criminal would regard himself as the victim and would justify his act by appealing to his egocentric morality, so he would feel obliged to inflict upon his partner the punishment she deserved. This process of self-justification took place very consciously, unlike in other crimes.

At the root of these different methods of asserting their demands, jealousy as a passion plays a fundamental role. It would be pointless to define the different forms of jealousy. In some people it creates suffering that reaches such proportions that it can give rise to suicidal thoughts. People who cannot produce a system of self-defence against their violent passions allow themselves to be drawn into an endless process of destruction.

Crimes committed out of jealousy, which are a recurrent theme in literature, also belong to the real world. The Michaud affair, referred to by journalists as 'the Othello Jewellery Shop Case', is a reminder of this. The character of Emile Michaud, an honest working-class man from Belleville, does not have the depth of a Shakespearian hero, yet he was the perpetrator of a crime of passion. The course of his jealousy illustrates brilliantly the process of re-evaluation of the loved one, of honour and of virtue.

Emile Michaud, an illegitimate child, was born on 5 June 1847 in the Jura region. At the age of twelve he left his native village and went to Paris, where he got a job as an apprentice jeweller. From 1871 onwards he worked as a jewellery maker in the workshops of Monsieur Chevallier. This was a growing sector of the craft industry and affected the urban sections of the population which benefited from industrial growth. The average employer had about fifteen male and female workers, and, according to the survey carried out by the Chamber of Commerce in 1860, it was a large cottage industry, since the percentage of employers with over ten workers was roughly 7 per cent. In Monsieur Chevallier's workshop Emile Michaud met Victorine, a pretty and hard-working young girl who supported her parents financially. In 1873 the two young people began to have intimate relations. Victorine went to see Emile every day at 154 rue des Maronites, unbeknown to her parents who also knew nothing about this relationship. According to the landlord's statement, she never spent the night there but had the key to the room.

Emile was her first lover – at any rate, this is what he claimed during the preliminary investigation and in his correspondence. On 15 August 1874, Victorine met Adolphe Goury, who was twenty-one years old and a currier by trade: 'Shortly after our meeting, I asked for her hand in marriage, and her family allowed me to visit her at home. I went to meet her nearly every evening at the workshop and accompanied her home.' The marriage was to take place only when he had been released from military service. Victorine had not yet broken off with Emile, and it was through a third party that he learnt of his mistress's engagement. 'For the past three years, Emile Michaud has been eating lunch at my house. Victorine's aunt came to tell me that her niece was going to get married. Emile Michaud was present, and he asked who she was marrying. It

was from that time that he started to look sad and to eat less. He said he was ill.'
Emile Michaud bowed to the choice made by his mistress, to the great surprise of
the presiding judge: 'You accepted Victorine's marriage to the other suitor?' 'I
had no choice, I had to. It made me so unhappy, I could have died, but I couldn't
stand in the way of this marriage.'

He did not try to make his mistress stay, or to change her mind. How can this
be explained? In all probability, Victorine had had no intention of marrying
Emile, who claimed that he had proposed to her at the start of their relationship.
Being powerless, he suffered cruelly from this choice but refused to admit it and
attributed his despair to the misconduct of his mistress. His jealousy was
exacerbated by the close watch that he kept over the engaged couple; and when he
discovered that Victorine had had intimate relations with Goury, he decided to
kill himself. During the hearing he declared, in tears:

I loved Victorine, and I still love her. I might have agreed to her marriage with
whoever she chose, but I couldn't get used to the idea that she had given herself to
another lover. Also, when I realized that Goury had merely succeeded me as a
lover, it drove me insane. I would never have been jealous of a husband, but I
was jealous of a rival right up until his death.

'You went out and bought a gun?' 'I only wanted to kill myself, and kill myself in
front of her.' 'Could you not do anything braver? You did nothing to make this
girl's situation respectable?'

I made her come into my bedroom and I said to her, 'you deceived me, you knew
that I loved you. You promised to be mine and you have a lover, it won't be long
before you have others, you are embarking on a fatal course. I beg of you, stop
yourself; I wouldn't have minded seeing you married, or rather I would have
resigned myself to it, but I can't bear the idea that you are going to run about
with a man like a worthless tart. I have made up my mind to kill myself, and I
have here what I need to do it with.' So I put the gun to my head.

'You held the gun as if you were about to fire, she rushed towards you and
grabbed your arm, and made you abandon your wicked plan.' 'Yes, sir, I loved
her, I still love her.' 'A fortnight later, you saw Victorine entering a building [in
the rue Merceur, one of those furnished lodgings which are rented out by wine
merchants over a fish shop] with her new lover. Did you not decide then to kill
her and to kill yourself afterwards?' 'No, it was only the following morning that I
thought of that, after having spent a night – oh, such a horrible night. The
previous evening, I was still beside myself and very upset.' 'Come now,
Michaud, it is obvious that there is a side to this affair which deserves pity.
There is reason to believe that you won't incur all the suffering which is reserved
for murderers, but perhaps you are exaggerating.'

With what unconscious skill did Emile Michaud, the deserted and betrayed lover, convince himself of his role as dispenser of justice which he must play in the name of grand principles! It was neither jealousy, nor resentment, nor dishonour that armed the future murderer, but his need to defend morality, his morality on which he placed an exaggerated value in order to justify his act: 'It was the idea of her setting off on a course of vice which upset me', he kept repeating.

The idea of ending it all and dying, by punishing this woman who was responsible for his misery, became a reality in his mind. The last scene in the furnished building triggered off the tragedy. In a letter written before carrying out the crime, Emile Michaud described the different stages that led him to the murder, while also justifying himself. This intimate letter, in which he bared his soul, was addressed to Monsieur Justin, Emile's employer. Did he write to him as a representative of authority? Or perhaps this gesture reflected the climate and the relationship between workers and employers, relationships which, despite the conflict involved, were not impersonal.

Sir,

I cannot live much longer with the suffering which afflicts me and which I shall explain here. On September 28th last, I was surprised to see Victorine looking so happy, as she had been crying every day for the past six weeks. She appeared to have a firm resolve. I therefore decided to follow her that very evening. I saw her in the arms of the man she calls her fiancé. I saw them go into a wine merchant's shop and climb up a small spiral staircase which as far as I could see, could only lead to a private room. To be absolutely certain, I went in immediately and I asked the manager if he had a room which he could put at my disposal for an hour or two. He replied that he did have a room but that only five minutes before it had been taken by a young couple.

Monsieur Justin, I don't know if you have ever loved one of your mistresses, but you can imagine what effect this man's words had on me. I can assure you that, if I had had something to kill myself with, there wouldn't be a crime today to reproach me with. The following day – I cannot find the words to express how I suffered. I contained myself in front of her so that she didn't suspect that I knew everything. I would smile at her, although my smile must have been a ghastly grimace, but you shall see.

I was obsessed, for I had to decide on something, since I couldn't sleep and I wasn't eating. The next day, I bought a gun with quite a high calibre, for I didn't want to miss my target; I wanted to kill myself, but I wanted my faithless friend to be at my execution. That is why I took her to my place the next morning. When we got there, I told her: 'My dear friend, do you remember a few days ago you told me – "I'm going to get married, my future husband comes to fetch me every evening and so I want to break off with you" and I therefore agreed with her. I said to her: 'Since this is the last time we will see each other, let's spend the day together.'

She willingly agreed, and it was the first time we had missed going to the workshop together. But part of that day was spent in tears by my friend. I asked her what the reason was and she replied that she thought she was at least eight days pregnant, and she was in fact, for everything I gave her afterwards should have brought back her periods.

So from that time onwards she came to see me every morning. Tired of seeing her always crying, I said to her: 'Try and get married earlier', so that she wouldn't have any difficulties. As she knew how I felt about her marriage, she never spoke to me about it.

In short, on September 28th, she decided to give herself to that boy so that he would think she was pregnant by him. Now I come to September 30th. I said to her: 'You didn't keep your word, you swore that you wouldn't have any other lovers but me, unless it was a husband. You deceived me. The man who was your fiancé has become your lover today. I loved you sincerely, I would have been happy to see you married, but you have another lover, so I shall die because of this.'

She made me promise that I wouldn't carry out my plan, but now I am suffering too much and I can no longer bear to see her give her caresses to another, and so that she doesn't drag herself through the mire like all fallen women, we shall leave this world together. I bid you farewell and I beg you to come to our burial.

After writing this letter, he went to the workshop:

At about eleven o'clock his friends commented on how pale and agitated he looked. When they questioned him he didn't answer, he seemed exhausted, and there was a frightening expression in his eyes. Unfortunately, Victorine, who is employed in the same workshop, came and sat beside him at his bench. Then, without any preliminaries, without any provocation, without any threats, without a sound, he moved towards her and shot her at point-blank range. The bullet struck her forehead. Almost immediately, in the same cold-blooded way, he fired a second shot at himself and was wounded quite seriously.[5]

The ties that had kept him alive had been too weak, and had become loosened under the pressure of jealousy. With no hope of persuading his mistress to return to him, he let himself be tortured by the spectacle of love betrayed. Throughout the preliminary investigation, Emile Michaud carefully described this process of self-destruction, which he was unable, or unwilling to control. Slowly, he had headed towards his final decision.

This drama of jealousy culminated in a very theatrical gesture, without the artifices of verbal and physical violence. The crime ended in a second failed suicide attempt. However painfully, Emile had to come to terms with the loss of the woman who had been unfaithful to him. Victorine was killed instantly, but he escaped death, although he was crippled. Members of the jury sentenced him to ten years' hard labour.

The Crisis Point

The idea of committing the crime develops into a final stage when the murderer lives through a period of withdrawal, and is unable to consider the future. He lets himself go, resigns himself to circumstances and is indifferent to his own fate. The crisis is marked by specific signs, such as loss of sleep and appetite and a lack of interest in work. Auguste Barreau, a twenty-three-year-old baker, was having an adulterous affair with Anna Gendis, the wife of a wine merchant. Barreau took his meals at the Gendises' home. On discovering his wife's unfaithfulness, Gendis forced her to break off the affair. Auguste was unable to cope with this rejection, and five days later he tried to kill his mistress. Adèle Baton, Auguste's employer, made the following statement describing his behaviour on the eve of the crime:

He told us he was leaving; the poor boy was like a madman. He didn't know what he was doing any more. He once told me that he had a blow in his head. I asked him what that meant, he said he couldn't explain. He was completely shaken and he wasn't eating. He said that what he was going to do would dishonour his family, but he was mumbling so much that I couldn't make head or tail of what he was saying.[6]

In conflicts that last a long time, the criminal-to-be feels threatened by the woman who is making him suffer. He casts himself in the role of someone who is in danger and who has no choice but to kill. Murder then has the function of magically removing the threat that interferes with his life, and endows the crime with a tragic dimension. He lives in a state of heightened tension. The outburst, which is imminent, can be sparked off by something quite trivial, for the murderer reacts to the slightest shock as his susceptibility to emotion is exacerbated by his obsessional struggle to persuade himself to act.

With his mind clouded, he proceeds to the crime with a sort of automatism similar to a state of trance, without preliminaries, without even speaking to his victim. No insults, no threats – he carries out his crime with an indifferent resignation which makes his judges say: 'He acted in cold blood.'

In spite of his determination, the criminal cannot act without the intervention of outside forces which remove his inhibitions and trigger off the explosion that precipitates the crime. Criminals remember this moment, but are unable to describe the circumstances of the crime and simply say: 'I no longer knew what I was doing, I was like a madman.' Because the memory is too painful and too destructive, amnesia or simulated amnesia serves as a defence mechanism against the perpetrator himself as well as against other people. Loss of memory sanitizes the monstrousness of the act and makes it bearable.

Like the majority of factors responsible for crime, alcohol serves as a catalyst.

Whether it causes an occasional state of drunkenness or chronic alcoholism, alcohol actively contributes to the creation of a dangerous condition. Drunkenness reduces the self-control that the individual can exercise over his urges and is a powerful stimulant, forcing latent tendencies to the surface.

Through this double mechanism, aggressiveness is released and increased, whether it is fuelled by erotic desires, jealousy, rancour, injured interests, family animosity or old emotional traumas, all of which are barely conscious. Ordinary drunkenness is sufficient to increase susceptibility, irritability, and brutality, and to make quarrels bitter. But drunkenness can also be a stimulus to physical actions, genuine pathological states which are fairly comparable with the frenzy of an epileptic fit and often followed, as they are, by amnesia. In fact, alcoholism is responsible in about half the cases.[7]

Indeed, it was quite natural for such individuals, who were in the habit of going to the tavern every day, to go there before committing a murder.

Jean Pène and Mademoiselle Duprat met during the Siege of Paris; he was a shoemaker and she was a seamstress. They lived together and planned to get married, but she rejected the idea because of her lover's violent behaviour. Living together became intolerable, and so she made several attempts at separation; but, each time the poor girl gave in to his threats and pleas.

Finally, in August 1874, the break came. Jean Pène, who knew all his mistress's habits, waited in the street for her at the times when she usually appeared and pleaded with her again to come back to him. When she refused, he showered her with reproaches and insults, and threatened her by showing her an awl which he always carried. On 30 August he went to her house, threatened her, and shouted out: 'She has destroyed my life, now I'm going to ruin hers.' The following day at noon, he went to wait for her in front of the workshop where she was employed. When she came out to go to lunch, he started threatening her again: 'Just wait till tonight, I'll get her with my knife.' Mademoiselle Duprat confided in her companions about the sombre foreboding which perturbed her. At around five-thirty in the afternoon Pène went into a tavern, ordered a coffee and a small carafe of brandy, which he drank at a gulp. He did not conceal from those present who questioned him that his mind was made up: 'I'm going to do what I said', he kept repeating.

Mademoiselle Duprat went home at about eight o'clock in the evening. A neighbour tried to warn her to be on her guard: he called her; she came out of her room, but she had barely stepped through the door when Jean Pène, who had been hiding in the lavatory, rushed out on to the landing, and without a word struck her violently several times with his awl, on her arms and on the left side of her chest. She fell at his feet. He was about to strike again when a neighbour, Monsieur Chointin, intervened and managed to overpower him. Jean Pène was sentenced to eight years of forced labour.[8]

In the case of the Charles Lecomte affair, the criminal denied being an alcoholic: 'I have never been a drunkard. In the morning I have a drop of rum with a croissant for my breakfast, in the evening I have an absinthe with gum and always ask for more gum than absinthe.' Lecomte lived under the crazed illusion that his lover was deceiving him; it took him a year to take his revenge. After the crime he blacked out for ten minutes, during which time he had abundant evacuations from his bowels which gave off a strong pharmaceutical smell. The preliminary investigation ascertained that Lecomte had taken laudanum and then absinthe in order to fortify himself for the crime.

Besides the criminals who drank 'to give themselves Dutch courage', there were men and women who were in a state not of occasional but of daily drunkenness. These chronic alcoholics, these 'drunkards', as the judges called them, were very often the habitués of taverns for the desperate and the destitute. Such people were the likely candidates for the inexorable physical and mental degeneration caused by alcohol. Such was the case of Jacques Billet, who declared that he did not drink more than two litres of wine each day, and of Marie Prudhomme, who as early as five in the morning went to the tavern to drink her first glass of Calvados brandy.

Yet this commonplace crime of alcoholism was nothing compared with one case that was widely talked about: the case of the woman who was cut into pieces. The man accused of this crime was Sébastien Billoir. This is a description of him published by *La Gazette des tribunaux*:

He is aged between fifty-five and sixty, of average height, stiff and impassive like an old soldier. He has an ashen complexion, his hair is greying, but his small moustache is still brown. His face looks tired. He has been ill and in the infirmary for the past few days. He wears a dark blue overcoat and has a white scarf around his neck. He no longer wears the military medal ribbon with which he was once decorated.

Sébastien Billoir was born at Blécours, near Cambrai, in 1819. At the age of fourteen he went to Paris, where he stayed with his brother and learnt the carpenter's trade. In 1840 he decided to join the army. He stayed in the army until 1869, when he retired as a non-commissioned officer with a paltry pension of 512 francs per annum. As a civilian once again, he looked for work in Paris. He was first employed as a bank messenger, later as a night watchman at the Gare du Nord. In 1875 his brother took care of him, giving him his board and keep and a little money in exchange for his doing all sorts of odd jobs. On the death of his brother, his sister-in-law got rid of him, as, according to her testimony, he got drunk too often and then lost his temper and became dangerous. Penniless once more, he got a job as a supervisor in a factory. He was seen drunk on many occasions and was dismissed. He eventually worked in an employment agency, in the rue du Faubourg-Poissonnière, which was run by the widowed Madame

Moreau, who offered to feed him in exchange for his doing some clerical work. There, in September 1875, Sébastien Billoir met Jeanne Lemanach, Bellengé's widow, who was unemployed and homeless, but was in possession of the sum of 1700 francs.

Sébastien immediately offered her hospitality, and without hesitation, Jeanne accepted this invitation to go and lodge in a stranger's house. She was twenty-six at the time: 'She was a small serious woman who was uncomfortable on account of her stoutness, who walked with difficulty, and was dirty and slovenly in appearance'; to complete this flattering picture, 'she was idle and not very bright'.

As far as her character was concerned, witnesses described her as a gentle, inoffensive woman, affectionate and devoted. The daughter of poor Breton peasants, she found a job as a maid at the age of fifteen. With a heavy body and an uneducated mind, barely able to read or write, she would have difficulty earning her living.

In 1871 she had moved to Le Mans, and worked as a maidservant to a rag dealer. Two years later she married Monsieur Bellengé, a locksmith who was thirty-two years older than her. He died in March 1875 and left her 1700 francs. After his death, her brother-in-law Rémi Bellengé, a pedlar, offered to take her to Paris in his carriage; she accepted and left Le Mans. She left her landlords 900 francs for safe keeping as well as a few possessions. After a short stay in Paris with some relatives who received her coldly, she returned to Le Mans and then went to Brittany.

Later in the same year she returned to Paris, and the widow Moreau found her a situation with the Bayer couple; but they dismissed her because they were not pleased with her work. It should be borne in mind that her weight and her problems with her legs prevented her from working quickly. After leaving this job, she met Billoir at the employment agency. According to the bill of indictment, Jeanne Lemanach confided in Billoir on the very first day they met how much money she had. Naturally, the prosecution developed this point to show the purely mercenary nature of the invitation made to Jeanne. Although there was a difference of thirty years between them, she 'thought him magnificent in his uniform and perfect in every respect', according to her own words. Seduced by Billoir's imposing bearing and by a dubious promise of marriage, she shared her money with him and lived in his room in the rue Feutrier.

The neighbours did not care much for Billoir and said he was addicted to absinthe, and that drunkenness made him insolent and rowdy. After many complaints, the landlords told them to leave. They moved to the rue de Clignancourt, then to the rue Christiani, and finally to the rue des Trois-Frères, to a tiny room which was so cluttered with furniture and possessions that three people could barely be in it at the same time.

The couple lived there, without working, and spent a lot of time in cafés. When he was questioned by the examining magistrate, Sébastien explained that he went to cafés 'to form relationships'. Sébastien and Jeanne went out every evening and came back late; Billoir was often so drunk he would sometimes roll down the stairs. Sébastien could not tolerate Jeanne's presence in the cafés with him. He once said to her: 'You'd be better off leaving, you're sitting here like a cow, you look like a slut, you're a disgrace to society.' Jeanne would lower her head. Sometimes she got up, went to the door and then went and sat down again without saying a word.

According to Monsieur Bellengé's brother, Jeanne had very little charm. Apart from her thick head of hair and her white teeth which always showed when she laughed, she was remarkable for her carelessness, and her lack of cleanliness: 'She had the misfortune of having smelly feet – the smell when she took her shoes off at night was unbearable. She often took snuff.' On the day of the trial, Billoir added that 'she had weak legs and that she sat with them wide apart like a man'. He knew that she was dirty: 'I had got her accustomed to water so that she was no longer afraid of it and she had learnt to attend to her toilet.' He added that 'she would break out into fits of laughter and that her laugh was so noisy that people would stop and stare at her.' Sébastien Billoir always refused to admit that he had set up house with her out of self-interest: 'I had her to stay at my place out of pity, and since I had no money it was agreed that she would pay her expenses.' No, she did not keep him; furthermore, he shared the housework with her: 'While she was alive I did as much housework as her; I used to go and fetch the water from downstairs.' From the evidence, the judges refused to believe that their relationship was based on mutual support.

Nevertheless, Jeanne's savings did not last for ever. When the money ran out, they had to resort to the pawnbrokers. Sébastien wanted Jeanne to find a job. She could not come to terms with having to leave the man she loved and called 'my uncle'. She preferred to endure small humiliations and reproaches, often in public, rather than risk losing him by alienating him.

Jeanne made several attempts to get a job, but without any luck. Finally, Madame Gervais agreed to take her on as a maid. She was to start work on 29 October 1876, but suddenly changed her mind and did not turn up as agreed. Billoir was not very happy about her unwillingness to work, especially as they no longer had any money.

On 2 November 1876, towards the end of the afternoon, when Jeanne came home she found Sébastien there already. While undressing, she knocked over a glass he was very fond of. She bent over to pick up the pieces when, furious, he kicked her in the stomach. Suddenly she collapsed. He thought she had fainted, but she did not regain consciousness. Billoir spent the night beside the corpse. He had just killed someone, and his act frightened him. The following day he decided to get rid of the body by cutting it into pieces.

After carrying out this terrible act of mutilation and throwing the various parts of the body into the Seine, he moved out of his lodgings. The crime would have been perfect, but the criminal was found out several weeks later. On 8 November, while playing along the embankment of the Seine at Clichy, some children noticed a strange package floating along the river. Frightened, they called for help. A neighbour managed to take the strange object back to the bank:

It was the upper part of the body of a woman, whose legs and abdomen had been removed; the head, which had been completely shaved, was wrapped in a coarse cloth, and the trunk was wrapped in a piece of a printed calico skirt; both arms were at the front and folded on her chest. . . . Several hours later, three hundred and fifty metres up-river, a fisherman discovered another package which contained the lower members of the same body.

A description of this woman was published in the newspapers, and the police sent around photographs. Mademoiselle Lemanach knew very few people, but the habitués of the Café Charles, in the boulevard Ornano, recognized her immediately.

When he was arrested, Billoir denied the events; the last time he had seen Jeanne was on 2 November before she started work as a maid.

This was a barbaric and spectacular crime; its sensational aspect made the judges forget the reasons for it. 'What were the motives?' asked the lawyer. If the accused had wanted to get rid of Mademoiselle Lemanach, was there no way of doing so without risking the death sentence? 'It is not possible that, given a choice between this woman and the guillotine, this man should have chosen the guillotine', he concluded.

The question of a choice did not arise in this way. Sébastien Billoir hit Jeanne; he was undoubtedly angry with her for having encroached on his life without respecting the contract that she had agreed to when she had moved in with him. With no money and no future, stupified by alcohol which often made him violent, he did not have the means to support a woman, and yet, he told the examining magistrate that he had ended up by becoming attached to Jeanne. If she had not refused to work, 'as they had agreed', then the quarrel would not have broken out so violently.

The public, who attended the trial in great numbers, were not surprised to hear the verdict which sentenced 'this monster' to death. An honest man may claim the role of upholder of justice, but to get rid of one's victim by cutting her up into pieces smacks of the despicable and the horrific. A criminal's perversity disturbs the public and alienates their support. The manner in which the murderer kills is largely responsible for the view that is formed of him; he is described as a hero or a monster depending on the circumstances. By hiding and by refusing to admit to his crime, Billoir provoked the dislike and animosity of the public. The complete reverse of the image of the 'good criminal', Billoir came across as a bloodthirsty monster.[9]

Committing the Crime

Alcohol alone does not always provoke a murder; it is necessary for a related circumstance to occur for the murder process to be triggered off. Among the factors that are capable of having this function are the reactions and provocations of the victim: real verbal aggressions or those interpreted as such by the criminal – these are the alarm bells. A rejection, an insult, a sign of contempt, an act of bravado, can be the last straw which provokes this impulsive outburst, this sudden and spectacular explosion of violence which is so peculiar to crimes of passion, whose execution goes beyond merely dispensing justice. Men who only a few hours before lacked the courage and the boldness to carry out their threats are themselves astonished by their own explosive behaviour.

The following is an example of a situation that was perceived as a provocation. On the eve of 27 March 1876, Médard Savary went to visit his wife who was living apart from him: 'I entreated her to come back to me and she gave me several blows with the handle of a toy.' After this scene he threatened her in public. The following morning he happened to meet her and shouted at her: 'Today's the day', and he then said to a neighbour: 'I'm going to spend an unpleasant quarter of an hour with your neighbour.' At about one o'clock in the afternoon, he went to the market in Cours-de-Vincennes where she sold food, and asked her for ten centimes' worth of butter: 'I came to buy some butter from her; it was she who pushed me away; she threw my money on the ground and grabbed hold of my shirt; it made me lose my temper and I don't even know what I did.' He rushed towards her and pulled out a carpenter's chisel which he had hidden under his shirt. His wife tried to grab him by the collar but collapsed immediately. Savary had dealt her two blows in the stomach with his chisel. Later he remarked: 'I hit my wife when my mind went blank.'

Crimes are rarely so spectacular; very often, a few wounding words are enough to provoke. On 16 June 1876, Jean Marié, armed with a gun, went to see his wife twice in one day and begged her to return home. He even insisted on going to see the room which she was renting to check there were no male belongings in it. He did not find anything, and so they went downstairs; a domestic quarrel broke out during which the young woman apparently provoked him. Here is the statement made by Jean Marié: 'She told me she didn't want anything more to do with me, that she was free, that she would take her pleasure where she found it and that it was none of my business. This is what provoked me and made me lose my head.'[10]

During the stage of 'articulated acquiescence', the criminal-to-be perceives the provocations as providing the moral and physical authority to succumb to the need to punish. The more or less involuntary role of the victim reinforces the mechanism of self-justification: 'If, at that precise moment, he or she had not acted or reacted in that way, I would not have killed.' Is not the spontaneity of the attack proof that responsibility lies with the victim? These were the arguments used by the accused to justify and rationalize their actions and to prove their innocence. Criminologists, judges and members of the jury echo the criminal by sharing the same perception of the role of the victim who is seen as actively instigating the crime. From the penal point of view, provocations are implicitly accepted as extenuating, even legitimate, circumstances in the case of a wife's adultery in the marital home.

As early as the end of the nineteenth century, judges recognized the relationship between victim and criminal. Several decades later, criminologists created the notion of the 'penal couple'. They pointed to the active participation of victims as well as to their predestination to become victims; there were, in a certain sense, 'born victims'. This theory was often used to justify some acquittals.

*   *   *

Although crimes of passion have always existed, methods of killing have differed and follow historically determined fashions. The choice of weapon and the manner in which the act is carried out reflect changing attitudes. The context in which the crime is actually committed partly explains methods of killing which are specific to crimes of passion. Such crimes are rarely planned, even if they have been contemplated for a long time, or rather wished for; and they are committed in a horrible frenzy. The emotional shock that releases the criminal drive can happen anywhere and at any time. Interestingly enough, these dramas of domestic life take place in public places as well as in the home.[11] Far from worrying about the consequences of his action, the perpetrator of a crime of passion acts without concealing himself, 'in broad daylight', to quote Enrico Ferri,[12] and is just as likely to attack his victim in a tavern as in the street.

It is also probable that living conditions were a contributory factor. These men and women from working-class areas spent most of their day outside their homes, and it is not surprising that arguments and assaults took place in public just as other events in their lives did.

The weapon used to carry out the crime was also indicative of lack of preparation. Work tools, such as awls, hammers or knives, were often produced as evidence in cases.[13] Very often the spontaneity of the act meant that the criminal grabbed the first object within reach to use as a weapon against his victim: 'She refused to come home with me, she insulted me. She got me in a temper, I struck her with a knife just like I would have slapped her. I deeply regret what I did.' Nevertheless, there was a not inconsiderable use of firearms. Generally speaking, these were acquired before the criminal process began and were not intended for any particular crime. As far as this was concerned, anyone in possession of a firearm proved that it was easy to obtain one, even though it was illegal to carry a weapon. The choice of a sharp instrument made the execution of the crime far more dramatic, and at times reached a point of indescribable savagery. Sometimes the incident was brief – one or two blows dealt haphazardly, with no serious effect, gave the victim time to run away, or else the criminal was stopped by the intervention of neighbours and could not finish the job. The incident may be a bloody struggle during which the murderer lacerates his victim relentlessly; in this case the number of wounds are uncountable and defy the imagination. (One victim received eighteen blows with a knife.)

This rage, this cruelty, which is interpreted by public opinion as a sign of perversity and insensitivity, reflects the criminal's panic. The physical cruelty inflicted testifies, in a certain sense, to the violence that the criminal himself experiences in order to carry out the crime.

This frightening battle is the last attempt to regain that body which has resisted the desires of the partner and escaped. It also represents the will to destroy that body so that it can never again belong to another – a will expressed very clearly in these threats, which provided momentary relief from suffering:

He replied that he wanted to go home and that if I did not want to, he would kill me. I told him: 'You can kill me if you like but I'll never go back to you. I no longer wish to live with you, I am going to find a job.' He replied: 'Don't you worry, I'll find you; you must have me back, otherwise I'll kill you and myself as well, which means that no one will have you.'

In his role of dispenser of justice, the criminal wanted to leave his mark on this guilty body: 'I never meant to kill her, I wanted to scar her forehead, her and her lover', as one criminal told the examining magistrate.

In the fantasy of the criminal, the sharp weapon is symbolic of the fury of the avenger. The idea of stabbing the victim with a knife which penetrates the flesh is largely reflected by the language used in these threats: 'If you ever go with another woman, I'll run you through'; 'I'll do you in'; 'I'll bleed you like a chicken'.

This allusion to close physical contact suggested by crimes committed with the help of a sharp instrument disappears when the criminal shoots his victim. The action of aiming at one's victim removes a certain form of violence and physical closeness, and gives the crime a 'cleaner and more civilized' appearance. Gradually criminals began to prefer firearms. According to statistics recorded in 1930, two-thirds of crimes of passion were carried out with a gun.

The gun, in making the act more acceptable, did not completely remove cruelty and savagery, which were expressed in a different way. Is today's murderer, who does not stop at one victim but kills a whole family, really less barbaric because he uses a gun?

Part II

Tales of Men and Women

4

The Break

At the time of the tragedy, most couples have broken up. It seems that the break, rather than jealousy or the other passions linked with love, is responsible for the decision to kill. Being deserted is almost always perceived as a failure, all the more bitter since it exacerbates already unhappy personal circumstances. The loss of emotional and financial support means being one step closer to misery for the majority of people. Their stories were often a catalogue of disasters and failures of every kind: reversal of fortune, illness, imprisonment, alcoholism, solitude, etc. They found the emotional failures and lack of career success difficult to bear and interpreted them as social injustices. Emotional anguish made poverty and the feeling of having failed all the more bitter for those who felt powerless in the face of such difficulties. It was then hard to face emotional emptiness which emphasized the precariousness of their lives and sowed the seeds of destruction and revenge.

Separation, for both partners, revealed the demands and expectations of couples with regard to each other's behaviour. Women were, more often than not, responsible for the separation, and were anxious to justify the reasons for their departure, which often looked more like flight. By explaining their motives – physical violence, alcoholism or laziness – they exposed the lack of reciprocity in the commitments made by partners or lovers before living together. The expectations of these women were frustrated, and they were pessimistic about the prospect of an improvement in their situation, so they reclaimed their freedom.

A Question of Money

Money was the main source of discontent. Suddenly, the financial equilibrium established by each partner would be destroyed. Women would fiercely expose financial problems, refusing to stay and keep good-for-nothing men, especially as the latter not only lived at their expense, but also mistreated them. Virginie Jouault experienced this situation so painfully that she decided to end twenty years of married life.

Louis Jouault had married Virginie Maison in 1852; he was thirty-seven and she was nineteen. Six years later they moved to Paris with their two children. In order to earn a living, she became a bread deliverer and he worked in a number of small trades. At the time of the tragedy he was working as a rag-picker – at least, when he was capable of working. According to his wife, 'My husband was never a good worker, but he was always a good drinker! Night and day he was drunk and used to hit me and insult me.'

More than the blows and the scenes of violence, during which he actually pursued her with a knife (the first time on 26 September 1872 and the second time on 21 October 1872), it was his laziness that persuaded Madame Jouault to ask the courts for a legal separation. On 24 October, she left the marital home in the avenue des Gobelins to go and live in lodgings in the rue de Lourcine. This is how she expressed her request:

To the Public Prosecutor:

Sir, I have the honour of telling you that since I have, for many years, been subjected to the bad treatment of my husband, Monsieur Jouault, residing at number 259 in the avenue des Gobelins, I beg you, Sir, to grant me a full legal separation so that I may escape his acts of violence, and a settlement whereby I may manage my affairs, since I am at present without means and am forced to feed my husband on pain of being beaten. His laziness is only equal to his lack of moderation with drink.

The day before yesterday, as he wanted some money again, he used a skeleton key to force the lock of my chest of drawers where I keep the few savings which I have painstakingly put aside. As you can see from the work I do, I'm a bread deliverer. My husbands expects to do nothing and wants me to feed and clothe him on my meagre salary – otherwise I get a beating. That's what happened the night before last at eight o'clock, and what forced me to put myself under the protection of the district Police Commissioner, who summoned my husband to tell him that his behaviour towards me was liable to bring the law down on him.

Therefore, Sir, I formally request permission to obtain a full separation, without which I won't know which way to turn.

With respectful regards,

Madame Jouault

In exasperation, Louis Jouault started to spy on his wife. On 3 November 1872, while she was at work, he waited for her at the wine merchant's, opposite the baker's. When she appeared in the street, he ordered her to return home with him; but again she refused. At that moment he brandished his gun and fired two shots. Luckily, Virginie was saved because of her corset, which prevented the two bullets from entering her flesh. While he was held, Louis Jouault tried to kill himself; this was regarded as simply play-acting on his part by the judges. In addition, on the day of his trial he made the mistake of denying that his act had been premeditated, after he had already confessed to his murder plans when he was arrested. Then he invented all sorts of implausible accusations to compromise his wife and to make her shoulder part of the blame. Finally, he added: 'She resented me, I was too old for her.' This created a very bad impression, and the members of the jury sentenced him to twenty years' hard labour. Differences of age, laziness and violence were sufficient to jeopardize married life; when a woman decided to leave, it was inevitable that a dramatic turn of events should occur.[1]

For their part, men complained of wasted money and spendthrift wives. Typically, they would reassess the money they had given and regret their generosity, convinced that they had been doubly betrayed, in their affections and in their money. Such was the case of Charles Balade.

This affair draws us into the shady world of lower-middle-class corruption. This young man of twenty-two owned an umbrella trimmings factory and lived quietly with his family. One day in August 1877, he went to a *brasserie* in the faubourg Saint-Denis and met Marie Thiéron, a '*serveuse*' (waitress), or rather a '*verseuse*', as these girls were called by customers.

The '*brasseries* with women' described by Maurice Barrès in *Les Déracinés* started to appear in Paris towards the end of the Second Empire. They were very fashionable and grew in number from 40 to 125 between 1872 and 1893. The waitresses, who were young and pretty, and often dressed in folk costume, sat at the customer's table, kept him company and made him buy drinks. Through their charm and seductiveness, they were trading their bodies. Parisian youth, in particular the youth of the Quartier Latin, the regular customers, created an atmosphere of endless festivity in these establishments. The *verseuses*, unlike street prostitutes, gave the impression that they were choosing their lovers and were generous with their words of love and tenderness. From the day Charles met Marie Thiéron, he started to neglect his work. His family begged him not to get involved with her, but then, unable to bring him to his senses, they broke with him.

Free at last to indulge his love for Marie, Balade let his mistress persuade him to go to Russia. On the eve of their departure, which was planned for 1 January 1878, Balade placed his money under his pillow and went to sleep with Marie by his side. Early the next morning he awoke to find himself alone and realized he had been deceived when he saw that the 400 francs had disappeared. In a mad rage, and at the same time in despair, he learnt that his mistress had returned to her parents in the Ardennes. He decided at once to seek her out. He caused an uproar when he found her, threatening her in public with a gun. As she was frightened, she agreed to go with him but refused to accompany him to Moscow. They eventually agreed to go to Brussels. While Balade was looking for a coach to take their trunk, Marie used the excuse of having to do some shopping at the perfumer's to run away again. She had the following letter delivered to him: 'My dear Charles, I do not want to go to Brussels. Go, and as soon as you have found a job, write to me and I will follow you.'

If Marie thought she had got rid of Balade, she was mistaken. He managed to find her and this time gave up his travel plans. He went back to his mother's house and Marie started to work at the *brasserie* again. In about April, she settled in Clamart with an old lover, and carried on her affair with Balade, who did not like this new arrangement. He wrote to her on 18 May 1878:

Marie, I think you have forgotten my address; if that is the case you could have asked my friends. I think it would be nice if you contacted me and told me what you mean to do, unless you prefer me to find out for myself at Clamart. I have no need to say any more, you should understand.

[He added in a postscript:] Marie, you know how much I have loved you, and how much I still love you. Well, take care that my love does not turn to hate, for then I will be merciless. I will avenge myself by all the means at my disposal, not against the person you are with – no! I have another, better revenge.

In July, Marie asked him for money. Balade stole some bonds from his mother and bought some clothes for his mistress, who promised to stay with him. But she did not keep her promise and, as usual, stole his money and left him. At the end of the year, finding herself alone, she spent several days with Balade, then they quarrelled again. On 15 December, she started work as a waitress at the Brasserie Pompadour, in the rue de Turbigo. It so happened that Balade used to frequent that establishment. For the first few days Balade chatted with Marie; then he asked her to be his mistress again.

On 20 December Balade seemed very nervous; he spent the entire evening in the *brasserie* playing cards, and waited in the street for Marie to come out. She seemed anxious, and Balade offered to accompany her home; she declined and went towards her lover who was waiting for her. Balade claimed that she started to laugh and scoffed at him. He followed the couple for a while and then suddenly fired five gun shots at Marie and ran off. Marie's life was saved by her corset and her thick clothes. In the rue Saint-Martin Balade met two policemen and gave himself up, confessing his crime.

In his defence, Balade claimed that Marie had sworn that she would sleep with him that night. During the cross-examination he explained: 'I acted in a moment of anger and madness. During the day I had been to the *brasserie*, I had spent a long time talking to Marie, in a very friendly manner, we had played cards together and she had promised to sleep with me that night.' The Thiéron girl replied: 'It's not true; he did come to the *brasserie* during the day, we talked, but I couldn't have said that I would sleep with him that evening because my lover was coming to fetch me.'

The judges were undecided. In addition, it was difficult to prove premeditation since the accused had the habit of carrying his revolver with him every evening, 'for his own protection'. The only point in Balade's favour was Marie's conduct. She was a girl of ill repute and had debauched an honest man, deceived him and finally left him. The accused saw himself as a victim: 'I spent a lot of money on her and, because of the expenses she involved me in, I was forced to leave my place.' Seen in a new light, the money he had wasted emphasized his feelings of injustice and suffering since he had lost everything. He bore Marie a grudge just as much because she had ruined him financially as because she had abandoned him. He was tried in April 1879 and acquitted.[2]

* * *

To break their financial commitments only threatened the economic stability of the couple; to renounce sleeping together, which is one of the few things shared by both members of a couple, is more distressing because it signifies the symbolical negation of the existence of the couple and is the material sign of the break-up. The importance attached to money and to furniture suggests that, as in the eighteenth century,[3] whether a union was lawful or not, it must of necessity develop into an economic unit or risk being precarious.

Etiennette Monchanin put up with being beaten by her lover, who was having affairs and threatening to leave her, but the day he went as far as spending the money that had been saved to buy a bedstead, she decided to avenge herself. According to the bill of indictment,

She had been living with him for four years; they frequently quarrelled. Monsieur Grange complained about his mistress's jealousy; for her part, she reproached him for squandering her money in taverns [she was an umbrella maker and he was a travelling salesman]. They were in a state of great penury and only had one table, two chairs and a straw mattress made of seaweed in their room. On July 19th, Monsieur Grange was out all day. Mademoiselle Monchanin was very angry about this; she reproached him furiously, and after a violent quarrel that evening, she bought some vitriol to throw in his face. Nevertheless, she spent the night hesitating about whether to carry out her plan; but, rummaging through Grange's pockets, she discovered that he had spent 40 of the 50 francs which were intended for buying a bedstead. At the same time she remembered that he had threatened to leave her. And so, while he was still dozing in bed, she threw the vitriol in his face and left after double-locking the door.

On the day of her trial, she did not feel it necessary to justify herself by describing the way in which her victim had ill treated her. Surprisingly, it was the judge who, during the cross-examination, exposed the brutality to which she had been subjected:

'You came to Paris together?'
'Yes, four years ago.'
'Did you live as man and wife?'

'Yes, Sir.'

'How much was your lover earning?'

'150 francs each month and 2 per cent discount on sales.'

'And how much were you earning?'

'I was earning between 3 and 4 francs a day from my work, and running a home at the same time.'

'You are hard-working. Grange wasn't, was he?'

'He did go out to work but he wasn't successful.'

'Did he come home late?'

'Yes, I could never get him to come home at a decent hour.'

'Did he drink?'

'Yes, a lot. He never told me how much he was earning. In all, he didn't give me more than 20 francs.'

'And he wasn't faithful either?'

'He used to see other women.'

'And you put up with these infidelities?'

'I put up with them for the sake of my family honour.'

'For your family honour? It was about time you thought of that. Although you put up with his infidelities, you reproached him severely about his behaviour?'

'Yes, sir, and then he answered back rudely.'

'He did more than that, he used to hit you and ill treat you, did he not?'

'Yes.'

'And despite this, or because of this, you stayed with him. The beatings you received at his hands made you cough up blood, is that right?'

'Yes, I was ill from it for three months.'

'Did you care a lot for this man?'

'I couldn't bring myself to leave him and I was also staying with him for the sake of my family honour.'

'Please do not mention that any more. Did you give your lover all the money you earned?'

'Yes, but as I told you, he went and spent it all. I suffered a lot. I wanted us to have a little home, I had decided not to live in lodgings any more. We took a small room but it was unfurnished. I wanted to save money so that we could buy a bed. He had always promised to marry me.'

This umbrella maker dreamt of having her own home, modelled on the *petit-bourgeois* home; she hoped to put an end to the peregrinations that were so typical of the working-class way of life.[+]

* * *

At the time of separation, each partner wants to take his or her possessions and go and live elsewhere. But the move takes away all hope and is a provocation to the partner who, powerless, watches the other leave. This act of dispossession, which is both material and emotional, is painfully perceived as an insult: 'You don't want to stay with me; well then I'll kill myself.' This was Georges Solhart's threat, the day his wife moved out with her possessions.

Solhart had married Désirée Normand in 1865; they were aged twenty-nine and twenty-one respectively. They had four children, but only one, a girl, survived. The Solharts sold butter and eggs at the central market. The accused frequented taverns and was involved in fights on a number of occasions; he was sentenced three times, once for disturbing the peace and twice for assault and drunkenness.

In May 1872, Désirée caught her husband *in flagrante delicto* with her daughter's wet nurse. During the preliminary investigation the accused denied this, and no enquiry was carried out to ascertain the truth. Gradually the couple's discontent grew. When she was questioned, Désirée Solhart accused her husband of having been the cause of their disputes:

Our relationship became increasingly difficult; he kept telling me that he did not want anything more to do with me and argued with me. At the beginning of last August, he got it into his head to go and have dinner in the restaurant although I had prepared food as usual, and as I refused to give him the money he asked for, he insulted me and punched me. I reported this to the police commissioner.

The accused replied:

It's me who should be complaining about her, because she spends the money from our business as she pleases and provides herself with numerous amusements such as walks, country outings, going to the theatre, without including me. I was obliged to go and eat in the tavern because she didn't prepare any meals for me at home. One day she threw me out and I didn't come back for about a week and lived off the money I earnt. She's turned everything back to front when she says that I hit her; it was she who hit me because I said that a 50 *centime* piece which was on the floor belonged to me.

In June 1873, Désirée decided to leave her husband. She went to live with her mother, and then, when she found lodgings, she wanted to remove the possessions that were still at her husband's. This took place on 17 August 1873. While she was in the middle of moving her things out, Georges Solhart shut the door, saying: 'So, you don't want to stay with me? Well, I'm going to kill you!' He broke a carafe over her head, then a crystal cup, and hit her with a chair. Finally, at the height of his anger, just as his wife was going towards the window to call for help, he rushed forward to push her out. But this scene was interrupted by a neighbour who had come to the rescue. Georges stopped attacking his victim then and, grabbing a knife, tried to kill himself. The prosecution stated that Solhart's life was sufficiently jeopardized for the suicide attempt to be taken seriously. Although Solhart made this bid in a moment of anger and had tried to kill himself, he did not go completely unpunished; the jury sentenced him to five years' hard labour.[5]

In theory, the law required women to obey their husbands; but in practice it did not condemn women who refused to comply with their conjugal duties, and, provided they did not have a lover, it granted them the right to leave a difficult husband or to make him leave the marital home. During these trials, judges rarely upbraided women who reclaimed their freedom; they did not refer to the married woman's duty, something described by a witness in the following statement:

Madame Kemps often confided in me about the violent treatment she received at the hands of her husband and told me that at Passy he had gone after her with a knife in his hand. This woman was so unhappy that she told me about her plan to leave her husband. It was me who talked her out of it and told her that it was a married woman's duty to remain at home, and that if she was desperate she could take refuge with us, but that she must only do so as a last resort.[6]

*   *   *

While leaving one's partner was expressed in practical terms by moving out, the request for a legal separation made the break official and definitive, and was even harder to bear since it meant paying alimony. Before divorce was reintroduced in 1884, couples who no longer wished to be together had recourse to legal separation and to a settlement (for property and possessions). It was not difficult to obtain this; it did mean, however, that the couple was unable to remarry. In 1876, a law was passed which allowed the poor to obtain legal aid so as to be able to begin this process. This provision made it possible for the poorest working-class women to be officially given their freedom without worrying about the financial cost involved. It was a move that was inevitably accompanied by violent scenes during which anything could happen. In many respects, the Descombes case followed the scenario common to this type of situation.

In 1857 Claude Descombes married Augustine Sarot in Mâcon. A few years later the couple moved to Paris, where they ran a wine business; there a daughter was born. According to the bill of indictment, Claude Descombes 'took to drink, was jealous and violent. He often insulted his wife.' Because of these scenes, Augustine suddenly decided to leave her husband on 18 August 1872. The very next day she asked for a legal separation, and to support herself she took over a drinking establishment, at the rue d'Angoulême.

The request for a legal separation was accepted by the law court, which ruled that Descombes should give his wife an advance of 300 francs as well as a monthly allowance of 120 francs during separation proceedings.

On 15 January 1873, Descombes received a letter from the lawyer notifying him of a distraint the following day. The same day he went to the rue d'Angoulême armed with a revolver. He went into the drinking establishment run by his wife and asked her to withdraw her request for separation. She replied that she intended to pursue it. 'Since you insist,' he said, 'here is your separation', whereupon he shot her.

She did not die from her wounds. In his defence, Descombes claimed that his wife's conduct was 'trying', and that she had behaved immorally with a boy from the shop. He explained that he did not plan his crime but had simply succumbed to a fit of jealousy, and he accused his wife of threatening him, insulting him and pushing him too far.

Descombes was sentenced to twenty years' hard labour. A journalist writing in *L'Evénement* explained that Descombes had received this sentence 'because his bestial face and his insensitivity throughout the hearing had not roused any sympathy'.[7]

The judicial ruling granting separation meant dishonour for the man; his wife had won, he had lost. He then had to come to terms with desertion, and especially with the destitution that was now his fate.

After the legal action taken by his wife, Antoine Couturier found himself homeless. Humiliated and desperate, he took his revenge by murdering her. The circumstances leading up to this crime were similar to those in the majority of crimes of this kind. According to the bill of indictment, Couturier, born in Poligny in Côte-d'Or on 12 August 1818, had run a drinking establishment in the rue de Vaugirard since 1868 with his wife, the widow Taffin, whom he had married in 1865. Possessing a violent nature, he had increasingly taken to drink and had obtained money from their business by intimidating her; the slightest hint of opposition made him flare up and threaten her. Living together became so unbearable that, after asking the police for protection against her husband's ill treatment, Madame Couturier was granted an order by the police commissioner preventing her husband from living with her. She then applied for a legal separation.

But events moved on rapidly:

'Did you rely on your wife to feed you?'

'Never. She didn't want me to sleep at home any more. So I asked her for our bed back; it belonged to me because it had been given to me by my previous employer. [Antoine had worked in a funeral parlour for thirteen years.] She refused. I said to her: "You have thrown me out of the business, you've had your own way, and this is how I'm rewarded." We talked some more, she asked me for a written document from my former boss. I was irritated and I hit her twice, saying: "Here's the document." She collapsed and I carried her to the cellar. I immediately regretted my act but it was too late, the deed was done.'

'You rose at four in the morning?'

'Yes, at four o'clock as usual.'

'What did you eat for breakfast?'

'I had a piece of bread and a drop of brandy.'

'After hitting your wife once, why did you not stop? Didn't your hapless wife offer any resistance?'

'Yes, but I couldn't stop myself. I said to myself: now that I've started, I have to finish. I was sorry I had started, but I couldn't stop myself from finishing.'

'You had already come to collect the furniture armed with a hatchet?'

'Yes, it's true; but I kept putting off the crime, in the hope that she would end up by listening to me. I wouldn't have killed her if only she had returned the furniture.'[8]

*   *   *

These different instances of separation are indicative of the independence of working-class women. Contrary to a certain image of the 'proletarian's proletarian women' – woman subjected to male authority – these testimonies show linen maids and costermongers forcefully demanding their freedom when the limits of what is bearable were reached. They were neither rebels nor revolutionaries; they simply wanted to live their lives. They opposed male power by refusing to compromise, and in so doing they sometimes risked their lives. Whether these women thought about their decision for a long time or took it on the spur of the moment, they did not hesitate to face loneliness and financial difficulty, in spite of renewed threats from husbands and lovers. In the majority of cases, separation took place in various stages; women did not turn their men out, but left instead.

Sidonie Breton did not let herself be intimidated by her husband's violence; she fought back and lived her life as she pleased. When she decided to leave him because he no longer wanted to work regularly, he tried to murder this woman who had shared his life for the previous thirteen years:

I met Sidonie Coppée in 1863. I was thirty-one, and she was eighteen. She was a children's maid and I often saw her in Montholon Square. [As she was an orphan, the mayor of her village had placed her in a convent which she had just left.] I became her lover and she had a child by me, Eugénie. We had been living together for two years, and to make the child legitimate we had recourse to the Société de Saint-François-Régis.

The wedding took place in 1866; they had four more children but only two survived. The couple lived at the rue des Jardins-Saint-Paul and paid an annual rent of 250 francs. Eugène worked as an assistant baker. His employer sang his praises: 'He was an excellent worker, he had spirit and was punctual; he worked from seven o'clock in the evening to five o'clock in the morning and earnt his wage' [about eight francs a day]. However, for no known reason, Eugène gave up his job, and his wife was then obliged to provide for her family. She went to a charitable organization which supported them for two years, and also gained permission from the town hall to become a costermonger.

According to the bill of indictment, it was a known fact that her husband ill-treated her. One evening in the middle of winter he forced her to stay out on the landing for several hours. But Sidonie was not completely powerless in the face of her husband's brutality and, according to statements from her neighbours, she knew how to defend herself. Madame Martin stated that 'she often argued with her husband, and people said it was because she found him too old for her.' Madame Hamm and Madame Menon claimed that they witnessed Madame Breton insulting, and even hitting, her husband.

And as for the concierge, she had witnessed one of these scenes when Madame Breton hit her husband with her shopping bag, but the concierge admitted that he was holding her by her hair at the same time.

Sidonie not only knew how to answer his beatings and his insults, but she liked having a good time at the wine merchant's, to the point of sometimes being 'drunk' and of being arrested by policemen from the Chaussé-d'Antin police station.

Eugène Breton was not only violent, he was also jealous. He suspected his wife of having adultery with a married man (assumptions that were shown to be without foundation by a police enquiry). Sidonie now supported her husband, and, tired of his scenes and his violence, she asked for legal aid to gain a separation. In May 1875 she moved to the rue Ticquetonne. Her application for a legal separation was turned down, on account of a letter sent by Breton where he stated that he intended to use all his rights as a husband to make his wife come back to the marital home. He implored Sidonie until she finally agreed to live with him again, but this only lasted until July 1875; she then took her two daughters with her and moved to the rue Marie-Stuart and later to the rue Pierre-au-Lard. From this period onwards Eugène started to hound his wife and make death threats to her; on one occasion he was found lying in wait for her, hidden behind a hand-cart, with a knife in his hand. Sidonie, who carried on with her small business, lived at the rue Pierre-au-Lard, in such poverty that she received charity from several ladies. In February 1876, one of her daughters died. Eugène was not invited to the funeral; he blamed his wife for the death of the child through negligence.

On 28 February 1876, Breton lay in wait for his wife; when she went out to go to the wine merchant's at about eight o'clock in the morning, he went in with her. There was a scene; he slapped her, then followed her outside. When they reached the rue de la Grande-Truanderie, he stabbed her in the heart and in the stomach and she collapsed, crying out: 'My child, my poor child.' Although seriously wounded, she did not die. Here is the statement of an eye witness to the crime: 'I heard her say to her husband: "I'm not scared of you"; he replied: "Me neither". I then saw the woman pick up a heavy object which she held up to her husband's neck, but I cannot confirm whether she wanted to hit him or to defend herself.'

*　　*　　*

Once women have made up their mind to leave, no moral or financial obstacle can make them change it. The determination shown by Madame Leclerc, who was pregnant by her lover, demonstrates such strength and resourcefulness. The man in question was called Dréville; he was thirty-one years old and worked as a day-labourer at Saint-Denis. In 1869 he left his wife and went to live with Madame Leclerc, who was also married and separated. Dréville was violent, and it was not long before he made life impossible for her and did not hesitate to ill-treat her although she was pregnant; one day he tied her by her hair to a door handle. Being jealous, he accused her of having fictitious lovers and threatened to kill her if she dared to leave.

In March 1872, as she could not bear this ill-treatment any longer, she decided to leave and found a job as a charwoman for a man whose mistress she soon became (a situation commonly found in the record files). A month later, on 23 April, her ex-lover managed to get into her room. Since she refused to obey him, he stabbed her with a knife four times, and then rushed down the stairs, shouting: 'I don't give a damn, you've had enough, now it's done.' During the trial, the accused claimed that he never intended to kill his mistress but simply to frighten her; then he added: 'If she had agreed to come back to me, I wouldn't have killed her. She was pregnant by me and I said to her: "Come on, come back", but she did not want to come back.' His victim made a complete recovery from her wounds, and the jury sentenced Dréville to ten years' hard labour.[9]

The Vulnerability of Men

The strength of these women lay in their ability to provide for themselves and to cope with loneliness if forced by circumstances. Conversely, their strength highlights the vulnerability of men. The men involved in these conflicts wanted to be looked after materially and emotionally; they were men who begged their partners to come back and not to leave them alone.

The image of the deserted, destitute woman corresponds to a social reality which was often described by nineteenth-century novelists and moralists. Literature has not devoted the same space to her male counterpart, with whom only journalists writing for La Gazette des tribunaux seem to be familiar. During the preliminary investigation and the trial, these men openly advertised themselves as victims of female desertion, without however enjoying the unqualified compassion of the public. What emerges from these crimes of passion is the role of dispenser of justice assumed by the perpetrators, men whose honour had been belittled since their wives had left them.

The murder attempt committed against Marie Breistoff on 30 May 1877 was the act of a man in indescribable despair since his mistress had left him. The man in question was Léopold Gassion. He was forty-two years old when he fell in love with Marie, a twenty-two-year-old who worked in a tobacco factory and had two children to look after. She met Léopold, who worked for a colonel – in recompense for his services to the French army during the Crimean War – when visiting her father who was a patient at the hôtel des Invalides.

For this former soldier, the return to civilian life had not been easy. First he was recruited as a town policeman, and then as a country policeman; later, he was employed in a number of firms. Unable to settle anywhere, he would leave jobs on a sudden impulse – or else be fired for bad conduct because of drunkenness.

Gassion's unsettled life-style reflected the difficulty he experienced in adapting to civilian life after retirement. According to the principle of conscription by drawing lots, the unlucky ones who could not 'buy themselves a man' to replace them had to spend seven years in the army. Over this long period, many conscripts forgot everything that they had learnt during their apprenticeship. They ceased to be skilled workers, and it was therefore difficult for them to pick up work in their trade; as they did not know what to do next, they renewed their contract with the army, where they remained until retirement. This was a difficult period for the majority of them, as they were unable to come to terms with the sudden change. Their paltry pensions forced them to look for unskilled work, such as lowly administrative posts. Furthermore, the drinking habits which they had developed during their military career exacerbated any circumstances that were already unhappy. Léopold Gassion, an absinthe drinker whose condition was so serious he had been hospitalized for a while at Saint-Anne, had several epileptic fits and tried to kill himself twice.

Gassion was very much in love with Marie and courted the young woman for several months; eventually, on 28 January 1874, she became his mistress – he could remember the exact date, which was quite unusual. Marie did not move in with him; she carried on living with her mother until August 1876: 'She became pregnant, her mother threw her out, and she came to live with me', said Gassion. He claimed that he never promised to marry her; Marie maintained the opposite: 'I lived with Gassion for five or six months. I met him three years ago, he was interested in me. He told me that he was widowed and wanted to marry me. I explained my situation to him and told him that I would accept, but had two children. In the end I gave in to him.'

Shortly after the birth of their child, Marie discovered that it was unlikely that she would ever be able to call herself Madame Léopold Gassion: another woman, a seamstress Gassion had married in 1861, bore that name already. Far from being a perfect husband and father, Gassion had left his wife twice when she was pregnant, leaving her to support her two other children, and had reappeared from time to time, when he wanted to eat. Eventually his wife had had enough of this situation, and in 1868 she made a request for a legal separation which was granted to her.

When she found out the truth, Marie decided to break off with Léopold and to go back to live with her mother. But Léopold did not accept the situation. He constantly badgered his mistress, who stood firm. He felt powerless and completely at a loss in the face of her determination. He started committing acts of violence, and even hit the concierge in the building where Marie lived, in order to get in and speak to her. He kept a close watch on her in the street and publicly threatened to kill her. Marie was worried and tried to frighten him by threatening to go and complain to the police if he did not stop; he replied that 'he couldn't care less about the police and that he would take the law into his own hands'. After their separation he gave up his job at the Invalides, and a month later, in May 1877, he decided to leave Paris. As he did not have enough money to travel, he stole three watches at his landlord's and fled to Rambouillet. But before he left, he wrote a letter to his mistress which showed his tormented state of mind.

Paris, May 23rd 1877

My dear Marie,

Now, more than ever, it is all over after the crime which I have just committed – I was out of my mind with pain because of you especially since our meeting on Saturday last (19th inst.), and as I was deserted and rejected by everybody, this morning over breakfast a ghastly thought struck me all of a sudden: in a word, I robbed the very man who was feeding me. As I write I don't know what to do with what I have stolen and where I will go.

I am branded now, dishonoured for ever, so it is a farewell to life that I am making. Don't ever tell our child that his father was a thief.

My beloved, do not think that I want to make you responsible for my crime; no, but I am afraid that I might commit a greater crime if I stay by your side, the crime of taking your life, as I told you last Saturday and which was my firm intention. You no longer need fear me, for before long I will most certainly be arrested, but at least it won't be near you, I am leaving Paris and I do not yet know where I am going.

Farewell, Marie, you whom I have loved so much, be happy and be sure to love our unfortunate child. Oh, where has my head led me? But I loved you so much that I couldn't survive being separated from you.

I am lost, dishonoured, and a thief! Oh my saintly and worthy mother, if you were alive today what tears would you shed? God has been kind and has spared you the sight of my dishonour.

So it's all over this time. Oh, Marie! If I don't have time to kill myself before I am arrested, I can never hope to see you again, for I would never dare to show myself to you. So, farewell, be free and happy but sometimes in your dear heart think of the man who loved you so much, even if he is a criminal.

So farewell, Marie, farewell!

After a short stay at Rambouillet, he returned to Paris with the sole intention of seeing Marie:

Paris, May 25th 1877

Marie, dearest,

. . . Yes, I wanted to run far away but I had to come back. Whether I am dead or in prison, I want to be close to you, my poor Marie. Did I have to end up like this?

Yet I would dearly love to see you again, for the last time in my life. You won't come – I know it. Well, tomorrow evening, at six o'clock, I will be in a cab at the corner of the Esplanade and the rue Saint-Dominique, near the Bazar. Marie, please come, I beg you on bended knees, come with your daughter . . . . Afterwards I will hand myself over to the police where I will receive my just deserts. Forgive me, I beg you Marie, forgive Léopold who loves you so much. Take pity on me Marie, for although I am a criminal and a thief (what a word!) I will be unhappy; yes I will hand myself over to the police on Sunday evening or Monday morning but no one will know, either in your neighbourhood or in mine. . . . Oh! My head, Marie! My poor head, I walked so much last night along endless roads and I slept a little in fields – I'm cold Marie, yes I'm cold and I'm tired. I lost some of the money which I stole. I pawned the three watches. Oh! I am so miserable and dishonoured, I am degraded!

I am going to have my beard shaved and take off the ribbon which I have dishonoured, I am no longer worthy of wearing it. Farewell, Marie, I love you too much, that is why God is punishing me. Until tomorrow, if you wish.

I don't know where to go and sleep tonight. God, I am mad and lost! Farewell my beautiful and dearest beloved. Tell me to die for your peace of mind and I will do it, for I am no longer worthy of you. Farewell.

Marie did not go to the appointed meeting-place. She was afraid for her life, and took Gassion's letters to the police station. On the evening of 29 May, Léopold told a friend that 'something funny would happen'. The following day he spent the night keeping watch over his mistress's movements. At about six o'clock, as usual, she went to the cigarette factory at the rue de l'Université. He immediately followed her. When she saw him she panicked and ran up to a policeman to have Léopold arrested. Just as she began speaking to him, Gassion managed to catch up with her and stabbed her in the shoulder. The wound was not very deep, and was not serious. He was immediately arrested. Passers-by stopped; when Gassion saw the friend he had spoken to the night before, he cried out: 'I told you yesterday that I would do something funny; well, I've done it, I had to end it all.'

Gassion felt disgraced. It was becoming an obsession to see Marie again. He later told the jury:

I didn't know what I was doing any longer. There was something like a buzzing in my ears; I was tormented. I wanted Marie to come back to live with me, I didn't want to kill her when she asked the policeman to arrest me, I succumbed but I was furious with this girl for what she did, so I struck her.

This man's suffering did not move anyone. Given his past, he deserved his fate; he had been a bad father, he was an alcoholic, and he had an unstable character: Léopold was unlikely to receive the goodwill of the jury. In addition, as a former soldier, his presence in the dock was a disgrace for the army.

'It would have been better for you not to wear your ribbon in court', the judge said referring to his military medal. 'I have worn it for a long time and I do not want to be parted from it. Anyway, I hope to be acquitted.'

The accused's arrogant attitude infuriated the jury, which sentenced him to ten years' hard labour.[10] A man who has the temerity to give way to despair out of love, and has shown himself to be vulnerable and emotionally weak, cannot be forgiven.

Unrequited Love

To kill because of jealousy or hatred is still a man's crime. The same also holds true of crimes committed because of the heartache caused by the rejection of a marriage proposal. These are situations that encourage criminal vengeance, and they led six men and one woman to murder the person who refused to marry them. They had no defence against the unswerving determination of the object of their desire, and so they preferred to take revenge rather than accept rejection. Thus, unrequited love played a major part in these tragic stories. These feelings of love, which might have been touching, even sublime, lost all semblance of romance and were, instead, transformed into jealousy and dishonour, which provided an explanation for this type of murder by rationalizing it.

Nevertheless, this category has proved to conform most to the image that we have created of crimes of passion. First, these crimes were not planned in the sordid and degrading atmosphere of desperation – reeking of stale alcohol – which was experienced with all the violence that poverty, both spiritual and financial, can generate. Unlike the other accused individuals, they stand out because of their youth and their apparent social stability. They are neither lazy nor alcoholic, and thus have nothing in common with the men and women whom we have already seen.

Disappointed and upset, they do not play at being heroes, or dispensers of justice, or even distracted lovers. The law did not, of course, give them much scope to be demonstrative about their feelings.

Disappointments in love are not a valid reason to kill someone with impunity – this, at any rate, was the public consensus, which rarely took much interest in, or showed much sympathy towards, the accused. The many suicide attempts that followed the retribution meted out to the victim did not prompt the usual indulgent response from juries. The attempt to make the object of one's love submit to one's will, by threats or blackmail, did nothing to ennoble this type of crime and make it worthy of compassion. Judges and juries were not taken in; except in the case of one woman and a father, they punished the rest of the accused.

The story of Isidore Trouvé shows the typical ideal perpetrator of a crime of passion, as described by nineteenth-century criminologists. Trouvé was an honest young man whose behaviour was determined by the torment of love: he dreamt of marrying his cousin Augustine, but she did not want to live the life of a Thérèse Raquin; despite the ties between her and Isidore, she refused to marry this man who wanted to impose his mother on her. According to a journalist writing in *La Gazette des tribunaux*, Isidore was 'a plump, rosy-cheeked boy, with a red moustache and an unprepossessing appearance. He does not "look nasty", as common parlance would have it', and his cousin was 'rather large and dry, and there seems to be a certain confidence in her bearing'.

It all began in 1863, when Isidore's mother took Augustine in. The episode was related by Madame Vincent, a neighbour:

One day the police brought in a little girl of six or seven; this was Augustine. She had lost her mother and father. She had been abandoned and the poor child was in rags and was crying. She was dirty, she had spent all night in the Vanves quarries and was black all over. When the police commissioner took off her bonnet we saw that her scalp was covered in eczema. She was a pitiful sight, totally neglected. The commissioner had asked the family to take care of her, but none of her relatives wanted her. They were about to take her to the foundling hospital when Madame Trouvé said: 'Well, the poor little child can't be abandoned like this. I'll take care of her', and she took the child home with her . . . . Whenever I went to their house, I found Madame Trouvé behaving like a real mother to Augustine.

Isidore and Augustine were brought up together as brother and sister. In 1873, when Augustine was sixteen and Isidore twenty-five, they became lovers. Was she in love? We will never know the answer. The examining magistrate suspected Isidore of taking advantage of the situation to have sexual relations with the girl. Whatever the case may have been, Isidore decided to marry his cousin, who was by then a consenting adult. This plan received the approbation of Madame Trouvé, who was delighted at the prospect of their marriage. Life would carry on as before. Not only would this union maintain the relationship between mother and son in the future, but it would also give her the right to watch over her daughter-in-law, who, because of the past, owed her obedience.

During the same period, Isidore, who was an office worker, was sent to Le Havre for several months. During his stay there, he wrote several letters to his fiancée where he described their future together, and continued to mention his mother's happiness.

September 12th, 1875

My dear Augustine,

Your last letter has cheered me up. I am working eagerly, thinking of you all the time, for it is impossible for me not to think of the one I love: morning and night my thoughts are in Paris.

My darling, your letters are charming and I see that I still occupy the most important place in your heart. Hope returns to me when I think that very soon you will be my wife, a happiness that I have long dreamt of. That day, my dearest, will be the best day of my life, for the two of us will be able to pay back my mother for all the care she has taken of us over the years. . . . I only await the day when we will be married so as to be able to make our mother happy. Look after her well.

My dearest, I kiss you and adore you.

Your cousin and fiancé

This was the first declaration of love, written with fervour and sincerity. Isidore had given in completely to his passion. But the happiness to which he aspired so impatiently was closely linked to that of his mother.

September 22nd, 1875

My dear Augustine,

My dearest, I think you are beginning to forget me in your letters. They do not seem to be as long as before and yet you know that if I am away like this it is so that our wedding may take place as soon as possible and also in order to make our mother happy. She has the right to rest now, and it is up to us, after we are married, to make sure she has a rest from the constant hard work she has endured for us over the years, and the countless deprivations which she has suffered in order to keep us. . . .

My dear Augustine, you cannot imagine how happy I am when you say in your letters: 'Your little future wife is taking good care of her mother and is thinking of her fiancé, for I cannot forget you. Take heart for I think only of you.'

Isidore seemed to be more concerned with his mother's happiness than with that of his fiancée. Filial love of this nature is suspect. At times it seemed to be a way of exerting pressure on Augustine: she was never allowed to forget the debt she owed Madame Trouvé, and the best way to pay it back would indeed be by marrying her cousin. His love for Augustine was, however, beyond question, as can be judged both from his letters and from what he confided to Marie Delarue during his stay at Le Havre: 'He told me that he couldn't live without her. He kept kissing her photograph and seemed entranced by her.'

On his return to Paris, however, Augustine's attitude and feelings for him had changed, and '[in spite of] his passionate entreaties, she refused to give in to his desires again'. In order to escape family constraints, she left the Trouvé household, and on 13 January started work for Madame Thévin, a bookseller in the rue Vieille-du-Temple.

The rejected fiancé was upset and jealous; he followed her and became very threatening: 'I'll kick the guts out of both you and your boss', he declared, convinced that Madame Thévin had influenced Augustine, and he said that 'if they heard two gun shots in the house, they shouldn't be surprised, for he would have fired them'. The same day, he went back to Madame Thévin and tried to make her think that his mother was dying and that Augustine should go home.

Threats, blackmail . . . . Augustine refused to obey him and no longer wanted to see him. When he felt too unhappy, he would go and see a friend, Annette Ambroise, a forty-eight-year-old woman of independent means, and talk to her about his beloved:

Isidore used to confide his thoughts to me, he would cry and say: 'I beg you, get her back for me, I need her, I love her too much.' When he was going through a bad period, I felt sorry for him. He would grovel at my feet. He behaved like a demented man and he would say to me: 'If only she would say something to me, anything, I don't care what she says, so long as she answers me.

On 22 February 1876, at about seven-thirty, he went to the bookshop. Augustine was standing beside her employer; without a word, he hurled himself on her and stabbed her in the back, prevented her from running away, and then wounded her again on her hand.

Hearing shouts, the police arrived on the scene and arrested him. At the police station he expressed regret at not having struck his victim in the heart. To justify what he said, he later told the judge: 'I couldn't control myself, I don't know what I said at that moment. I was overcome with jealousy. I loved her, I had always counted on our getting married and she had consented. My poor mother was also waiting for us to get married.'

Augustine survived, but the jury sentenced Isidore to four years' hard labour.[11]

The law proved to be more indulgent towards a young woman who had been deserted. Elisabeth Prévost, a criminal who was just as headstrong as Isidore Trouvé, used a 'more female' trick to win over the love of her life: 'She said she was pregnant by Monsieur Jarretié so that he would marry her.' She was a very determined young woman with a rather lively and passionate temperament, prepared to do anything to achieve her aims. To a certain extent, her story is more interesting than the crime of which she was accused. Elisabeth was born on 19 April 1852 at Meurthe-et-Moselle. Her mother died of cholera two years after she was born. She was brought up by nuns and given a job as a maid at the age of fifteen. She was charged for the first time on 22 May 1868: her employers had found some money among her possessions, although, according to them, she had entered their household 'without a penny'. The court sentenced her to three months' imprisonment.

After this episode she went to Paris, where she worked as a salesgirl in 'Les Trois Frères', a shop in the boulevard du Faubourg-Saint-Martin, and rented a room in the same street. Later she got a job as a seamstress working for Olympe Bayard, head seamstress, at the rue Notre-Dame-de-Nazareth:

The Prévost girl came to work for me on April 1st 1874 and she left on May 10th. I had wanted to give her the sack, anyway, as I wasn't happy with her work – she didn't work hard and she told the other workers that they were over-worked. She also boasted that she had two lovers.

Her first lover, Monsieur Dupuy, a twenty-nine-year-old ironmonger, testified: 'I had relations with the Prévost girl from September 1874 to August 1875. We were both quick-tempered so we broke up. Anyway, I had had cause to feel jealous, although I couldn't pin it down. We never saw each other again.'
 Elisabeth met Antoine Jarretié in the same period. This is his statement:

I had known Mademoiselle Prévost for about nine or ten months, while she was still with her lover. She used to come and see me with a friend of mine, Marie Lejard, who was my mistress. Elisabeth Prévost complained that her lover did not give her enough to eat and that she was unhappy. I suggested that she should come and eat at the same time as my mistress. She told me that my mistress was cheating on me; that was when I left her and started living with Elisabeth. She moved in with me in a house on the rue Aubry-le-Boucher. She left her lover and we moved to the Quai des Grands-Augustins. Then she expressed the desire to have a home of her own. I bought a wine merchant's shop in the rue Saint-Martin. I slept at that address until June 3rd. I had stopped sleeping with her because she had threatened to come to my place, if I didn't marry her, and to smash all the bottles of wine in my cellar. A few days earlier, she brought some linen to my house and, all of a sudden she felt ill; I carried her to my bed and left her alone; when I returned I found her with a gun. She told me that she wanted to kill herself and did not threaten me personally that day. I made her promise not to use the gun. She had a lively character, was hot-headed, and used to drink. She wanted to become my wife and she talked about it all the time. I didn't want to marry her because she didn't behave properly.
 On June 8th, she was drunk and we had an argument; I categorically refused to marry her. On June 9th, she came to ask me to help her open her door because she had lost her key.

Elisabeth desperately wanted to get married, but this plan did not involve any commitment to be faithful. She was careless and cheated on Jarretié with a hairdresser. This is his testimony: 'I met this girl on the staircase, she asked me if I wanted to do her hair. This meeting took place at about eight o'clock in the morning. I came back that evening at about five o'clock and we started having relations. This happened on a number of occasions until her arrest.'
 Jarretié was suspicious and quarrelled with Elisabeth because of this: 'Eight days before the incident, they had a fight because Jarretié had discovered the hairdresser in Elisabeth's room. There was a scene, the Prévost girl was shouting

and getting angry with Jarretié; she said she was her own mistress in her home' (statement made by a neighbour).

In spite of these arguments, Elisabeth wanted to get married at all costs, and to get her way she said that she was pregnant, and blackmailed Jarretié by threatening suicide. This had no effect on him. On 9 June, Elisabeth spent the evening with her other lover at a *café-concert*, and afterwards at a *brasserie* at Châtelet. Later she went to Jarretié's house and, claiming to have lost her keys, asked him to accompany her home to open the door. A violent argument broke out between them in the corridor, then a shot was fired. Witnesses who heard the noise saw a man leave, his face stained with blood.

In her defence, Elisabeth completely denied that she had intended to murder Monsieur Jarretié and accused him of wanting to kill her; then she contradicted herself by producing several versions of the story. Some letters addressed to Jarretié during her detention prove her guilt. The members of the jury generously acquitted this young woman.[12]

* * *

Although they were not unpleasant, Isidore and Elisabeth were murderers who lacked calibre; they were candidates for failure in everything, and thus even failed in their criminal ventures. They were childish rather than sinister, and were unlike any of the other accused, for their distress involved only love and their crime was completely motivated by passion. The members of the jury showed clemency. This was not the case for Adam Helfrich. The determination that this industrious and honest worker showed in matters of the heart did not move anyone.

Adam Helfrich, a navvy of Bavarian origin who was forty-two, had lived for the previous year on the same floor as Madame Langot, a widowed mother. Many flattering statements attested to the fact that Helfrich was an honest man and an excellent worker. He had set his heart on his neighbour, and would quite happily have married her, but had never formally proposed to her. Unfortunately for him, Madame Langot did not share his view of the future. The following is her version of events:

My husband died in 1871. I resolved to devote myself entirely to my children [two girls of twelve and six]. However, I had nothing to live on except my work [she was a charwoman]; but thank God, it was enough to meet my needs. For the past year, Adam Helfrich has been living on the same floor as me. I have known him ever since he went to pay a visit to an ailing neighbour, at the same time as me. He used this situation and our meeting by Madame Giroux's bedside to allow himself to greet and speak to me, and to embrace my children. He asked me to darn his linen. I agreed and he paid me scrupulously. He also got into the habit of coming to see me, something I wasn't entirely happy about because, although he never said anything indiscreet, he spoke in such a way that I could see he had marriage in mind.

And so, at all times, he pretended to feel sorry for me, said I worked too much, that I was accepting too heavy a burden by trying to bring up my children by myself and that it was impossible for me to continue to live alone. Nevertheless I was careful to reply that I was firmly resolved never to remarry.

Her employer's statement also testifies to Madame Langot's determination:

She told us that Helfrich had indirectly proposed to her. My husband urged her to consider these proposals, because of his high opinion of Helfrich, but Madame Langot was determined to remain a widow, and expressed her intention of seeing less of him. To this end, she asked my permission to spend her evenings at my home.

Madame Langot did not care much for her neighbour's constant attention and tried to avoid it by every means:

As this kind of conversation was tiring me, I managed to get Helfrich to play dominoes with my little girls so that we didn't converse. Recently I have even been eating early and spending the evening at a neighbour's house so as not to be at home when Helfrich goes back to his room.

Helfrich was at first oblivious to this change. He then started to behave so strangely that Madame Langot, frightened, did not dare go out alone. Unfortunately, her fears were well grounded. On 26 July, at about eight-thirty in the evening, just as she was putting the key in the lock, he rushed upon her, an axe in his hand, and struck her on the head. She collapsed, and he continued to strike her like a madman. Madame Langot, who did not die from her wounds, described the scene as follows: 'Without uttering a word, and gasping for breath, he looked like a woodcutter hacking away at a tree.'

Adam Helfrich did not express himself very well in French; throughout the preliminary investigation and the trial he refused to confess the real reason for his crime and invented an unlikely story of persecution. According to him, Madame Langot had wanted to get him dismissed; when the judge referred to his marriage plans, he replied: 'I wanted to spend my evenings with her, I wanted her company.' The members of the jury saw this in rather a different light; the unremitting attention and the brutality of this man, who was a foreigner into the bargain, was not viewed with any indulgence.

Looking at all the evidence, Helfrich's crime did not have any of the characteristic features of similar cases. He was unprepossessing and inarticulate, and thus unable to express the passion that lay behind his attempted murder. Outside the context of love, it looked like a contemptible act of revenge, especially since the way it was carried out made it all the more barbaric.

Adultery

During the nineteenth century, the scandalous story of the betrayed husband who catches his wife committing adultery and kills the unfaithful woman or her lover thrilled the public in court and made the front page of newspapers, which sometimes devoted entire pages to satisfy the curiosity of their readers who were always eager to read these news items. These accounts provided a special source and a favourite theme for the playwrights who had hits in the popular theatre.

This obsession with these sinister love-stories accounts for the erroneous association often made between crimes of passion and adultery. Out of eleven people who were accused of this type of murder, four were members of the bourgeoisie: François Duc, a doctor, Charles Leroy-Dubourg, a man of independent means, Frédéric Smeyers, a furniture dealer, and Marie Pourcher, the wife of a contractor, who was unemployed. This was the only news column where members of the bourgeoisie appeared. This observation gave ammunition to all those who savagely condemned adultery as the scourge of the bourgeoisie: 'While background and upbringing are responsible for leading working-class girls to prostitution, they are responsible for leading the bourgeoisie to adultery.'[13] The guilty party was, naturally, to be found among women, who were a source of corruption in society. Out of all the motives given, adultery provided the absolute criterion for being lenient towards perpetrators of crimes of passion.

During both the preliminary investigation and the trial, the accused would repent; some would even weep. In order to explain their behaviour, they spoke of jealousy, of blindness. Nevertheless, they did not consider it necessary to justify themselves: the misbehaviour of the victim seemed to them justification enough. While the protagonists of these dramas were always the same, the intrigues were different. As for how the crime took place, there were three main types of scenario. First, there was the crime committed on the spur of the moment, the *flagrante delicto* – this was the crime that Enrico Ferri described as 'ideal', and for which he demanded acquittal. The second type was when the accused tried to catch his unfaithful wife; he would keep watch, spy on the lovers for a long time, plan a trap, and take his revenge after he had confirmed his suspicions of adultery. In the third and last scenario, the betrayed man, no longer able to stand the infidelity and desertion, would resolve to take revenge.

Literature turned adultery into a typically middle-class crime. The reality of the courts was somewhat different. Members of the working class were equally quick to react to conjugal infidelity. Nevertheless, the behaviour of criminals and victims differed according to social class. This difference can be seen mainly in the attitude of working-class women, who were not only unfaithful but also deserted the marital home without shame. While their husbands sometimes tolerated the indignity of being 'cuckolds', when their wives deserted them this was too painful a humiliation for them to bear, and triggered off the tragedy.

The Tronché couple had a marriage just like any other. He was a factory worker and she was a seamstress. One day, in December 1871, she met the man who was later to become her lover. Two months later, on 12 February 1872, she moved in with him, leaving her husband and her child. Antoine Tronché could not come to terms with the fact that his wife had left him and pursued her: 'On a number of occasions my husband tried to make me come back and I always refused to go with him; he even threatened to kill me.' On 27 March he went to see her at the house of some friends where she was having lunch and ordered her to leave with him: 'She refused to go with me and insulted me. I lost my temper. I hurled a knife at her in the same way as I might have slapped her across the face. I deeply regret what I did.' He received eight years' hard labour for her murder.[14]

François Shenk was unable to keep his wife, a seamstress: she had gone to live with her lover the previous fortnight. This was the account given by the betrayed husband, who was thirty-six years old and a joiner by trade:

My wife left me with the child. [For the past fortnight she had been living with her lover.] I did everything I could to bring my wife to her senses, but for a long time she had been misbehaving, and wasn't working and was reading bad books. . . . [After his wife deserted him, he went and bought a larding needle to 'lard his wife'.] . . . I met her with her lover with whom she had spent the night and that was enough to finish me off and make me lose my head. I only struck her once, I wanted to mark her, her and her lover.

Shenk was acquitted.[15]

In the Couzimié case, at first the deserted husband lodged a complaint and proved that there were circumstances of adultery *in flagrante delicto*, on 22 May 1876. This afforded him little consolation since it did not bring his unfaithful wife back home. On 24 June of the same year, Couzimié noticed Monsieur Joubert, his wife's lover, in a tavern, entered, went up to him, and violently picked up a bottle which he proceeded to break over Joubert's head; he then kicked him several times in the stomach. Joubert died the following day as a result of an intestinal perforation. According to the accused's allegations, he claimed in his defence that he had been scoffed at by the victim and that it was a totally spontaneous act of revenge, not against his adulterous wife but against her lover, a target rarely aimed at by betrayed husbands – unlike women, who more readily attacked their rivals.

Following a pattern identical to that found in the crimes described above, Antoine Dée's revenge exploded equally suddenly. Suzanne Dée, aged thirty, was a shirt-maker who lived in Belgium with her husband and her son. Tired of being ill-treated, she ran away:

'He used to beat me for no reason. There were times when my head was as black as a stove. He used to get angry without rhyme or reason.'

'You left the marital home with your lover?'

'Yes, that is true. I was wrong to do so, but I had suffered so much. When you have felt like I felt, you start to let yourself get carried along by everything. Emile [her lover] was leaving; I asked him if I could go with him for the journey.'

Antoine Dée lodged a complaint of adultery, and then withdrew it and entreated his wife by letter to grant him a reconciliation, which she did. Antoine and his son joined Suzanne and Emile, who were already settled in Paris. The couple started living together again and the lover moved in on the floor above them. The two men worked together as street cleaners. One morning, when Emile had just knocked on the door to wake them up, Suzanne asked him the time and suggested he come in, something which incensed Antoine: 'I thought it was improper. I told her off; she told me that she had a higher opinion of her lover than of me. I was very excited and I lost my head.' He threw himself at her to strangle her, then stabbed her several times. Emile rushed into the bedroom to help his mistress. Antoine Dée then said to him: 'What are you doing here, it's none of your business. If I want to kill my wife, I'm free to do so.' He was acquitted.[16]

To be sure of being acquitted, it was necessary to catch one's wife committing adultery *in flagrante delicto* in the marital home, a fairly rare occurrence. During the nineteenth century, society violently condemned female licentiousness, and article 324 of the Penal Code confirmed the conviction that women should be faithful. In the following case, the murderer-husband satisfied the necessary conditions to justify his act and to receive a pardon, particularly since he looked like an honest man. His story was related by one of the journalists writing for *L'Evénement*:

Law Reports. Bessières is an honest coppersmith, almost an artisan, a handsome brown-haired man aged between thirty-four and thirty-six who, a few years ago, married a young girl, a quite remarkable beauty, but a Parisian from the suburbs, that is to say badly brought up, with no education, corrupt, already accustomed to loose relationships, and indulging in dangerous liaisons, and with a pronounced taste for spirits and tobacco. With these natural tendencies, the Parisian girl of the people is usually happy in a dive or in a student's room; she can pass for a lively and agreeable mistress to the innocent boy on whom she can try out what she's learnt in a trivial love-affair.

Bessières was unlucky enough to meet this type of woman. He was simple, ignorant, naive and superficial like all good, hard-working men who have had neither the will nor the time to observe women at close quarters. He began by adoring this woman, and, without knowing anything about her, he chose her for his life's companion. It was lucky she did not mind complying to the will of a coppersmith . . . .

Madame Bessières, for her part, had only made a marriage of convenience, and it can be said that she gave only her hand. During the first months, the appeal of novelty, of relative comfort, the pleasure of ruling over something, of being mistress somewhere, kept her fairly well occupied. . . . This new, healthy atmosphere filled her heart and for a time subdued her fickle instincts. But the situation could not last. Gradually, the prostitute's character was to emerge from the woman. Soon, her idleness and her solitude, which encouraged her to fantasize, awoke her sexual instincts. The memory of her last fling returned. She imagined her old lovers in procession and she was seized by lewd excitement, fever.

Yet she was already a mother. Her maternal duties did not stop her. She sent for spirits, started to get drunk again and to indulge in every sensual fantasy. In each man she saw a seducer, for each of them barely figured in sentimental terms. However, the unfortunate Bessières finally suspected that he had rivals. He had become aware of the disorder of their household, of the sometimes debauched and drunken behaviour of his wife – he realized that Léonie had indeed shed her modesty. He reprimanded her gently at first, then came more violent reproaches; but Léonie continued to sink deeper into her life of prostitution, protected by marriage.

Lastly, giving up all shame and restraint, she even befriended a young tenant in the house, a fair-haired philosopher, a fop, who used to receive her every day in his attic room. Her husband used to leave early to go to work. Léonie would get up and go up to the sixth floor wearing the flimsiest of garments; there, in the arms of the blond dreamer, she would resume her interrupted sleep and have a 'lie-in', as they say. On the stroke of eleven, she would go downstairs in her slippers, and prepare her lover's lunch in her own kitchen. . . . This had been going on for a long time, when one January morning Bessières suddenly came home between eight and nine o'clock; as there had not been enough to do in the workshop, the foreman had sent him home.

Naturally, the house was empty. At first he thought his wife had gone to the market. But he did not fail to observe that not a single piece of her clothing was missing and that even her shoes were there. Then, a terrible suspicion, which had already crossed his mind, overwhelmed him again. He went up to the sixth floor and there, on the landing, his ear pressed against the attic door, he listened.

He immediately heard the sound of kissing, of words exchanged in a quiet voice – in short, all the noises which could inform and distress the most obtuse and the most stoical of husbands. Despite the terrible emotion that choked him, he managed to restrain himself. So he went downstairs and simply waited for his unfaithful wife outside the door of their rooms. She kept him waiting for a while. But she finally appeared. She was in a hurry, no doubt, to cook a delicious meal for her Monsieur Alphonse.

Her clothes were indescribably untidy. . . . When she saw her husband, who stood waiting with a vengeful look, she went horribly pale and looked down. But suddenly her base nature reasserted itself and she immediately looked up and, confronting his reproaches, confessed everything with a cynical arrogance, showering her husband with the most vulgar of insults, as if he was the guilty party and not she.

This time Bessières, carried away by a fierce rage of jealousy and love, could not overcome his indignation and his anger. He suddenly grabbed his knife and, throwing himself at the horrible creature, struck her several times. Fortunately the neighbours saved her from his wrath. Her wounds were not fatal, and Madame Bessières quickly recovered. She appeared in the assize court today, as a witness. She is tall, rather thin and she has a listless, slouching bearing. Her face bears the marks of debauchery and vice. She looks like a portrait of lechery, sketched in charcoal in the manner of Callot. Bessières's attitude, on the other hand, was as good and as kind as possible. One could read in the facial expressions of the members of the jury their impatience to free this man as quickly as possible. Moreover, the judge and the assistant public prosecutor virtually urged his acquittal. Thus the verdict and the judgement were a pure formality.

By giving a very exaggerated description of Léonie Bessières, this misogynist journalist was attacking the freedom that working-class girls enjoyed: they were 'fallen girls', 'suburban weeds', who would never be able to become the model wives which the bourgeoisie would have liked the workers to have.

A certain amount of voyeurism is apparent in the attitude towards female adultery, which blackens the image of working-class promiscuity; the sensuous appetite of women of leisure who found a handsome young lover to satisfy their desires and their need for gratification, without the slightest feeling of love, was condemned. Was this simply a male image being projected on to women's sexuality, or a journalistic perversion?

Working-class people speak of wounded pride, of personal slights, whereas the bourgeois person kills out of jealousy but is concerned about lost family honour. Working people doubtless share the same feelings, but they do not express them explicitly: the fury, exasperation and blindness which they experience because of certain affronts speak for themselves, as far as they are concerned, and explain their acts.

François Duc was an aggrieved husband who took the law into his own hands after drinking a few glasses of absinthe; he fired a gun at his unfaithful wife. This pedestrian story is interesting in so far as it is a source of information about marital relationships and the way of life in bourgeois milieux. Whereas working-class women were more likely to leave the marital home because they were having a love-affair, middle-class women were more reluctant to do so and often did not dare leave their husbands. The fear of losing their comfort, of adopting a position that was financially inferior and of becoming social outcasts was a difficult obstacle to overcome. You needed guts and energy to cope with prejudice and to find a job worthy of your social class if you had been kept first by your parents and then by your husband. Madame Leroy-Dubourg and Madame Duc certainly expressed the desire to get a separation, but they eventually gave in to their husbands' will.

Moreover, the way the Duc case developed is revealing of the view taken of this type of crime if the accused, who was a respectable citizen, could demonstrate that he had behaved irreproachably.

On 18 January 1860, François Duc, a respectable doctor, married Alexandrine Boulanger, the daughter of one of his patients. He was forty and she was seventeen. Two girls were born of this marriage, which continued untroubled for twelve years. In 1874 it became apparent that there was discord in their relationship. Madame Duc, feeling neglected by her husband, who was frequently called out, did not resist the amorous attentions of a young man whom she had met in the street and who was to become her lover. The bill of indictment summed up the result of this affair:

The accused gained proof of infidelity through two letters which his wife had written and which left no doubt about her adultery; he was told about these letters on 11 June 1874 by an old servant who had been dismissed. He acknowledged that during that period the idea had first come to him to commit the crime of which he stands accused today. His brother and one of his friends intervened, advised him to restrain himself and managed to bring about a reconciliation between the two spouses. This reconciliation was sincere on the part of François Duc, but his wife did not respect the commitment she had made, and it was not long before she was unfaithful again. . . . She was not even scared to confide in her servant, Raulin, the secret of her correspondence with several young men, to whom she had even allowed access to her flat.

On Thursday, 16 July 1874, Madame Duc went out to visit a woman friend whom she went to see every week. The accused had lunch alone and was served by Raulin, who, when he questioned her, admitted everything she knew and exposed her mistress's loose living. This new revelation infuriated Duc, who armed himself with a revolver and announced that he would be avenged before nightfall. The accused indulged freely in alcohol so as to reach the necessary state of excitement to carry out his plan, and went to wait for his wife at the place du Palais-Royal.

Here is the version of events given by Madame Duc in her statement:

Unfortunately, when I reached the place du Palais-Royal, I saw that my husband was waiting for me. I wanted to avoid a scene in the street and I got off the omnibus. I tried to ask Monsieur Duc for an explanation, but he replied that he did not owe me one, that I was to go home with him, and that if I did not obey him he would kill me in the street. On the way back he said curtly that I had three lovers and that I received them at home every day. When we reached the house I had just taken off my hat when I turned to my husband to explain things to him; he replied that there was no explanation, that he was going to kill me and, at the same time, from his left trouser-pocket he pulled a revolver, which he fired at me.

François Duc prided himself on having been a happily married man, at least until 1872. His wife's admissions to the investigating magistrate showed that she had not shared in this happiness:

I no longer loved my husband and found his presence disagreeable. I would have liked to leave. . . . For the past year or so I have forgotten my marriage vows and had intimate relations with a young man. . . . From then on we started to have problems together, and I often suggested to my husband that we part, but he would never agree.

On this subject, Monsieur Duc explained: 'My wife did indeed ask me for a separation but I did not agree to it because I didn't want her to drag my name, and my children's name, through the mud.' This wish for a separation was passed over in silence in the bill of indictment and throughout the trial. It was feared that talk of divorce among the general public would be revived; it was very important that this young woman's behaviour should not be condoned.

For some time, François Duc had observed a change in his wife's behaviour:

I noticed greater coldness on the part of my wife, more stiffness towards me; she became smarter and was more attentive to her dress, but there was no deterioration in our conjugal relations. . . . She had taken a great liking to going out. She would go out on some pretext or other and often did not return until very late at night. Her cares and her attentions became increasingly rare and the attention which she did pay me seemed forced at times. I reproached her very severely for her behaviour but I could not get her to change her habits. She made excuses about going out which did not satisfy me at all.

'You do admit that you too had become very irritable and difficult to get on with?'

What was I to do? I was terribly worried about my wife's determination to go out so frequently. The slightest thing made me suspicious, touchy and violent. I was jealous and had a feeling that something strange was going on that was jeopardizing my honour and my marital rights.

Before the members of the jury, he took up these arguments again so as to present his crime as a brave act committed by a man who had the right to take the law into his own hands.

Moreover, the role of servants in this drama should not be underestimated; it might never have taken place had it not been for the intervention of one of them. Unlike other workers, servants were dependent on their employers, with whom they shared their daily lives. They were completely isolated, and if there was any conflict they had no choice but to take their own measures, which usually took the form of an act of revenge such as denunciation or theft. The day François Duc dismissed Adèle, in June 1874, his wife made a mistake for which she was to pay dearly:

I wanted to dismiss our maid because she was idle; my wife was reluctant; finally she agreed to it, but by a strange turnabout she refused to give her a certificate of good behaviour. One day, this much embittered girl came to see me while my wife was out and said: 'Monsieur, I cannot bear it any longer! I must tell Monsieur everything. Madame is a hussy and has lovers.' As proof of these infidelities, she handed me a note and a letter.

This incident testifies to the strong bond between masters and servants. To be waited on implied other conditions of servitude, too. Indeed, the private lives of their masters did not escape the prying eyes of servants whose silence had to be bought through giving presents or conferring advantages. The new maid, the Raulin girl, who was disgusted by Madame Duc's behaviour, also exposed her. Her admissions were to prove fatal. Before the judges, she disguised this act of revenge by talking in very moralistic terms about female virtue: 'Monsieur Duc was a good husband and it was painful to watch his wife deceiving him. Anyway, I was always out running errands to deliver letters and I didn't like it. And then when the third lover appeared on the scene, that was the last straw, I decided to warn Monsieur Duc.' Judges were familiar with the practices of servants, which is why the judge was surprised that Monsieur Duc had not been wary: 'You accepted your maid's denunciations without checking them?' As daily witnesses to the private lives of the bourgeoisie, domestic servants were dangerous and cunning individuals.

The assistant public prosecutor, whose job it was to support the indictment, described Alexandrine as a 'wretched creature' who was unworthy of her husband's affection, and he paid tribute to François Duc's noble feelings and to his honourable past.

The verdict did not come as a surprise to anybody, for an acquittal had been anticipated. The articles in the press once more confirmed the public's indulgence towards a certain type of perpetrator of crimes of passion:

The assize court of the Seine, usually so serious and austere, had a slightly festive air about it today. Everyone seemed happy and it looked like a gathering of friends who were there to pay tribute to one of their number, to a genial character, to one of those good personalities who attract the crowds and keep them under the spell of their ability to communicate [sic]. For it is indeed a rare occurrence for an honest man, an unknown, a modest benefactor of humanity, to be standing trial.

As usual, when the doors opened an enormous, busy, and wealthy crowd of people who were all dressed up in their Sunday best and consisted mainly of the worthy Doctor Duc's patients, rushed forward in a split second into the court room.

A few moments later, Monsieur Thévenin, the able assize judge, and his two assessors took their seats and the accused – forgive me, the martyr – was brought in. [*L'Evénement*]

The victim's guilt was beyond doubt for this journalist writing in *Le Petit Journal*: 'He is an honest man who has been deceived in the most vulgar, the most base manner by a creature unworthy of his affection; the real accused is not him, but her.'[17]

*   *   *

The accused sometimes actually *was* a woman, as was the case with Marie Pourcher, a thirty-six-year-old mother of two. This young woman, who was poor but dignified, received a very proper upbringing in the house of the Legion of Honour of Saint-Denis. Before getting married, she had even worked as a milliner. Her husband, an ordinary working-class man, managed to rise through hard work to the rank of master locksmith. The marriage was going well, as was business, until the day in 1877 when Pierre met a *brasserie* girl called Augustine Meunier. Augustine was the stereotype of the clandestine prostitute with her kept *petit bourgeois* manner. A medical student even claimed that he had spent 60,000 francs on her.

Before making Augustine his mistress, Pourcher courted the young woman and then set up house for her; this was typical of the extra-marital affairs of the *nouveaux riches*. Indeed, the infatuation with this sort of prostitution, which grew throughout the nineteenth century, can be explained by the economic prosperity enjoyed by the bourgeoisie. Keeping a woman was a means of advertising one's wealth, and this 'little extra' was part of the way of life and the expenses of a gentleman.[18] According to Maxime Du Camps, 'Nowadays everybody wants to have a mistress, just as everyone wants to go hunting, to take the waters, and to bathe in the sea.[19] A mistress also meant carnal pleasure. Nineteenth-century society played on two very powerful images of women: the mother, and the courtesan. The former had to give herself, body and soul, to the family; she stayed at home and devoted herself to motherhood. This conception of women, associated only with motherhood, excluded any form of sensuality and caused the husband to be attracted towards the courtesan, the object of sexual enjoyment.

Faced with this dualism, which was imposed by bourgeois morality, the courtesan made it possible to remove the guilt of sexual pleasure, by offering men the opportunity of living out some of their fantasies and sometimes even of creating other forms of sociability in their mistresses' drawing rooms. The woman of easy virtue was not a common prostitute who would sell her charms to the first man who asked her, for she gave the man who kept her the illusion of love and seduction.

Monsieur Pourcher's liaison might have remained a secret had he not spent too much money and neglected his business. Because he was unable to explain the large sums of money that he had spent, his wife started to suspect him. She kept watch over him, and it was not long before she discovered the existence of Augustine and found out her address.

From then onwards she only had one idea in her head, and that was to meet her rival in the presence of her husband. To this end she tried to enter the building when her husband went to visit his mistress, but the concierge prevented her from doing so. After trying in vain again, she decided to speak out, and during a squabble, she told Pourcher everything she knew and demanded that he arrange a meeting with Augustine Meunier, on the pretext of wanting to see the furniture he had given her. Monsieur Pourcher agreed to this, but Augustine categorically refused. So as to appease his wife, he approached a justice of the peace in order to get back the furniture. Naturally he did not follow up this request; and, so as to avoid a scene, he stopped going to visit his mistress and met her only in public places, or in hackney carriages, all the while continuing to keep her.

His wife was not deceived. As she did not know what to do next, she decided to have recourse to the law with the aim of officially establishing circumstances of *flagrante delicto*; but the police commissioner told her that this was not a suitable case for an official report and advised her to go and see the Public Prosecutor. She was helpless and gave up the case. During this period matters continued to go badly and she felt utterly desperate.

On 2 February she went to Augustine's home and waited in the street until Augustine decided to come out. After several hours, she appeared. Madame Pourcher accosted her, blamed her for ruining a family, and threatened to kill her. In order to get her to leave off, Augustine promised to break off her relationship with François Duc.

Three days later, on 5 February, Madam Pourcher followed the two lovers and then witnessed the rendezvous that they used to have in carriages. The following day, when her husband left her to go and see Augustine, she took the terrible decision to put an end to it all:

At that moment I felt something, I don't know what, go to my head, I saw that everything was lost, me, my home and my daughters. I made up my mind to avenge myself on this girl who was causing a decent family so much unhappiness. At about nine o'clock, not knowing how else to avenge myself, I took a revolver out of my husband's desk and I went and waited in the rue Saint-Jacques for Augustine to come out so that I could shoot her.

When Augustine came out, 'I reproached her for having taken my husband away from me, for taking the food from my children's mouth, and for boasting that she had made my husband spend 75,000 francs and that she would ruin us.'

Suddenly, Augustine Meunier pushed away the weapon which Marie Pourcher was aiming at her and ran off as fast as she could shouting: 'Help!' Madame Pourcher pursued her and shot at her. The bullet struck a man who, at that very moment, had placed himself between the two women; he was slightly wounded in the arm.

Marie Pourcher's jealousy towards Augustine Meunier was exacerbated by the promises she had made, but never kept, to break off with Marie's husband, and by the length of the liaison, during which 'her husband neglected her and his children'.

The accused felt that Augustine was leading her husband astray and that she was corrupting him by preventing him from working and earning money.

Far from denying the importance of the financial aspect, Marie Pourcher used it to justify her crime: it was because her husband's business was no longer going well that she was worried, and it was because Augustine 'was taking the food from her children's mouth' that she went as far as trying to commit murder. She focused her claims on the furniture given to Augustine, a present whose symbolism did not escape her; she wanted to see it and to own it, since it represented the marital love that she no longer had. Not only was this woman of ill repute a financial liability for the Pourcher family, but she was also destroying their security. 'I saw everything lost, me, my home and my daughters.' Betrayed husbands talk of honour and of rights – Marie Pourcher thought of her home!

The members of the jury had very good reasons for acquitting this 'honourable woman'.[20]

Marital Hatred

Many couples are pushed to committing a crime of passion after an accidental outburst of marital hatred. These stories, which are fairly commonplace, reflect the reality of everyday life as experienced by the majority of people; but under the magnifying glass of the law such very ordinary tales of life became sordid, and only the blood that was shed makes them distinctive.

Physical violence, quarrels, alcoholism: these three recurrent themes punctuate each of these dramas prompted by criminal motives.

First and foremost, marital squabbles between husband and wife play a decisive role in the criminal process. They break out because of reproaches and insults caused by something trivial, maybe an evening meal not ready on time, or someone being late. With few exceptions, these quarrels were caused by a temporary disagreement. The couples in question were not in situations where there was no escape, and they were not on the verge of breaking up; it is very likely that, if these altercations had not accidentally taken a tragic turn, their stories would not figure in criminal records. When criminologists of the Positivist School describe the ideal crime of passion, they are referring to the impulsiveness of the act and to a lack of premeditation. In so doing, they are thinking of adultery and not of domestic quarrels. Considered unworthy of interest, verging on the despicable, this type of motive has never been the subject of a specific study. And yet, it has all the so-called ideal conditions, such as the spontaneity of the act which occurs in the violence of the altercation, during which the couple exchange blows without thinking of the consequences. If they use a weapon, they do not choose it but grab the first object within reach. This violence is never premeditated; there is no threat, no trap and no surveillance. A verbal or physical provocation is enough for criminal violence to be used.

The Douard couple, who had been married since 1859, owned a seed shop in the rue Montmartre. Aréna Douard was forty years old, his wife Marie-Henriette was thirty-seven. According to many witnesses, the husband as well as the wife often came to blows. Aréna had been convicted several times for his violent ways. One day Marie-Henriette stabbed him in the stomach with a knife, but he did not want to lodge a complaint. After this incident the violence disappeared from their day-to-day relationship, but the discord continued to exist.

In January 1877, the Douard couple engaged the Marmontel girl as a maid. According to Marie-Henriette's statement, the event took place in the following manner:

On February 8th, I found the young girl at the door and she explained that my husband had treated her with disrespect. I took her side. My husband was furious and quarrelled with me on a number of occasions because I had given in to the entreaties of this girl, who had asked me to keep her until she found a new position. On February 20th, he came home a bit drunk and, on seeing the maid, he wanted to send her away immediately. The Marmontel girl replied: 'No, I won't leave, you lazy lump, you big good-for-nothing, you great bastard, not before I have broken my clogs on your ugly mug.' I intervened and told the girl to go to a neighbour's house and said that she could then go and stay at my mother's while she was looking for a situation. Afterwards I reproached my husband, saying that you had to be a real coward to treat servants without respect.

At these words he became angry and went upstairs, only to reappear with a revolver.

He aimed at his wife and fired two shots. She was slightly wounded and took refuge with a neighbour. Meanwhile, Aréna went back to his bedroom and said to his servant, who had followed him in, 'It's all over now. I feel that I have behaved badly. Take a cigarette, this will be the last time that we smoke together.'

Marie-Henriette, who had recovered somewhat from the trauma, returned home. She went straight to the bedroom where she found her husband. As she crossed the threshold, she saw him aiming the gun at himself. Before she could intervene, he had shot himself in the head. This suicide attempt ended in a broken jaw and a completely disfigured face. At the trial his wife gave a very restrained statement; indeed, she would have liked charges to be dropped. During the preliminary investigation, Aréna Douard admitted that he had had the sudden 'desire to end it all' with his wife, but during the trial he retracted this and denied any intention to murder her. The intervention of his wife and the failed suicide attempt were in his favour: on 26 July 1877 the Seine assize court acquitted Aréna Douard.[21]

Whether it was justifiable or not, this open defiance is the enactment of working-class married life, which is conducted in accordance with the activities or fantasies of each individual and does not reflect their life as a couple. People would come home at whatever time they wanted without a thought for their partners. Nevertheless, when certain limits were exceeded, latent tensions would be grafted on to the slightest deviation in behaviour, which normally would have been tolerated. It was thus that Anna Delafosse's lack of moderation triggered off a violent argument.

Jean-Claude Brazier had been working for the previous sixteen years at the Government Printing Office. The information about him was very favourable. Although he was accustomed to living alone, in 1875 he decided to set up house with Anna Delafosse, a seamstress paid by the day who had been widowed since 1871. Several accounts suggest that her reputation was not unblemished. Apart from her aggressive behaviour, her excessive drinking was severely criticized. Anna denied this accusation to the examining magistrate. When the judge asked her, 'Were you in the habit of drinking?' she replied: 'Since my husband died, I take the occasional glass of wine, although I shouldn't as it makes me dizzy; but our quarrels have never been caused by drink.'

On 29 December 1875, Anna came home at about eleven o'clock, and Jean-Claude about half an hour later. She reproached him for being late and for having been with women. 'I was not drunk that night; the concierges were mistaken when they said that I was not in my normal state.' An argument ensued; the neighbours heard raised voices. Brazier announced to the examining magistrate: 'I hit her because she grabbed me by the collar and wanted to start a fight. I said to her: "I can see that you want to spoil everything, but I won't let you." Then, when we were on the ground, I tied her wrists together.' Then he shouted: 'Try and undo that', and at the same time he pushed Anna out of the window. Fortunately her fall was cushioned by the branch of a tree.

Brazier maintained that Delafosse was completely drunk and that she threw herself out of the window, which is not at all plausible, given the height of the iron bars in front of the window. In spite of the evidence which suggested intent to murder, Brazier was acquitted. Anna's bad reputation played its part in this verdict.[22]

*　　*　　*

Something trivial was enough for a marital quarrel to break out; the mundane character of the motives concealed more serious tensions. These banal altercations should not, however, have degenerated into criminal violence. Such frequent outbursts suggest that couples were accustomed to blows and shouting. There was neither ulterior motive nor perversity in the individual who suddenly flew into a rage. The spontaneity of this violence continually reflected the harshness of their lives. The intensity of their tensions was such that they sometimes had to be given expression, even if it meant killing their partners.

This violence highlights the problem of battered wives. Four women were battered to death between 1871–1880. There were a great many badly treated women who were subjected to physical brutality, and who, from an instinct to survive, managed to put an end to male violence. These four women evinced an extraordinary silent resignation, a submission to spiritual misery and to fate which, however, should not be interpreted as a weakness on their part: children or the hope of a change got the better of their desire to leave the madman who was beating them. Out of a sense of dignity, they concealed the marks of violence on their bruised bodies, sometimes running away only to return a few days later, and attempt to survive their married hell.

This was Mathurine Lebersorg's situation. In September 1868, at the age of fifteen, she married François Lebersorg, a maker of caps, who was fifteen years her elder. Mathurine's mother told the examining magistrate about her daughter's agony:

I was against this marriage because I thought she was too young. Before long I could see that she was not happy. She did not complain to me, but I could guess what was going on. She had a very affectionate, very childish nature. She loved her husband greatly, and would always find excuses for him and defend him. On September 4th 1870 she came to me in tears. She had been beaten, she didn't want to say that it was her husband who had done it. In October she took refuge in my house again. Then they made up. Towards the end she became unwell and part of her body was paralysed; her left hand trembled. On the morning of the crime, she complained to me about her suffering. The following day, the accused came and told me that my daughter was ill; my poor child was dead.

Two women who worked in François Lebersorg's small workshop confirmed this statement: 'On September 4th, I saw the accused beating his wife; he was running after her with an iron in his hand. He was furious with his wife; she hid behind me and I got punched in the process. Madame Lebersorg was very affectionate towards her husband, who always rejected her and often insulted her.'

On 21 November 1870, François did not just beat his wife; he fired two bullets at her with a revolver because, on that day, when he came in at noon, 'she was sitting down, her clothes filthy as usual, and everything was in a mess, so I went out to eat and I came back at one o'clock.' These were the reasons which this man dared to give the examining magistrate to explain his crime. Furthermore, he did not even try to help his wounded and dying wife, but simply remained by her side. The neighbours did indeed hear the groans of the poor girl calling her mother, but they thought it was one of their usual domestic quarrels. Nevertheless, their indifference was astonishing given the noise caused by the shots. At the end of the afternoon François went out and left his wife; on his return at about ten o'clock he became apprehensive about his wife's condition and finally decided to take her to hospital.

Without intervening directly, Madame Philippe, a neighbour, took the initiative of warning the family:

On November 21st, I heard a shot and some groans. I heard Madame Lebersorg say to François: 'Ah! I forgive you.' I informed the concierge but she refused to go upstairs. I went to my step-mother's house but she wasn't in. I went home again but I could hear the same wails. She was crying out: 'Mummy, mummy.' In the evening, when the poor woman was taken downstairs, she said to me: 'I hurt myself while I was playing.' And as her husband was crying, she said to him: 'François, don't cry, I'll be back soon', and she added, 'Don't worry, I shan't say a word.'

Mathurine died several hours later at the hospital. Her dying words testify to her resignation and her piety: 'He quarrelled with me. He fired two pistol shots at me. He did not look after me and left me in a pool of blood, but I forgive him just as I ask God to forgive me as I will soon appear before Him.'

During the preliminary investigation, Lebersorg continued to pretend that it was an accident, that his wife had wounded herself with the pistol which she kept hidden on her person. In addition, he had the temerity to accuse her of stealing money from him. In the face of the insensitivity of the accused, the members of the jury were severe and condemned him to hard labour for life.

Another woman, who was literally trampled over by her lover, experienced some atrocious suffering without the neighbours, accustomed to frequent domestic quarrels, reacting to the screams. Was this indifference on their part, or were they really inured to daily violence?

As a rule, neighbours were sensitive to distress and did not hesitate to come out in order to save victims; this has been observed on many occasions. But in the case of battered wives, there is, inevitably, a certain weariness in the face of repeated violence. Such was the case of Madame Yvon, who had lived with Louis Perdriat for seventeen years. She was born in Chartres in 1841 and came to Paris in 1854 and worked as a laundress. Louis Perdriat was an assistant butcher in the slaughterhouse of La Villette. He was dismissed following a squabble during which he threatened a butcher, who had given him an order, with a knife.

According to the judge, 'this habitual criminal showed a disposition towards evil from a very young age; this brutal man, who was given to drunkenness, had become increasingly violent towards his common-law wife since his last arrest.' Indeed, this man, whose past was, to say the least, unruly, did not gain the jury's sympathy. For a theft carried out at the age of twelve, he had spent six years in a remand home. In 1859 he was again sentenced to six months' imprisonment for theft, and then, in 1864, to thirteen months for theft and fraud; in 1866 he was sentenced to a month in prison for insulting behaviour to the police, and on 20 September 1875 he was sentenced to three months for beating and wounding his common-law wife, Louise Yvon. After forcing her to the ground, he belaboured her body with kicks.

In order to justify himself, Louis Perdriat complained to the investigating magistrate that his wife did not work and spent too much time at the wine merchant's. If he beat her, it was because she 'created a scene when he came home a bit excited from drinking'. On 30 December 1876, he went home at about nine o'clock in the evening: 'Supper wasn't ready, the stove was not lit and she was in bed.' They quarrelled, and then, suddenly he hurled himself on her and began to hit her wildly. Despite the screams, the neighbours did not intervene. After half an hour, they heard two piercing screams, then a prolonged silence; the young woman had died.

On the day of the trial, the judge laid great stress on the strange behaviour of the accused after the crime: 'Perdriat, when you killed her the butcher's boy inside you came to the fore. You took the body, you carried out on to the landing and you washed it like an animal which has just been bled at the slaughterhouse.' 'I don't remember.'

And yet the body of Louise Yvon was found dressed and laid out on the bed with care. When he was arrested, Perdriat asked whether he could be decapitated for this. The members of the jury sentenced him to hard labour for life.

The use of physical force is not a male prerogative. Women often resort to it. Some do not hesitate to strike first, and sometimes even to tyrannize their husbands. The following article which appeared in the 'Law Reports' column of L'Evénement, recounts the crime of Madame Charrier. Although this affair was treated with humour and derision, a man was nevertheless completely disfigured. The detached tone demonstrates that women's violence was not taken seriously: by poking fun at the domestic suffering of the male, the press was seeking to deny a reality that ran counter to the image of the submissive wife. Conversely, far more attention was paid to battered wives:

By a strange predestination, she was called Moutarde and she appeared today before the Seine assize court, not, it is true, for treating her husband with a mustard poultice against his will, but for thoroughly cleaning his face with vitriol. When one has a name that is as caustic as Moutarde, such treatment is hardly surprising. Charrier, the husband, alone was at fault for marrying, without thinking about it twice, a forty-year-old woman, especially if he had first read Balzac's detailed account of women at forty.

In short, last January, Charrier, a staid fifty-year-old, a former deputy sergeant in the police force, married Marie Moutarde with every appearance of devotion; and six months later, on July 14th, the honeymoon came to an end with the vitriol attack which today brings the wife to stand in the dock.

It appears that it was not long before Marie was making her husband's life a misery. According to him, she was revoltingly filthy and a dreadful miser. She literally starved him to death, and showered him with reproaches and maltreatment. Nevertheless he had resigned himself to eating his meals in a restaurant, to spending the day far from her and to only coming home in the evening. Finally she took it into her head to create jealous scenes; he had attended a baptism in the company of a young cook and she claimed that this cook was his mistress.[23]

Marie Charrier ill-treated her husband because she wanted to go back to her village to look after her ailing mother and he refused to go. According to him, the cause of their divorce was a child who was in his care:

I think I'm the father of this child, I've always looked after it; it was agreed that she would also take care of this child. There were arguments on account of this. My wife was nasty. I was not frightened of the enemy, I was only afraid of her. This woman has never loved me, she was dreadfully miserly; I was ashamed of her, she always went out looking disgusting and, worst of all, she was violent.

On the morning of 15 July 1875, Monsieur Charrier was sweeping the dining-room in the presence of his wife who was preparing some food for herself. A quarrel broke out: 'She said to me: "Go on then, go to the slut you were with on Thursday." I replied: "I don't need to go out to find what I already have at home."' They insulted each other; she left the dining-room, went into the kitchen and came back holding a cup, the contents of which she threw in the face of the accused. It was sulphuric acid. That morning, contrary to her custom, she had drunk a glass of absinthe.

Nevertheless, female aggression does not compare with male aggression, since it never reaches the same degree of cruelty or savagery. The inequality continued in so far as the 'battered' man rebelled and ended up by having the last word, as was the case with Jacques Billet, who put up with his wife's ill-treatment without protesting until the day he committed the crime. He told the judge that 'he had killed his wife so as not to be killed by her'. According to a number of accounts, Madame Billet often made her husband cry, and would hit him in public. She used to boast, among other things, that she 'had broken her brother-in-law's eggs by kicking him'.[24]

In the Paulmier case, the former common-law husband of Pauline Prudhomme described this woman's violence and confessed: 'Sometimes she wanted to beat me, but as we are the same age, I rebelled.'

It was often the case that the first blow served as a provocation, enraging the wounded man. Thus, when Madame Brossier violently pushed her husband away by scratching his face, he was unable to contain himself: 'I looked at myself in the mirror, I saw that my face was covered in blood, and then I lost my temper.'[25]

5

The World Upside Down

The Working-Class Woman as Martyr?

Deserted or rejected women have other means of avenging themselves than murdering their lovers or their unscrupulous husbands. The women who appeared in the assize courts were victims – victims of the brutality of men and of their own destructive instincts. As such, they provide a series of portraits of women who are not as different from one another as they might appear.

Apart from the fact that the majority of them belonged to the lower classes and worked, the powerful common denominator of these women was their desire to destroy themselves. Indeed, in many cases they succeeded in asserting themselves, refusing to resign themselves to living with a man they no longer loved or one who was making their life together unbearable. In other cases, they rejected an irksome suitor or were unfaithful to their husbands. They dealt blows during domestic quarrels or suddenly left the marital home to lead a different life. All of them demonstrated their strength and their needs individually through their day-to-day resistance to male power, by resolutely fighting to have freedom over their bodies and time for themselves.

Too busy defending themselves daily to contend with financial or emotional difficulties, they were ignorant of the struggles being fought against sexist laws by a handful of feminists.

For working-class women, problems of equality between the sexes were posed in different terms; for, while equality did not exist in law, these women tried to establish it in practice. This freedom was relative, however, especially as it came up against restrictions which were difficult to define, and which varied according to each woman.

Penury was particularly hard to bear during a period when glaring social disparities made the lot of the disadvantaged even harsher. It is difficult to grasp the positive aspects that poverty could offer; indeed, the very suggestion seems improper. And yet, these profiles of women, these 'slices of life' that have been scrutinized in the archive dossiers, differ markedly from the images of working-class women conveyed by the sociologists and humanists of the period, who did their utmost to expose the exploitation of women. A title such as *Les Vierges martyres*[1] made explicit such writers' vision of the lot of working-class women.

These images of women who were oppressed by men, who were the victims and the martyrs of capitalism, and were corrupted by work, were reinforced by Marxist ideology, which asserted that capitalism, far from having emancipated women, had made them slaves to machines and to men. The working-class woman was the 'proletarian man's proletarian woman', doomed to prostitution because of the inadequacy of women's wages. While people like Paul Lafargue or Jules Guesde were demanding the right for women to work and to receive equal pay, the trade unions, which regarded women workers as competition, wanted legislation which, disguised as social protection, would have put women back in the home.

The inhuman working conditions of some workshops, the lack of financial security and the lower wages of women are indisputable, as is also the reality of their fate, which at times was inexorable. The most vulnerable were ready-made candidates for suicide; others did indeed resort to prostitution; and the luckier ones struggled so as not to allow their lives to be determined by fate.

Through these criminal cases, it is possible to examine the means of struggle that these women chose; their way of life forces us to revise the traditional view of working-class misery, as endured by women. It seems difficult to identify these portraits with the negative and depressing images which, whether deliberately or not, have concealed the existence of energetic women, who had their share of pleasure.

These linen maids, these factory workers or charwomen, correct the images of tired sad women, doubled over under the weight of their fate as slaves. There is a need to show that, despite financial constraints, working-class women were able to thwart the snares of male oppression, and to assert themselves in both public and private life by demonstrating their will, their moral strength and their independence. As one reads in the archive dossiers about their daily struggle, their positive and distinctive qualities emerge, namely their freedom in matters of the heart and their sexual freedom, and especially a formidable instinct for survival, which at times was accompanied by a certain warmth and exuberance. This freedom which was so often eradicated, was sometimes described by moralizers who presented it in a degrading light by associating it with vice and licentiousness, which they considered typical of working-class habits.

What distinguished working-class women was the spontaneity of their amorous relationships, which were dependent on chance encounters, and were rarely subject to matrimonial arrangements. Their setting up house with someone did not result in their being alienated; they knew that the emotional and financial ties that bound them to a man could be broken if necessary. This advantage enabled them to establish a relationship of strength and to ensure that some of their rights were respected, even though they might be beaten by their companions. Although they might refer to physical violence to justify breaking up, they did not describe it as a determining factor unless the threshold of tolerance was exceeded. Their inurement to violence was significant.

Their freedom was also reflected by the events and the acts of everyday life. Indeed, they would dine in small restaurants, spend the evening at the wine merchant's or frequent the *cafés-concerts* and public dances without having to account for it, and especially without worrying about their reputation, since there was nothing to reproach them with in their behaviour. It should not be forgotten that this freedom was not the prerogative of single women alone; married women also took advantage of it, without concerning themselves with the possible jealousy of their husbands.

*   *   *

All the observers of the working class have criticized women's low wages which made women financially subservient to men by forcing them on to the path of debauchery — in other words, prostitution. And yet women's wages, which everyone regarded as pin money, gave them sufficient financial independence to allow them to live alone or to provide for the couple for a while. In many cases, they could not rely on the regular income of a husband or common-law husband whose work depended on the seasonal fluctuations of certain jobs, or on the goodwill of a worker who decided to leave his employer if he felt unfairly treated.

With these paltry wages, some women even claimed to support their men. Such was the case with the widow Lagache and her lover, a mechanic. According to a neighbour, 'he worked from time to time when he had something to do; if he didn't have enough it was his fault because he was intelligent'; and since she always saw him lolling around, she assumed that the widow Lagache was supporting her lover.[2]

Financial resources provided, above all, freedom. For the widow Langot, her wages as a charwoman assured her complete independence. Since the death of her husband, this woman had brought up her two daughters single-handed and had no plans to remarry.

Marie Gautré, an ordinary laundress, climbed up the social ladder by marrying a self-employed cabinet-maker. Fed up with being badly treated, and wishing to lead her life as she chose, she preferred insecurity to an unhappy existence. This is how she replied to her husband, who was begging her to return to him:

'Won't you come back?'
'No.'
'You're making a mistake; you'll be unhappy.'

'Oh! Don't you worry about me, just leave me in peace. I'll manage to earn my living.'

'Then it's my life that you'll destroy.'

One of Marie's companions, also a linen-maid, advised her to go back to her husband: 'My child, you may find yourself short of work or fall ill.' 'That might happen', Marie replied, 'both my brother and my father died in hospital, so I too may end up there.' This was a last challenge to destitution which she preferred to face rather than to stay with 'a man who made her unhappy'.[3]

While women could compensate for the lack of their husband's wages for a while, the situation became critical when men threatened to become permanent burdens. This, at least, is one of the reasons most often given by women to explain their decision to leave their partner. To survive, they had to balance their budgets; the slightest problem involving money was enough to make the couple focus on this aspect of their lives together. Each partner expected the other to be able to make a personal contribution and to be able to support him- or herself financially. This mutual expectation explains the attitude of women when they realize that their partner no longer wishes, or is no longer able, to work.

The ubiquitous theme of money was used in the indictment by judges who wished to reduce the crime of passion to a sordid act. Statements such as the following were typical of this mentality: 'You killed because you wanted her money and no longer wished to work.' The point of this approach was to prove the mercenary character of the crime, thereby negating any excuses: the accused had killed not out of despair in love, but because they could not accept a separation that left them without means of support. This motive had the advantage of clarifying the situation by simplifying the complex background of the crime. Thus rationalized, the crime of passion could be more easily understood, and ceased to be a source of fascination. Emotional suffering was then demystified in favour of base material concerns.

To this end, the accused were questioned about their personal means and their expenses, in the hope of finding compromising details. Information on this subject is difficult to make use of and does not tell us how the working-class household was managed and whether it conformed to any specific practices.

Some examples suggest that the role of managing the household was left to women. Victor Parizot adored Anastasie, his mistress, a twenty-eight-year-old married woman who was separated from her husband. The two lovers met at Chagny in Saône-et-Loire. In accordance with Anastasie's desire, they moved to Paris. Victor clearly submitted to Anastasie's wishes: 'I told her that I would follow her everywhere she went and I gave my mistress all the money I earned.' But one day he suddenly decided to return to his home town and to take back his savings. Furious, Anastasie warned him never to try and see her again.[4]

In the Marié couple the wife managed the finances with no concern for her husband's opinion: 'And when I used to ask her what she did with the money which I gave her and the money which she earned, she would reply that she didn't throw it out of the window. I never succeeded in getting her to do any accounts for me.'[5]

In the Langlais case, the betrayed husband trusted his wife implicitly: 'Léonie has been unfaithful to me for a very long time with Langlais; it is a great sorrow to me . . . I have never refused her anything, nor deprived her of anything, not even money for she was always the one who kept the little we had at home.'[6]

Women seemed to value this right to control the household money. In the Gaudot case, a young florist friend of Léontine commented on it to her: 'I urged her to stay with this young man who had a great deal of affection for her and who, unlike many men, gave her everything that he earned.'[7]

* * *

Nineteenth-century society dreamed of women who dedicated themselves body and soul to the admirable task of raising a family. Through their work, humanists, scientists and politicians, who were convinced that the ideal woman's role should be confined to that of being a good wife and an exemplary mother, exalted the virtues and blessings of a happy home ruled by a woman. It was a role that was made to measure for her, and one that suited her nature so perfectly! Middle-class women colluded in this family policy; they applied themselves to being exemplary wives and excelled in their roles of women in the home. Nevertheless, the retreat into domestic life occurred mainly in well-off homes. Working-class women were more resistant to this tendency; the majority did not, in fact, have any choice, since their circumstances were precarious.

Indeed, the reality of the working-class world went against this idealized view of womanhood. Material conditions, far from encouraging these women to stay at home, forced them to spend the greater part of their day outside it and to frequent public places. Their cramped living quarters and the lack of furniture reduced the time they spent on housework; they never complained about being oppressed by their household duties or by looking after their children, who were often entrusted to child-minders until the age of five or six.

Parisian working-class women avoided the domestic slavery of a second day's work by taking advantage of the highly developed network of services offered by tradesmen; the variety of small trades made it possible to meet all one's daily needs. The laundress and the clothes mender took care of the washing; and it was pointless to do one's own sewing since the wardrobe dealer offered second-hand goods that were less expensive. As far as food was concerned, by looking at one of the standard budgets given in books on working-class conditions, one can see that women bought ready-made food or food that required little cooking.

For all these workers, the prospect of spending the evening in a cold and cramped room after a day's hard work was not very appealing. In this restrictive world a hot meal in a small restaurant or at the wine merchant's offered relaxation and escape, to which was added the luxury of being waited upon. The café and the tavern were still not exclusively male territory, and women frequented them freely as habitués, just like men. The expression, 'I went to my wine merchant's', was included in a great many statements and confirmed the role of such a practice. The café acted as a living-room, replacing a second room which was lacking in small lodgings. Although there were *assommoirs* or bars, where you became stupefied with the fumes of alcohol, the café provided, above all, a place for socializing. People went there to relax with their families, as can be seen from the following account:

I went to Perbos's house and found him getting ready to go out with his mistress and his little girl who is six years old. I accompanied them to the rue des Trois-bornes to a pub where we spent the rest of the evening laughing, drinking and singing. Madame Biard, who was very merry, sang, and Perbos accompanied her on the guitar.[8]

One should not jump to the conclusion that the working class did not also aspire to spend the evening in the cosiness and comfort of their own homes. Imprisoned for ill-treating his wife who wanted to leave him, Savary tried to persuade her to stay with him. He wrote to her, praising the attractions of conjugal bliss: 'There's still time; stay at home, I'll work in my trade, and you'll work in yours. When you come home in the evening, you'll find a nice fire to warm you up and a real friend to relax with.'

As he had no reply, he wrote again to reproach her and to recommend establishments which she should frequent:

As you stay at the wine merchant's until ten o'clock at night, you've plenty of time to write me a note. Why do you always go and eat at that wine merchant's where prostitutes go with their pimps? I'd like to see you leading the life of a respectable woman; why don't you go and eat at Dubois's? Then you'd see some good examples.[9]

Working-class women's lack of interest in their home and their lack of eagerness for household duties runs counter to the precepts taught to young middle-class girls. Conscious of this wide gap in behaviour compared with prevailing models, the accused felt implicitly encouraged to play upon this negative aspect to discredit the victims in the eyes of the judges. They would complain, claiming that they did the housework themselves.

These complaints and regrets were legitimized by the ubiquitous praises and urgings to promote women in the home. The working-class man, the workhand, was also entitled to dream of this female ideal. Towards the end of the nineteenth century, working-class men expressed a very clear aspiration towards the marital home based on wife and child, in imitation of the model of the bourgeois family. This tendency towards domestication and moralizing, which was reinforced by employers who were keen for their workforce to be stable, took place initially in large industrial centres. The integration of family life of the Parisian working class proved to be more difficult. The praise of the housewife had still not convinced the majority of wage earners. The itinerant life-styles, the insecurity and the economic activity of women were the main obstacles. It was not until poverty was reduced that it was possible to realize these working-class aspirations, and for these portrayals of the household angel – that reassuring image, bearer of order and symbol of prosperity – to become a reality.

As they were free to wander about town during the day, as well as at night, women wanted to spend their work and leisure hours as they pleased, without being restricted in their movements by an over-inquisitive companion. If they came home later than usual, they did not consider it necessary to give any explanation. Some men criticized their wives' behaviour in front of the judges – for example Poujat, who wanted his wife to respect him: 'She used to stay out very late, several times a week. She talked to me as if I wasn't her husband.'[10]

Madame Breffeil never left the tavern at the same time as her husband and openly declared her independence: 'Instead of leaving so as to be at home with me, she only came back two hours or two-and-a-half hours later. I didn't like it. When I told her so, she replied that she wanted to be her own master.'[11]

Madame Shenk had the same attitude and did not think it necessary to justify the frequency with which she went out:

For ten years she did everything she wanted, making me turn round like a weathercock, and answering me back all the time. On the evening of June 19th, as I could see she was going out despite the rain and was pushing away the child, after helping her prepare dinner as usual, I asked her where she was going. She replied sharply, as was her habit: 'If anyone asks you, say you have no idea.' She came back the next day at eleven o'clock in the morning.[12]

Monsieur Gautré reproached his wife for going dancing and for singing at the glee club: 'She used to go wherever she pleased, I don't know what she did. All I know is that she used to leave the house in a rush and that she stole money from me.' He used to beat her, but she defended herself: one day, two witnesses saw her grab a cooking pot and throw it at her husband's head. At the trial, Monsieur Gautré complained about his wife's nastiness: 'I put it down to her frequent visits to the public wash-house. They said that I was earning money, that you had to enjoy yourself, that if I grumbled I should be sent to bed . . . Ah! I know the nonsense they talk at the wash-house, oh, yes! and at the laundry.'[13]

The wash-house, that specifically female place, aroused the curiosity and mistrust of men. It was not by chance either that female connivance expressed itself precisely in places as symbolical as the laundry or the wash-house, where the private life of each was exposed to the penetrating stare of women who faultlessly interpreted the domestic life of others from their dirty linen. Washing your own linen or someone else's in public provided an opportunity for gossip and allowed one to settle one's accounts. The violence described by Zola in a scene in *L'Assommoir* was not pure fiction. This is testified to by the serious altercation during which Madame Gautré is said to have grossly insulted her mother.

If men proved to be too much of a nuisance, or even if they were jealous, women refused to bow to male authority, and at times freed themselves from these companions who hindered their movements. When Madame Bessières returned home drunk one night, she did not take her husband's comments very well: 'After I had told her off, she left our lodgings and only came back the following morning.'[14]

Léontine, Gaudot's mistress, only ever 'did as she pleased': one evening she went out dancing and only came home the next morning. Gaudot demanded an explanation: 'I want to know where you stayed all night.' And, as he was pressing her for an answer, she replied: 'I was with César; now leave me alone, you know that I don't want to stay with you.'

For the examining magistrate, Léontine's behaviour was simply the result of the bad upbringing which working-class girls received. Brought up in an atmosphere of vice and permissiveness, with bad examples under their eyes, they were necessarily drawn into a life of immorality. The judge showed little surprise at Léontine's infidelities and was contemptuous of Gaudot, criticizing him for going with a girl of such easy virtue: 'What right had you to reproach her for her bad behaviour; you picked her up at a public dance. You should have realized that she would never be a decent girl.'[15]

This behaviour reflected the attitude of the bourgeoisie towards the working class, which they considered to be inferior and beyond redemption.

Julie Marié was annoyed at being watched over by a jealous husband and decided to leave the marital home on 21 March 1876: 'My wife left me three months ago after I reproached her for her behaviour in her parents' presence. She had been coming home late, at about two in the morning, and I demanded to know where she was spending her time.'

In his written statement, he complained about how frequently his wife went out:

I can tell you that for the past year she never came home until eleven o'clock, midnight, one o'clock, and even half-past two on the day of the carnival, and that was two, three or four times a week. And if I ever reprimanded her she would shout loudly, on purpose so as to wake the child, and so that I wouldn't say anything else; for she knew I didn't want to upset our child who loved his mother more than she deserved. One day when I had told her to come back early so as to fetch the child from school, as I had an errand to do after work, well! she came home at one-thirty in the morning and said that she wouldn't bother herself anymore. So I hit her. I think I had the right to do so.

Although the preliminary investigation could not prove it, she was presented as an unfaithful wife, a judgement based only on the repeated accusations of her husband:

I would have preferred her to tell me frankly that she had other men that she liked better than me, rather than to say she was leaving because I treated her badly. She knows better than anyone else that I only hit her once: a slap on the back of her head on the day I told her to come home early to fetch the child from school . . . . Only a wretch would wish me dead in order to be completely free, although she is not at all worried – she even told me before she left that she wanted to be free. But I hope that the information that is collected about me and her will mean that I am set free as soon as possible, as I need to work to bring up my child since she is such a bad mother as to abandon him. But I'll take care of him. When a woman holds her mother and father in contempt, then it is not surprising that she scorns her husband.

A woman who did not submit to the patriarchal order, and who did not even fulfil her duties as a mother – here were edifying arguments to excuse the poor husband and condemn the victim. Another source of discord and exasperation was Madame Marié's refusal to have sexual relations since November 1875; if his wife was to be believed, this was the real cause of the conflict.

Everything went well for eight years, then he contracted a venereal disease and admitted it. For some time I stopped having any relations with him. That was when our rift began, and he claimed that I was the cause of his illness. He accused me of giving it to him. Since I have never had it myself, I urged him to get a doctor to examine me so that it could be established that his accusation was false, but he wouldn't agree to it, claiming that he did not want to be ridiculed.

On 21 March 1876, Madame Marié left her child and went to her parents at Arpajon. When she returned to Paris on 8 April, she rented some lodgings in the rue Puébla under a false name. Her husband managed to find her on 15 June. He tried in vain to persuade her to return to their home, but, faced with her obstinacy, he agreed to write on stamped paper a sort of commitment whereby they granted each other freedom. This was simply a trick on the part of Marié, who was not unaware that this agreement was void: 'If I wrote it on stamped paper it was, on the one hand, because I knew that this agreement was not valid, and on the other hand, because I wanted to test my wife right to the end.'

The significant abstinence of their separation increased Jean's exasperation. Furthermore, the preliminary investigation was unable to prove Jean's presumptions about his wife's infidelity, and it was clearly established that she lived alone after leaving him. On the day of the crime she made her independence very clear:

She told me to my face that she would never come back to me but that she wasn't under a vow of chastity, and that she wanted to be free to do whatever she pleased. That evening she told me, in the presence of Madame Chapuit, the grocer she worked for in the afternoons, that she would have as many other men as she wanted and that it was none of my business.

This was the final provocation which wounded Jean Marié's pride, and made him decide to avenge himself.

Célina Biard was equally determined to maintain her independence, and preferred to go out to work rather than to look after the home. Barbe Perbos, her lover, described her as a woman with a rather lively temperament and a very independent character:

She was flighty and I got involved with her despite the fact that she was extremely fickle [he proved that she was, in fact, having affairs with other lovers]; I would have married her if she had wanted to make our child legitimate, but she didn't want to; she said that she wanted to stay free. She would bring strangers to the house; I had to show three or four of them the door. I did what I could to prevent her from being unfaithful and to keep her at home but she used any opportunity to enjoy herself.

A witness added: 'Célina did not bother about the housework; she did not know how to work; her lover cooked, went to fetch the water and did the shopping.'

Julie and Célina were women of their time, who made the most of their freedom by defying, if need be, their family obligations. Their companions then had to take charge of running the household and looking after the children. In practice, male and female roles were not at all strictly determined according to specific models.

* * *

Sexuality, which was another aspect of female freedom, played a large part in these stories of love and passion. The claim to it, that is to say, the refusal or the desire of one's partner's body, was expressed indirectly in reproaches and grievances. Nevertheless, couples did not attach more importance to this than to other marital conflicts. During the preliminary investigation, the judges dealt with this matter without investing it with indirect implications. Sexuality had not yet supplanted jealousy in the interpretation of criminal motives. However, they never ignored so-called deviant sexuality, namely acts against nature, pornographic material and sexual intercourse before or after the criminal act.

Questioned about their sex life, the protagonists of the drama expressed themselves with a certain amount of modesty, using fairly allusive expressions, such as: 'I got to know her that night', 'I was united with her', 'I became acquainted with her' or 'I had intimate relations with her' – the word 'sexual' was never used.

While nineteenth-century moralists and scientists did their utmost to prove that women felt neither desire nor sexual pleasure, many accounts present us with women who not only denied these statements, but dared to express their appetites and their desiderata. Referring to these women, the neighbours said with restraint that 'they were passionate about men'. Far from being denied, female sexuality asserted itself in the dismal surroundings of the assize courts.

In a working-class environment, seduction followed neither strict social conventions nor moral and economic constraints. Encounters and conquests did not require the same preliminaries as in the middle class, and often occurred in a place as public and anonymous as the street, where women, very much in evidence, had to contend with male solicitation. But the street was not the only place for potential seduction; there were also the *café-concerts*, the theatres and especially the dances where people went to enjoy themselves.

Women went to these dances unaccompanied and allowed themselves to be accosted by the men who took their fancy. Since the period of seduction was not subject to the rules of matrimonial strategies, lovers gave in to the impulse of the moment. And because they did not worry about the cost to their virginity or their reputation, they rarely held back from doing as they wished.

It was common for a man and a woman to have sexual relations on the very day they met, and quite usual for young girls to agree to a rendezvous with boys that they had seen in the street only for a few moments and to form a relationship without waiting for an offer of marriage.

Throughout the Marambat case, the examining magistrate was surprised that Jeanne-Justine should give herself to her lover without having first received a proposal of marriage. Jeanne-Justine Marambat, a pretty young girl of eighteen, who worked as a linen-maid at the Panthéon shop, met an employee called Henri Robert. The journalist writing in *La Gazette des tribunaux* described him as 'a fat boy with a common appearance, but from a good family'. When he was questioned, he stated:

'During the first six months of my time at the Panthéon shop I never had the opportunity to speak to Mademoiselle Marambat. One evening, in October 1874, I met her in the home of one of her friends, Mademoiselle Héloïse Langlois, with whom I sometimes spent the evening and who lived on the same floor as me. That evening, Mademoiselle Langlois happened to go out and left us alone. We had sexual relations just like any other young people.'

'Did Mademoiselle Jeanne give in to you easily?'

'Yes, very.'

'Did you promise to marry her before she gave herself to you?'

'No, sir, never.'

'Did she give in to you out of youthful enthusiasm?'

'Yes, we both succumbed because we got carried away – we suddenly liked each other, and it was impossible to resist.'

Throughout the statement, Justine acknowledged that she gave herself freely to this boy:

'Did you know Mademoiselle Héloïse? Was her room a sort of meeting place for young people?'
'Yes.'
'Did you use to see Robert there?'
'Yes.'
'Did he court you?'
'Yes.'
'And did you not put up much resistance to his advances?'
'No.'
'And you gave in to him?'
'Yes.'
'Did he promise to marry you at that moment?'
'No, sir, that was later.'
'And thus you were both carried away?'
'Yes.'
'Without any special promise or agreement.'
'Yes.'
'Did you use to go to his room in the rue Boutebrie?'
'Yes.'
'You even spent the night there?'
'Yes.'
'Often?'
'Three times.'

In July 1875, on discovering that she was pregnant, she told Henri Robert, but he strongly denied paternity: 'That's false', he said. 'When she told me that she was pregnant, I did not believe her since I had taken every precaution so that it wouldn't happen as a result of my behaviour.' (There were murmurs of indignation in the courtroom, and several ladies covered their faces.) Henri Robert accused Justine of being a girl of easy virtue. According to him, she agreed to meet a certain Buyzat, the son of Monsieur Marambat's employer, in a carriage and apparently 'gave herself to him'.

Jeanne-Justine's version was very different: 'I agreed to go for a ride with him in a coach once, but I did not allow him to do what he wanted and I did not give in to him.' The judge added:

Monsieur Buyzat's statement does, indeed, correspond to your statement. He acknowledges that you refused to grant him your last favours. You must admit, however, that it was more than imprudent to go for a ride in the evening in a closed coach with a young man whom you should have assumed was forward – you were exposing yourself to grave danger.

Hackney coaches and private dining-rooms in restaurants offered very useful refuges for lovers. Thus Monsieur Pourcher, who did not wish to be seen by his wife, met his mistress in coaches.[16]

*   *   *

As they were free to love, women required men to fulfil their conjugal duties, and they did not hesitate to openly express their dissatisfaction. Mélanie Lerondeau told the judge who wanted to know why she was not sleeping with her husband: 'If he wasn't sleeping in my room it was because he didn't want to. If he hadn't distanced himself from me, I wouldn't have asked him for so many explanations; but he didn't care about his wife.' She later added: 'My husband wasn't a womanizer.' During a second cross-examination, she accused him of neglecting her: 'I was always calling him a coward and an idler who abandoned his wife all day without worrying about her getting bored.' Mélanie confided in a witness and complained about her husband's indifference: 'That pig, it's three months now since he last touched me.' She apparently even said that if she had to remarry she would choose a young man.

During the trial, several people confirmed these statements. First, there was police sergeant Gaubillart: 'She complained that her husband was not amorous enough with her.' Monsieur Guilpin, a close friend of the couple, took the side of the neglected wife:

I know the Lerondeau household well and it wasn't a happy household. I think I guessed the reason for this rift. One day when I came to their house, they must have been arguing because I heard Madame Lerondeau saying: 'That bastard, he's neglecting me!' I even felt it was my duty to make a comment about this to him, and I said: 'It's clear that you are behaving badly towards your wife. You're wrong to do this, as she often goes to Versailles, and she could easily find elsewhere what she doesn't find at home. You would be to blame if that happened.' But he didn't like this topic of conversation and I never mentioned it again.

During the trial, when the judge revealed these confidences, Mélanie Lerondeau was rather embarrassed, and denied speaking publicly about her sexual problems. 'You would have liked a younger husband. Did you not use to reproach him for not fulfilling his conjugal duty as often as he should have?' (The accused woman lowered her head.) 'Yes, but I only said so to him.'[17]

Louise Mellet also asserted her right to pleasure. In revenge for being badly treated by her lover, Auguste Vallaud, she taunted him about his sexual impotence. After leaving Vallaud, Louise set up house with another man, François Cherrier, whom she met at the wine merchant's. Auguste Vallaud, however, wanted to force her to come back to him. One morning, he managed to get into her house, and, after an argument, he plunged a knife into her throat.

He explained his act by referring to the victim's provocative attitude. 'You stabbed her in the throat with a knife?'

I only picked up the knife after she insulted me. She told me she had had a lovely night and that she preferred to stay with Cherrier rather than to go with me, as my natural instincts have failed for the past year because I suffer from bronchitis. This insult made me lose control. . . . I was frantic with pain, my lover refused to come with me.

(Auguste Vallaud forgot to describe Louise's financial generosity towards him; as for this 'young loafer', as he was called by a journalist, Louise's departure put an end to this financial support.)[18]

Women did not always express their amorous demands with such sudden brutality. Some criticized through hints only. Anastasie Faudot, for example, got on well with Victor Parizot, and yet: 'I cannot say I had any complaints about him all the time we were living together but I did sometimes reproach him for not showing enough interest.'[19] Others contented themselves simply with making allusions. Thus, when Bessières still had his baker's shop, he overheard a conversation between his wife and the maid about a young man who often passed by the shop and appeared to look at the baker's wife. Madame Bessières apparently said: 'When you get one like that, it's better than having a baker.'[20]

Submission and passivity, images that were all too often associated with women's sexuality, were belied by those women who refused to acquiesce to men's sexual demands. In the face of threats and the repeated supplications of their lovers or husbands, they resisted by fiercely defending their sexual freedom.

During an argument, the widow Biard insulted her common-law husband and said to him: 'You filthy swine, I'd rather die than sleep with a pig like you. I'll take you for a ride all the time, I don't give a damn about you.'[21]

In a written statement to the examining magistrate, Barbot displayed the cunning that was traditionally associated with wives wanting to reject the sexual demands of their husbands:

Apart from her indifference, I mean her obvious coolness, many times while I was lying beside her at night, I caught her touching herself indecently after having rejected my most persistent entreaties, on the pretext of some indisposition. Indeed, she rarely neglected to feign illness as she went to bed each evening, without however, losing her excellent appetite and her very regular sleeping habits.[22]

Among the reasons given for avoiding one's conjugal duty, the fear of contracting a venereal disease or getting pregnant were the most often mentioned.

While she was waiting to be officially separated from her husband, Madame Guillot slept in a separate room under the pretext of wanting to avoid a pregnancy:

I returned from Auxerre on October 1st. I found my house in the greatest disorder; everyone was master and doing as they pleased. My wife had forbidden the clerks to obey me. She was enjoying herself with Monsieur Boulet and she hid from me. I had forbidden her to go into the clerks' room, but she didn't listen. She and her mother only thought of creating a scene and arguing with me every day. So for about four months she slept with her mother, saying that she did not want to have any children. . . . Her uncle had for a long time told her to break off with me and to collect as much money as possible, and that once she was separated from me he would restore her in his name. I started to reorganize my house again, and there were always scenes with those three who said they would have me sent to the furthermost part of Brittany or to the Pyrenees so that I would never return. I said to her: 'You don't fling your arms around my neck like you do with your uncle.' She answered: 'I'd like a husband like him!' Her mother didn't want her to sleep with me.[23]

Men did not always dare publicly admit that they had been rejected by women; like Alexis Kemps, they preferred to remain silent of the subject of this rebuff which they interpreted as an insult and a rejection. Witnesses spoke for them: 'She did not want to have relations with her husband; I don't know what her reasons were, but it was a source of argument between them. He would hit her and she would hit back.'[24] Shortly before committing his crime, Alphonse Dupont wrote a letter to his parents explaining his motives: 'The idea of death came into my head the day she refused to kiss me goodnight as well as refusing to sleep with me.' Like Alphonse Dupont, many of the accused had resorted to writing down these rejections.[25]

Portraits of Women

The desire to improve the lot of women has, all too often, given rise to pictures of miserable, at times caricatured, living conditions. This approach, although it can be justified, has neglected the positive aspect of women's lives and, concentrating on their political struggles, has ignored their endeavours to be independent. According to these exaggerated descriptions of misery, the lot of working-class women was rooted in fear; but this seriously underestimates their potential energy to survive and to enjoy life. By looking at the details of their daily lives and examining the individual history of each woman, their tenacious resistance to different forms of oppression emerges. They refused to be disheartened and, on the contrary, asserted themselves and found ways of being happy despite the gloominess of their lives which were fraught with difficulty.

Like many other young girls faced with the harsh realities of life, Léontine Puthomme had to look after herself from a very early age. After the death of her mother when she was five years old, she was sent to a religious institution. When she was old enough to work, the nuns found her a situation as a maid. At the age of fifteen, all that Léontine retained of her childhood was a carefree attitude and a desire to enjoy herself. She met Charles Gaudot at a dance and became his mistress; the young couple at once set up house together. Léontine, however, had not made a vow of fidelity. She betrayed her lover and went to public dances, which made Charles jealous. In a long statement to the examining magistrate, he told his story:

I left home at the age of fourteen and since then I have worked every day of my life to support myself. I let myself get carried away like all the youth of Paris, and I met Léontine Puthomme at a dance, when I was eighteen. This proved to be a fatal meeting, for after speaking to her for a short while, I did what I wanted with her. As I could already see that she was lost, I wanted to bring her back to the straight and narrow, by asking her if she wanted to live with me, and she accepted without hesitation. This was when I advised her to give up the kind of life she was leading, and told her that a change in her life-style could only be for the better. She promised me this, and it was on the basis of this agreement that we started living together. She even told me that she would be only too happy to do so, as she didn't like the life of dissipation she was leading at that time. The day after we set up house together, I dressed her from head to foot. She was happy and I thought I had made an extraordinary conquest. But, unfortunately, shortly afterwards, a great change came over her. She was possessed by one of the seven deadly sins – laziness – and on several occasions, I had to do her housework. For a while I didn't say much about it, because I thought it must be a leftover from her bad conduct and that she might succeed in getting rid of it. Unfortunately this didn't happen; on the contrary, I saw that not only was she lazy, she was also dirty and greedy. I reprimanded her every day; she took no notice, and, since I loved her, I overlooked all this. She took advantage and, as she could see that I never said anything, she started to run around again. Since I was at work all day I didn't notice anything, and she used all the tricks she could to conceal her odious behaviour.

Two months later, she was unable to hide her behaviour any longer as she had caught a venereal disease. So I told her to get treatment for it, and, as her disease got increasingly worse, she was obliged to go into hospital at Lourcine where she was admitted as an emergency case.

After about eight days in hospital she sent me a letter saying that she was pregnant, and that she was convinced that motherhood would make her behave herself. . . .

She stayed in hospital for about a month and then came home. She behaved herself for about a month, until one day she decided to stay out all night. I severely reprimanded her for this the next day when she came in; she told me that she had slept at the house of one of her women friends. I suspected that she was lying, but I thought of the child she was carrying, and I turned a blind eye, wanting to do my duty right up to the end. She contracted another venereal disease on about December 27th 1877 and went into the Saint-Louis hospital again, and as I had caught the same disease I had to spend a month in the Midi hospital.

In April, Léontine gave birth to a boy, to Charles's great pride.

I loved that child with all my heart. She didn't feel the same way as I did, for shortly afterwards she realized that she was no longer free to enjoy herself, and she even stooped to hitting him, something that upset me terribly.

Then, in November, I told her – out of pity for the child and out of anger with her – that there are places where you could put a child if he was a nuisance. She didn't reply and the next day I went off to work; I came in at midday to eat. She was there with the child, and in the evening I came back from work and found her looking unconcerned, and I noticed that the child had disappeared. She owned up to me, and then I understood that she was going to start a new life. As there was nothing I could do I left her to do as she pleased. I even contained my anger because of the love I bore that child.

The day after she had taken the child to a home for foundlings, she went to a dance while I was out. I went to find her as I knew where she would be. I saw her in the company of a young man, and begged her to leave. She said that she was only my mistress and that she was free; at midnight I went home. She only came back to me the day after I had seen her with that man. She admitted that she had had a good time and that she couldn't bear it any longer. As she was hungry I went out to get her some food. I felt sorry for her until she had eaten. Then I lost my temper and I slapped her a few times; but I had never hit her before.

And so, Monsieur, you can see that I could no longer suffer this existence because of her life of debauchery. And as I couldn't bear to see her prostituting herself before my very eyes, I made up my mind to do the deed of which I now stand accused.

Although the self-satisfaction with which he described himself did not fool anyone, it does not detract from the validity of this statement attesting to the independence of women.

Many statements confirmed that Léontine's behaviour was very loose, but because of her age no one blamed her, except for Charles Gaudot, who was so jealous that he eventually poisoned his mistress using a very peculiar method.

Gaudot left the workshop every day to check whether his mistress had gone out. Léontine would outwit him and, accompanied by her friend Elisa, she would go to the café or to a dance. On 7 December 1878, the day the crime took place, she went to Elisa's house and told her: 'You know, Charles doesn't want me to go out; come and see me.' They sat and drank coffee; the landlord even heard them laughing and singing. At midday, Gaudot came in and again forbade her to go out. Ignoring his warning, the women went out for a walk, and they met two young men who invited them to go to a *brasserie*. Meanwhile, Gaudot returned home and, finding Léontine not there, cooled his heels on the doorstep. Léontine turned up at about five o'clock, in the company of the two young men, 'whose familiar and licentious manner were proof that they had obtained the favours which permitted such behaviour' (quoted from *L'Evénement*). Gaudot grabbed hold of her roughly, but she refused to go with him. Eventually he managed to persuade her to go upstairs with him. On the landing he slapped her. Gaudot admitted: 'I slapped her again and again. She didn't defend herself, she just kept calling me a coward, then she uttered the word "bastard". I kicked her on her left breast and in the stomach.'

He forced her to get undressed and to get into bed. She was at the end of her tether and shouted out: 'I'd rather die than suffer like this; if I had some poison, I would take it at once.' 'That's no problem,' replied Gaudot, 'I'll go and get you some. It will make you, as well as other people, happy; we won't have to watch you prostituting yourself anymore.'

He immediately went to a nearby paint shop, bought some copper arsenate, and went back home. He dissolved the poison in a glass of sweetened water and gave it to Léontine: 'Here, drink this; I can promise you that in an hour your suffering will be over.' In a final act of defiance, Léontine swallowed the poisoned drink in one go: 'I drank the poison of my own free will – I would be lying if I were to say the opposite. But I was so unhappy that I preferred to die – it was hellish in that house.'

Did she really wish to kill herself?

After a short while, Léontine started to feel the effect of the poison: 'When I told him that I was in great pain, and that he must help me, not only did he do nothing but he mocked me. He even said some words which I haven't the courage to repeat. He didn't stop insulting me and laughing at my suffering.' Gaudot prepared a second glass for her, but she refused to drink it. Léontine understood the implications of her response – she did not want to die. She complained: 'My head is spinning, my heart feels weak, I can feel myself dying. I'd like to write to my father, he's the only person I want to see.'

Her father was to refuse to see her. Ever since Léontine had left home, her relatives had behaved as if she did not exist any more. Gaudot went out to take the letter, after first taking the precaution of throwing his mistress's clothes on to a nearby roof so that she could not leave. Léontine pleaded: 'I can feel myself dying, don't go – I want someone to at least be by my side.'

On his way out, Gaudot asked the landlord not to let anyone go upstairs to see Léontine – in particular, not to allow a young girl in who was corrupting her. He then went to see Léontine's father and told him that his daughter was ill;

Gaudot gave him her letter but he refused to read it, saying that he had given up his daughter as lost, and that it would be a good thing if she were to die.

Meanwhile, Léontine managed to call for help. The landlord, who had heard some shouts, went upstairs and warned her that she could no longer stay there and that he did not want to see her any more. A neighbour lent her some underclothes and she got dressed and went to Elisa's house. It was not until the following morning that she was taken to the Lariboisière hospital, where, despite all the treatment she received, she died five days later. The members of the jury allowed extenuating circumstances for Gaudot, this twenty-year-old criminal, and sentenced him to eight years' hard labour in 1879.

*   *   *

The Shenk case is the story of a married woman who neglected her duties as a wife; she did not care what people thought, and left the marital home whenever she felt like it to be with her lovers. In 1862, Marie-Françoise, a seamstress, met François Shenk who worked as a carpenter. He was twenty-six and she was nineteen. Marie-Françoise moved out of her sister's house and in with her lover. A year later, she gave birth to a boy. It was not until 1868 that they decided to get married.

François Shenk had an excellent reputation; the bill of indictment presented him as a very sober, steady and thrifty worker who had always fulfilled his duty, apart from his attempt to murder his wife. Indeed, he was accused of buying a larding needle 'to run his wife through', because her lover used to come and see her while Shenk was at work.

According to François Shenk, Marie-Françoise had always misbehaved. In his statement he portrayed himself as the martyred husband of an overbearing woman who was lazy and debauched and did not run the home properly. A number of statements supporting Shenk confirmed the truth of his grievances: 'Her husband often came in to find his dinner wasn't ready.' Françoise was also a bad mother: 'When she gave birth there wasn't a rag in the house for the baby.' Far more serious was the fact that Marie-Françoise was, in the words of her own parents, 'mad about men'. This was a subject to which her husband could testify. He reminded the judge that when he had met Marie-Françoise she was having an affair with her brother-in-law:

The previous year, my wife had had unlawful relations with her brother-in-law for six months, unbeknown to her sister (while she was out shopping). They were caught *in flagrante delicto* and the husband was even sent to prison.

In 1864 she slept with the fifty-two-year-old Monsieur Moyen, while his wife was at the wash-house. In 1866 she went to stay at her father's house for a while with our child. After being away for two months she wrote and told me that she was going to marry her lover from that village. I went there immediately to take my child out of her clutches; I found him naked in the street while she was wandering about the town with her lover. I brought our child back to Paris; she

131

didn't want to see him before leaving. Finally, after her father had threatened her, she came back ten days later.

She always wanted to have her way and I had to give in to get some peace and quiet; from that time onwards everything was just about all right, apart from a few little arguments. In 1870 she forced me to leave my lodgings in the rue Sabat. . . . In 1871 she came back to my father-in-law's house every night at eleven o'clock. On the eve of my return to Paris she told me that she wanted to stay for a few days longer than me, under the pretext of keeping her father company. For three months she wrote me letters full of nonsense whenever I told her to come home.

On her return I gave her 300 francs which were my savings from work. Several days later she told a neighbour that if her lover from home came to Paris she wouldn't be responsible for her behaviour. . . .

[In April 1872 she had a new lover.] My wife, who has always taken advantage of my work and my weakness, took advantage of my absences to have unlawful relations, even in my home, with a man by the name of Bigon, the greatest scoundrel around; people should be warned about his constant double-dealing and thieving. I met this man on about the 9th or 10th June and I was still unaware that they were having relations.

While I was out at work, Bigon would come and spend part of the day in the house and my wife would then send the child out, saying: 'Stay out until six o'clock or else you'll get a beating' – this was the time when her lover left, just as I was returning. He would come back while I was there; they even made me go to a dance with them. He was living in the hotel in the rue Constance. . . . On June 19th, my wife spent the night in the hotel and left me to worry about the child. She came back the next day at eleven o'clock thinking I was at work. She had bought some stewing meat for me and some steak for herself. I questioned her and she eventually told me that she had slept at the hotel, since I had bolted the door – we didn't argue at all.

In the evening, I helped her to prepare dinner as I always did when I got back from work. Immediately afterwards, she got ready to go out and, contrary to her usual custom, she did not want the child to go out with her, supposedly because he was not behaving himself. The following day at three o'clock in the afternoon, she went out. I followed her and saw her meeting her lover at the hotel where she stayed for five days without returning home. I lodged a complaint with the Public Prosecutor. After six days the police commissioner sent for me to discuss this matter. I told him that my wife had come home the previous evening.

On June 24th, when she returned after six days, I forgave her everything as she told me that she would behave well in future, but the next day she sent all her possessions, and some of mine, as well as some of our private papers, to Madame Charron's house where she stayed for three weeks.

On Sunday August 4th, when I left work, I went to 24 rue de Maistre, where I had placed my child as a boarder with Madame Thénot while his mother was away; I wanted him to go to the school his mother had taken him away from three months before. I was taking care of the child's needs, and all I received were reproaches which were really nasty lies.

I saw my wife's lover in the street and followed him to Montholon Square where my wife had arranged to meet him and where she was waiting. I followed them and then lost them from sight. I was so overwhelmed with jealousy and grief that I no longer knew myself and I took leave of my senses. The following day, I was out of my mind and I drank a few glasses of wine – this is something I never do as I can't tolerate alcohol – and I apparently stabbed my wife several times with a knife, but fortunately it did no real damage. I have been told that she is all right.

On 5 August 1872, after obtaining a larding knife, François Shenk went to the Charron couple's house, and in their presence, he stabbed his wife eight times with his knife.

My wife was the happiest of all the workers in Montmartre in every respect; she could drink, eat, and come and go and do as she pleased. I used to give her my entire wages, between 130 and 140 francs, every month, and she squandered it, lent it and generally wasted it, she was so unselfish! Then our household would suffer while I was struggling to work and did not dare spend a single penny unless it was necessary.

Due to my wife's negligence, the house was in the greatest disorder. She would spend half the day and night reading history books, novels and Republican newspapers. She would copy out songs which she taught our child and which he now sings very well, instead of getting him to do his homework. While his mother was reading cards, our child did the washing-up and ran all the household errands, doing everything from memory or from his mother's written instructions.

So as to have a bit of peace and quiet, I was forced to put her completely in charge of the house. She treated me like a bear, and made me eat potatoes and beans while she ate red meat and eggs. She would push me to the limit and at times she provoked me to get into arguments and then I was obliged to tell her off very fairly, but to no avail. I got a lot of satisfaction out of my work as a carpenter. I used every means I could to avoid the disturbances which my wife caused and to bring her back to her senses by being kind to her.

On the day of the crime, she could see that I had taken leave of my senses and that I was completely out of my mind. . . . My intention was to scare them so that they should no longer deny everything, or to catch them *in flagrante delicto*. My wife can confirm that she gave me every reason to do what I did, and I can even say with certainty that, since these orgies were taking place before my very eyes, if I hadn't acted she would have considered it cowardly of me to tolerate her debauchery.[26]

133

Women, it would seem, face up to the facts. They are brave and remain so right until the end; they accept situations where there is conflict, without being afraid of setting up a relationship which in certain cases can become dangerous. As they are accustomed to looking after themselves as their circumstances change, they are more capable of resolutely defying male authority when their happiness or their lives depend on it. These women are perceived as dangerous and responsible for creating disturbances. They behave as it suits them; 'they want to be their own masters', and they come and go as it pleases them. They are a source of irritation for the judges who pronounce harsh verdicts and pass severe sentences on them, for they consider them responsible for instigating crimes.

The Freedom of Middle-Class Women

When the rich negotiated a marriage, love often took second place. The two parties involved were essentially looking for an equitable relationship which would guarantee that the family name and inheritance were passed on. In marriages for money or marriages of convenience, men willingly adapted to this situation as they knew that they could easily have extra-marital relations and that there would be no obstacles to prevent them from engaging in venal love or from having adulterous relationships. The same did not hold true for their wives, who had to sacrifice their lives so as to ensure peace and quiet and preserve the happiness of the family. Some, who were less high-principled, allowed themselves to be tempted by secret love affairs. Their faces hidden behind their veils, these unfaithful women went to their love trysts. In contrast to their husbands, who could flaunt themselves with impunity in the fashionable drawing rooms of coquettes or in the private rooms of restaurants, women had to constantly be on their guard and to behave discreetly so as to avoid a scandal. Nineteenth-century society severely censured female adultery, and many women paid dearly for having tasted this forbidden fruit.

In order to punish them, their outraged husbands did not always turn to the law, for fear of compromising their family honour; they preferred to banish their guilty wives to rest homes. Some women did in fact have to endure the odious revenge of unscrupulous husbands who, to humiliate them, made them suffer the indignity of establishing circumstances of *flagrante delicto*.

Fortunately, few women experienced the tragic fate of Denise Dubourg and Alexandrine Duc, whose confessions confirm the restrictions imposed on young middle-class women who did not enjoy complete freedom as they were constantly being watched. Socially, they had to look like paragons of virtue and honour. Their behaviour had to be exemplary. Their upbringing made them conscious of the role with which they were invested. If they successfully carried out the duties assigned to them, then society would honour them; otherwise, they would be censured. They were housewives and ruled supreme over their households, over their children and over their servants. When they went out they followed strict social conventions; they never lingered long, since street-life was alien to them and certain areas forbidden; there were also some public places where they could not go alone.

They were placed under the financial protection of their husbands, and were thus materially dependent on their goodwill. This dependency meant, in essence, that they were unable to leave the marital home or to make a request for legal separation, either because their husbands would not agree to it for fear of jeopardizing their reputation, or because they, as wives, could not face being condemned both by their family and by society. Such was the case of Denise, who was the 'heroine of the rue des Ecoles' and the victim of a jealous husband and sexist laws.

Like all young upper middle-class girls, Denise Dubourg received an excellent education in a convent, which was the institution best suited for protecting the virginity and innocence of these young ladies, while also developing their talents. When they reached a suitable age for marriage, they were sent back to the family home where they were exhibited in the drawing-rooms of the capital with the aim of finding a husband. During one of these society gatherings Denise met Monsieur de Précorbin. A romance began between these two young people, but there was no hope of their getting married since this young man, who worked at the prefecture of the Seine, had no private means and no prospect of a brilliant career.

In 1869 Denise married Arthur Dubourg, a twenty-nine-year-old man of independent means: 'The marriage was arranged very quickly by a friend of the family.' On the day of the trial, the judge commented on this:

Your marriage, like many marriages, was arranged very quickly; the negotiations took place in the space of a fortnight. On the eve of the wedding, your wife was so uncertain that her aunt, Madame Fourrichon, told her: 'There's still time to refuse if you're unhappy about the marriage.'

She finally agreed to marry him. The newlyweds left Paris and moved into the castle of Launay, near Courtomer, with Dubourg's father. Denise experienced her first disappointment as she bitterly learnt the meaning of conjugal duties. Several months later she wrote to her husband to ask for a separation:

Arthur,

What I am now writing is forcing tears from me and they are the bitterest tears which a woman ever shed. But I cannot bear it any longer; the day I gave you my hand I also sincerely hoped that one day I might give you my heart, but as time goes by life becomes increasingly difficult for me. Married life is hell when one doesn't get on, when the slightest thing causes arguments and creates a scandal and, therefore, suffering. You have always been good to me and suffer on account of my character – in a word, your life is a misery when it is united with mine. So . . . it's hard, but if you still love me, if you do not wish my downfall – my head is racing so much that I would be capable of anything – then let me live alone, honourably. My education and my principles will serve as a guarantee that I shall do so.

Let us part, Arthur, for hatred grows from contempt. Let us part with no ill feelings and let us live far from one another. Misfortune may remain with us, but it is better to suffer alone than together.

If you still think of God while you are thinking of me, then ask Him to remove from the earth the woman who has caused you so much unhappiness, and you will forgive me, won't you?

My life and my death depend on you. You are free!

Denise

A few more words. Arthur, I swear that I have made a terrible decision; if you do not want your name to be for ever ruined, then, for the sake of the friendship which you have shown me, do not let there be a scandal. Allow me to live alone and apart for ever.

Denise's husband did not share this view and refused to agree to a separation. The young woman tried to resign herself to the situation. As a distraction, they went to Paris for a brief stay. On her return to Normandy, Denise wrote a moving letter to a female friend where she described her aversion to her husband and contemplated her future with sadness.

Launay. Saturday, November 27th 1869

To my dear and true friend,

My return to Launay was silent. I preferred to keep quiet rather than speak with a heart overburdened with grief. Yes, what a life I lead! Everyone thinks me happy and yet my heart is shattered!

At the age of twenty-one, an age when one should be happy about everything in life and when one feels the need for affection, I am forced to say: 'No, there is nothing more for me, my future is over, all that remains is for me to run away or to weep every day because I am not in love.'

As I have spoken frankly to you, dear Madame, as well as to Monsieur X . . . , I will continue to do so. Why shatter everything when one is calm; the storm will start again before long, I prefer to wait for it and to avoid it if I can. This is what we have agreed: to see each other only at meal-times and when it is absolutely necessary. My husband hunts in the daytime; as for me, do I not have my room where, beside a good fire, I can read and write, work and cry! In the evening I play whist or a game of *écarté* with my father-in-law, and then my bedroom closes in upon me and my sadness, and opens only when I go downstairs for breakfast.

Perhaps I shall manage to live like this for a while. It's sad, I admit it, but I cannot say any more. I am sorry to think that I am making someone with a kind heart unhappy, for he is loyal and loves me. I have nothing to reproach him with, but what can I do? I have an aversion that I cannot overcome and above all he repels me strongly – this is the cause of my unhappiness.

Forgive me, dear Madame, for having importuned you so much with my grief. I only ask for a friend's advice that will serve me well.

With gratitude and affection for you and Monsieur X.

Denise

In 1870, during a trip to Switzerland, Denise was confined to a nursing home on the pretext of a nervous illness. As regards her stay there, Arthur Dubourg refused to give any explanations to the judge:

'Tell us what happened in Geneva.'

'I would like to dispense with that explanation. Please allow me to remain silent.'

'That's impossible; we need to know everything. What is required here is not silence, but the whole truth. But if you do not speak, I have documents here which will speak for you. They are two telegrams sent to your father and to your father-in-law. "Come quick," they say, "do not waste a moment, for the honour of the family is at stake."'

'Those telegrams were not sent by me, but by a doctor.'

'One of your friends' doctors?'

'I said a doctor.'

'Well, that is a word that requires some explanations which you will not give? You see that you must talk. Was your wife ill, then?'

'After a series of arguments she was suffering from a nervous complaint.'

'A nervous complaint? Does that justify the words: "The honour of the family is at stake"?'

'I can say no more, Sir. Spare me.'

'I would like to, but we must know the truth, however painful it is. Your wife must have been in a position . . . '

'I beg you, let me respect her memory.'

'I would like to. Nothing would please me more, but how can a verdict be pronounced if we are not enlightened on this matter?'

'It is impossible for me to explain further.'

'Well! The members of the jury will take note. They will make an effort to understand the implications of this case. Once your father and your wife's father were in Geneva, a doctor was consulted after which your wife was put into a nursing home.'

Madame de Boos, in whom Denise confided, provided some information on this subject: 'She confessed to me that she had other lovers in Switzerland and that her husband found out and forgave her.' The jury had to content itself with these unsatisfactory revelations; Denise's unfaithfulness did not explain the accused's deranged silence.

When she recovered, Denise left the rest home. The couple remained in Switzerland for a while until the Franco-Prussian War broke out. Arthur left behind his wife, who was pregnant, and went back to France to serve his country as a militia captain. Was it her pregnancy, or the distance, or perhaps the rest home, that suddenly transformed Denise's feelings for her husband? If one were to judge from the letters which she wrote to him, their marital relations would seem to have been fairly good:

Oh! Come! Come! out of love for me, come and kiss me if you are able to do so without risk. My poor friend, come! I await you. Your letter upset me terribly, and to think that my letter, which was written in a moment of sadness, was responsible! I regret it so much and would burn it if I could! Forgive me, I was so ill! I was so unhappy!

I shall be in despair if a word of affection from me doesn't reach you before you leave; I shall also write the same words to you in Paris and in Launay. For pity's sake, my dear friend, do not expose yourself to danger. What would become of me if something awful were to happen to you? I am sobbing as I write this! What would become of me? If that were to happen I would never go back to my family. Here I am, three or four months pregnant. Where will it end? The war will decide! Goodbye, my dearest beloved, forgive me! Love me with all your soul, for I love you, I love you! For pity's sake, write to me, or you will kill me! My poor friend, don't be angry with the one whose tears used to make you forget everything. Tell Villiers anything you like, but you know, my darling, that I cannot go there.

Affectionately, your poor Denise

Here is her husband's reply:

(*To be opened after my death*)

My dear Denise,

I am writing these lines to you, perhaps the last, with death in my heart: I have not heard from you and you may never hear from me again. I won't say that I have any forebodings; I don't believe in them anymore ever since I heard yours.

I thought at first that it was childish nonsense; you persisted, it was an obsession! You will not die when you give birth to your child; you will live for him. I want you to, I don't say for me, for I do not know whether it will help me, but you owe it to my family, who had only me. You will do what you must to make them happy. You will gain great satisfaction from fulfilling your duty. You must never leave them. You must always remain at Launay.

I hope, if this is also your wish, that you will find someone who is worthy of you and who will protect your child. Maybe we will be together again one day and then I will thank you for having carried out my last wishes.

138

By giving you everything that I can, I am speaking from my heart which has always belonged to you, and I am also giving you my blessing and complete forgiveness. Be resolute and good. Remember that one partner must make demands on the other in order to be happy. Do not be angry with me if I have hurt you in any way; I certainly never meant to. Do not ever hold any grudges towards your family who loves you so much. Make all the people who will be around you happy, and remember your Arthur's last kiss.

This letter, or rather this will, was meant to be an authoritative statement on the duties of women.

In March 1871 Denise returned to France to give birth and fell ill immediately afterwards. The couple went to stay in Paris at the house of a friend, Madame de Boos, so that Denise could rest and get medical advice. The arguing began again; Denise reproached her husband for coming in late at night and was adamant that she would not go back to live at Launay.

She was eager for her husband to go into business and make a position for himself in the capital, since their private income was not enough to allow them to settle in Paris. But Arthur had no intention of working; in despair, Denise tried to instigate separation proceedings. Arthur contacted a solicitor and, on his advice, he refused under the pretext of avoiding a scandal. During the same period, Denise happened to meet her first lover, Monsieur de Précorbin again.

The similarity between the fate of Denise and that of Alexandrine Duc is striking. Apart from suffering marital disappointments, the two young women were both faced with refusal when they attempted to reclaim their freedom. They were forced to endure married life and were unlucky enough to be the victims of jealous husbands.

It should be borne in mind that François Duc married one of his patients, without taking into consideration the age difference between them. He worked all day and was also absent in the evenings; he neglected his young wife who got bored in their flat in the rue Ticquetonne with her two children.

I married Monsieur Duc in 1860; I was young, barely eighteen, and I needed a husband who could look after me far more than he did. Although he was a married man, he did not give up his bachelor habits and left me to spend every evening alone at home. He seldom went out anywhere with me. We had two children; they provided me with an occupation and a support in my home, and I was thus able to forget the lack of attention which my husband paid me.

During the first twelve years of my marriage, I devoted my life to my children and to running the house. But you will understand that I wasn't getting the love that my husband should have given me, and gradually, the affection and devotion that I had had for him faded.

About a year ago I admit that I neglected my duties as a wife and had intimate relations with a young man whose name I do not have to mention; the letter and the note which you have just shown me were written to him by me.

The young man in question was Léon Renaud. They had met one another in the street: 'I noticed her and followed her, as young people do. I spoke to her and she allowed me to go back to her house with her. She became my mistress, but she never came to my house. I went to see her either between ten and eleven o'clock in the morning, or at nine o'clock in the evening.'

The letter referred to in Alexandrine's statement is evidence of her happiness. Without inhibition she gave free rein to her amorous passion:

My darling,

Yesterday evening, the first this week that I had gone without seeing you, was pretty dismal. Well, this morning, after a restless night, I hoped that seeing you would make me feel better. But nothing of the sort happened; I didn't see my darling child. That is why at this moment I am so restless. In a word, as I am very bored and I won't see you again tonight, I want to tell you this: 'You are a beautiful baby that I love will all my heart, just as I did yesterday and will do so forever.' I wish you could be here with me so that I could eat you a little.

You know, at the moment, I have a mad desire to kiss you which makes me shiver with pleasure all over, as I told you one evening. If you were here in my arms, just imagine what I'd put you through!

I'm still wondering why I didn't see you this morning. I stayed by the window until nine thirty. As you told me one day that the rain sent you to sleep I thought that you had let yourself be lulled for a while longer, and then you didn't turn up after all. Anyway, I'll find out what happened tomorrow evening, that is on Saturday – Oh, how long the word 'tomorrow' sounds. I'd rather write straightaway or else constantly; it would make me happier.

Goodbye, my beloved child. I am giving you a thousand kisses on your darling mouth.

Your very own Alexandrine

P.S. I'm so happy that I have you and can think of you; otherwise my house would be unbearable at the moment. Everyone is in a bad mood, but I have isolated myself from it all with the beautiful memory of you, and so I live happily.

This lover who received such adulation did not love Alexandrine with the same intensity. One day he disappeared from her life:

My marriage was never the same again after that. There were problems and I suggested that we get a separation, but my husband would never agree to it. About a month ago, when my husband was shown the two letters that have been referred to, I offered him an explanation. I told him what I had already told Monsieur Atrux, that is, that the letters were a year old and that I had not had any relations with the person to whom they were written for the past ten months. My husband forgave me.

140

I must say that since then I haven't had anything to complain about: he has spent every evening with me and has given me the attention which I have never had before. But unfortunately, I no longer loved my husband and I found his presence disagreeable. I would have liked to leave the house.

Shortly after this episode, Alexandrine started a romance by corresponding with a young man, Antoine Biderman, who lived in the rue Française:

My window is opposite Madame Duc's window. At the beginning of this month, I saw her at her window and I was struck by how pretty she was. Unfortunately I got it into my head to court her and she responded to my advances. We started sending one another letters through the maid. Madame Duc received me twice in her drawing room for about twenty minutes, but nothing shameful took place between us. Two days before the incident occurred, she arranged to see me on the following Friday, between two and three o'clock, near the Saint-Martin gate.

On the eve of the crime François Duc found out about his wife's infidelity from his maid, the Raulin girl. The next day he tried to murder the guilty woman. The press got hold of the story, embroidered the facts, and credited the ill-fated Alexandrine with having had numerous love-affairs.

Confronted as he was with this publicity, Antoine Biderman thought it advisable to deny a liaison that was beginning to damage his reputation. He wrote to his mistress's mother to tell her that, having learnt about Alexandrine's misbehaviour from public gossip, he had the feeling he had been betrayed and felt pity towards the 'poor husband'. In response to this boorishness, Alexandrine wrote him a very moving letter:

I felt hurt for two days. I managed to be alone and I forced myself to go into the drawing room so that you would see me and not be so worried about me. You saw me, I am sure of it. How did you thank me? By speaking to me almost insultingly. The wound inflicted by a bullet heals; you should have spared me the other wound that you have just inflicted on me. You believed the newspapers which said my husband saw me in the arms of a lover. It's not true. I was alone. Someone told him that we wrote to each other. I think the concierge must have talked.

You chose to doubt me and you are abandoning me at a time like this. I pity you for you do not know how to love![27]

In addition to being confined to the home, middle-class women were also prisoners there. Legal separation necessitated not only courage on the part of the wife but also her husband's consent, since disappointed love was not a sufficient motive for judges to consider their requests. Although these women were financially secure, they had to organize their day to the tune of boredom, accept their situation and, especially, forget their aspirations of love. Those who refused to accept the ideal of 'bourgeois happiness' very often had to take refuge in a world of dreams or madness.

Other women, who were determined to fight, rejected such situations. They were militant feminists and demanded rights for women; they fought to have the divorce law reinstated and to put an end to their marital servitude.

Old Mistresses

Some women reversed the order of things; these were the courtesans, who were immortalized in nineteenth-century literature. Unlike common prostitutes, they appeared to be free and elegant women. They shamelessly ruined their lovers and brazenly enjoyed themselves.

The crime committed by the widowed Madame Gras took place against a corrupt background; underlying the case was a suspect morality where passion and money were intertwined. It was a subject that excited, and one that was indicative of the amorous practices that middle-class gentlemen indulged in during the nineteenth century; their sexuality, or rather, their eroticism, blossomed in places other than the conjugal bed.

The highly stratified diversity of clandestine prostitution on offer contrasted with the prevailing climate of puritanism. Having a kept mistress was a way of avoiding the dangers of street prostitution, which was considered too vulgar. The status of these *demi-mondaines* changed according to the fortune of their lovers. They offered sexual pleasure with the additional guarantee that one would not contract a disease. This was a valuable asset at a time when everyone felt threatened by venereal disease. Such courtesans were devoted to carnal pleasure and thereby exercised another social function: they protected the innocence of young girls from good families, ever anxious to preserve their purity and their precious virginity until the marriage night. Families did not mind seeing their sons have their first sexual experiences with women of easy virtue, who had the temporary role of initiating them into love in exchange for financial remuneration. It was impossible for these adolescents to have a relationship with young girls from the same social background as themselves, and so they had no choice but to gain their experience of love with these 'waiting' women who were adept at making 'men' out of them before they settled down and founded a family. Society was grateful for this service and so tolerated clandestine prostitution. But once they had done their job, these women of ill repute had to disappear and let the sons return to their families; otherwise they would invite opprobrium.

In this respect, the Gras case enables us to examine male behaviour where venality was concerned. Although men paid for the favours that were granted to them, the money they gave was not a means of exerting sufficient pressure to subjugate these women, who had the power to turn their position as prostitutes to their advantage. Furthermore, men were eager to disguise the mercenary character of the relationship in order to delude themselves about the substance of their relationship, and very often they respected their mistresses. Thus, widow Gras's lover claimed that he never gave her money, a lie that enabled him to preserve his honour and the illusion of shared love.

The story of this courtesan also complements the careers of such working-class girls who raised themselves to the rank of wealthy women, who were free and worshipped by men. Since she had financial assets, Madame Gras could have looked forward to growing old, sheltered from worries and solitude. But things turned out differently!

Traditionally, these high-class kept women took their assumed names from the aristocracy; the most famous were Blanche d'Antigny, Liane de Pougy and Emilienne d'Alençon. Madam Gras had changed her maiden name, Eugénie Bricourt, to Jeanne de la Cour. She was born in Ménilmontant in 1838, in a concierge's flat. Her father, a hammerman, worked in a nearby factory. Their meagre income was not enough to bring up four children, and so, from the age of five, Jeanne resold fruit in the neighbourhood in order to bring in a little money. By a happy coincidence, a lady, the baronne de Pallault, noticed the child and took an interest in her. With her parents' consent she had her baptized Jeanne and sent her to boarding-school.

This was a start in life worthy of a serialized novel in the style of Eugène Sue. Yet there was nothing extraordinary about this fairytale story in itself; the baroness's good deed was part of a tradition of charitable works which virtually formed a bourgeois institution. When she was questioned by the investigating magistrate, the baroness gave a harsh judgement on her little protegée:

In her youth Eugènie was hard, miserly and, above all, incredibly arrogant. I took her to the country one day and she haughtily spurned one of the little girls in the village, saying that the daughter of a baroness (she maintained that she was my daughter) could not play with the daughter of a peasant. Besides, she never showed any gratitude for what I did for her.

This anecdote shows the consequences of breaking with one's background. For this girl from Ménilmontant, there was another world which she wanted to enter.

Unfortunately, Jeanne's dreams of grandeur collapsed suddenly. In 1848 her parents wanted her back, and so they took her away from her patroness. They sent her out to sell gingerbread near the gates of Paris. No unkindness was intended on their part; Jeanne was simply a source of considerable revenue. Later, she worked in a chenille yarn factory. When she was about sixteen, Jeanne left her parents and the factory and asked for help from her former benefactress, who responded generously. She gave her a trousseau and a dowry of 3,000 francs, and on 16 May 1855 married her to Charles-Victor Gras, a twenty-four-year-old who owned a small grocer's shop.

A year later, the young couple parted. This marriage failure was, in fact, the result of Jeanne's desire for independence; with her dowry she was now rich, and she launched into business. She started with a perfumery, then a paper shop, first in the Passage Vendôme, and later in the rue de la Rochefoucault. After these brief and unprofitable ventures, she gave up commerce, and in 1864 made her debut in the Théâtre des Folies-Marigny. This was her first step towards corruption. For the majority of cocottes, going on stage meant the opportunity to find a benefactor. It was not so much her talents as an actress as her physical attractions that made a rich Breton landlord notice Jeanne on stage.

Early in 1865 she moved into the comfortable surroundings of the rue Saint-Georges; under the Second Empire, and at the beginning of the Third Republic, high-class prostitutes resided in the districts of Notre-Dame-de-Lorette, the Madeleine and the Place Saint-Georges. For a while Jeanne lived in Paris and Brittany and led a life of leisure. But in 1871 her benefactor left her to get married. He was generous, and offered Jeanne a small estate near Nantes to thank her and to get rid of her. But this gift was not enough for Jeanne; armed with compromising letters, she blackmailed him and, over a period of about five years, extorted various amounts of money from him.

Meanwhile, this adventuress became the mistress of a young man of twenty who gave her an annual income of 3,000 francs, besides her rent. He parted from Jeanne for the same reasons as had her previous benefactor. He, too, was subjected to threats and had to buy his ex-mistress's silence.

During the same period, Jeanne saw Mathieu Gaudry again; as children they had played together in the rue de Ménilmontant. This chance meeting took place on Easter Monday of 1876. Unlike Jeanne, Gaudry had not improved his social position. He had become a father at the age of seventeen and had joined the army. In 1865 he moved to Amiens and married the mother of his first child; she was then pregnant again. Ten years later she died. As he was now alone, he decided to leave the eldest child in Amiens; he moved to Paris and lived with his mother who took care of the second child. At first, Gaudry worked as a moulder in an ironworks in Saint-Denis, and then as a day-labourer in a colza oil factory.

Jeanne, who was now transformed into a *bourgeoise*, made a great impression on this working-class man; every Sunday he went to visit her at 5 rue de Boulogne, where she had been living since 1873. He used to do all sorts of odd jobs for her, such as bottling wine, cutting wood and fetching coal, and then they would eat together. At the factory where he worked, his friends noticed a change in his mood: 'On Mondays he seemed to be sad and preoccupied.' He confided that he had met a childhood friend whom he was in love with and dreamt of marrying. 'She's not a worker,' he would tell his friends, 'she's a lady.' Eventually, this passion became so intense that whenever he looked gloomy or distracted, his friends knew why; they would say: 'So you've been to see your lady friend.'

He confessed these feelings to the examining magistrate as well:

'What was your relationship with her?'
'We were childhood friends.'
'Did you know the kind of life she led?'
'Yes, a little, in the early stage.'
'What was your intention in going to see her so often?'
'I had gradually fallen in love with her.'
'Did you want her as your wife or as your mistress?'
'As my wife.'
'In spite of her morals! Did you think she was rich?'
'I never thought about that.'
'We'll pass over that. You wore an overall, that was very respectable; but she wore finery which she had obtained by shameful means.'

What did Gaudry mean to Jeanne? He was more than simply a friend who could help her with her household jobs; he was a link with the past. After rejecting her background and modelling her behaviour on members of the bourgeoisie, she enjoyed the complicity and nostalgia of relaxing in the company of this man with whom she shared childhood memories. But Gaudry's role did not extend beyond this. He was never her lover, that much caricatured figure in the world of corruption. Moreover, Gaudry had to contend with a rival, René Martin de la Roche, Jeanne's last benefactor.

Jeanne and René met during an outing to the country at Bougival in 1873, and three years later, when Jeanne was single again, he became her official lover. This very rich young man had nothing else to do but enjoy himself. To live off an income at such an early age went against bourgeois morality; disapproval for this aristocratic life-style can be detected in the indictment: 'His idleness, just as much as the isolation in which he lived, made him defenceless in his relationship with Madame Gras.'

The portrait of Jeanne which was presented in court drew attention to the despotic power which she exercised over her lovers in order to dominate and take advantage of them. René came across as a victim, while Jeanne was the demon, the Machiavellian creature who was bent on profit and whose sole interest was to gain more and more money: 'The passion which she aroused in him was all the greater because it stemmed from habit and developed gradually. The accused had absolute power over him without his being even aware of the weight of this burden.'

Did the judges wish to ignore the fact that Jeanne lived off her physical attractions? If so, what was their real criticism of this prostitute whose life-style corresponded to her occupation? Kept women were submissive neither to their lovers nor to the social order; their freedom and their arrogance *vis-à-vis* men represented a threat. The judges could not digest the fact that Jeanne treated her lovers like objects and ridiculed them. The counsel for the prosecution, Monsieur Chopin d'Arnouville, based his summing-up on criticisms such as:

While she was alive she only had two aims in life: domination and self-interest. 'Men must be my stepping-stones', she would say, 'I know how to get them.' 'The world is just a chess-board and men are pawns that one must learn to manipulate,' she wrote. One of her lovers wrote to her and said: 'I'm the old man who loves you and who wishes he were the young man whom you love.' Thus, one of the first lovers whom she ensnared, Gontran, tried to poison himself so as to be free from her power. A note, written on paper with a black border around it, was found in her flat: 'Jeanne, I am dying because of you, but I forgive you. Max.' When she was questioned about this she replied: 'He's a German who I never bothered much about.'

And that wasn't all. In the course of twenty years of lust, this woman disregarded a great many of her victims. She made her lovers swallow hashish mixed with cantharides[28] and kept this drug hidden in her praying desk. This is the poem that she wrote to her doctor:

> For shame, naughty doctor
> You wanted to make fun of me
> And to laugh at my mistake,
> Force me to swallow
> A drug with no effect.
> You should have given me
> The Spanish Fly
> That I asked you for,
> After all, dear Sir,
> I am not going to overindulge
> In this divine poison
> But I would like to try it
> Without delay.
> Be kind to me
> Fear not for my health
> Doctor, and give me
> A night of pleasure
> A night of happiness
> A whole night of love.
> I beg you – hear me,
> My fate is in your hands
> To make a simple lover
> My hero for the morrow.

146

This vivid poem gives an idea of the expedients available to courtesans to encourage eroticism and the enjoyment of venal pleasures. 'To make a simple lover my hero for the morrow' – here was something to make the lover, subjected to a regime of marriage, dream.

Using aphrodisiacs was not Jeanne's only crime. Because of her stay in a rest home, the counsel for the prosecution presented her as a woman who suffered from hysteria; and into the bargain, she engaged in male activities: she speculated on the Stock Market. The counsel for the prosecution criticized Jeanne not for having been a kept woman, but because she did not conceal how materialistic she was: 'What was far more shameful than her depravation was this woman's motives – people said that she made a god out of money. One of her lovers, who lived with her for the longest time, even said that she was no longer a woman, but a symbol of cash.'

Society tolerated these clandestine prostitutes on condition that they were submissive and obeyed male authority. Courtesans had to give the illusion of offering love, and were supposed to make their lovers forget that they were prostitutes, as is testified to by this journalist's assertion: 'Madame Gras was not, therefore, an insatiable courtesan, but a trader of her body who granted her favours only for the price of bonds drawn up by a notary.'

René de la Roche was already enslaved by his mistress. Jeanne's maturity and experience attracted this young man who was completely subjugated to her. (He later admitted quite freely that she exercised absolute power over him, and he acknowledged her superiority.) René's family were fed up with seeing the relationship continue for so long, and they were very keen to get him away from Jeanne so as to be able to arrange a marriage. Jeanne was not unaware of this pressure, and, far from withdrawing, she tightened her grasp over René, who had to come to terms with the contradictions created by his desires. His correspondence with Jeanne during a stay at his family's home in January 1877 testified to his hesitations and his remorse *vis-à-vis* his mistress:

January 7th

This morning I received your sweet, kind letter, darling Jenny. I don't really understand why you want to go to the Opéra, and I can't see anything very convincing in your letter as to why one should spend an evening in that den of vice. [He is referring to the masked balls at the Opéra. Women of high standing were not allowed to go to public balls; nevertheless, wearing a mask gave a certain amount of freedom to those who wished to mix with the riffraff.] I will do as you wish, though, and we can go to the ball together.

But for that you must be kind and good, and I wouldn't dream of depriving you of a pleasure which you seem to want so much, my little darling. I've made a host of good resolutions since I've been here. You can judge for yourself. I thought that I have been behaving very badly towards you, my beloved Jenny, and that I was always leaving you alone and that you must be bored to death. I run around all over the place without thinking that I am leaving you to worry about me. I don't want to behave like that any more and, when I get back to Paris I'm going to spend more time with you. You love me enough not to get bored when you're with me, and you are everything to me in the way of affection. So it's bad of me to leave you like this and I no longer want to do it. We will live happily together. You'll continue to love me well, and I will give you all my affection. Isn't that how it should be? We'll spend our evenings either at my place or at yours. We'll go to the theatre sometimes. I won't be so tired as when I spend my evenings in low dance halls. When I always have your love near me I won't be so sad, and you won't be alone any more and you won't think of things that torment you. I don't know what would become of me if I didn't have your affection to protect me. So you must get better. My Jenny, your René sends you all his kisses.

In the following letter, he reassured her again about his feelings for her: 'As time goes by I become more and more attached to you, and I can hardly imagine life without you. I shall soon be back in Paris and then I'll take you to the ball. I shan't stir from Paris until the Spring.'

With these assurances, Jeanne should have had no more worries about the future; but this was not the opinion of the prosecution, which presented Jeanne as having no illusions about the rest of her affair with the man she referred to as her child. She was convinced that the outcome would be inevitable, and as she was aware that she was getting old, she understood that it was urgent for her to assure herself of René's faithfulness.

René de la Roche arrived in Paris on the Friday evening and spent the night with Jeanne at 5 rue de Boulogne. On Saturday, during the day he did some shopping, and in the evening he took his mistress to the ball, as planned. At about two in the morning, a cab stopped in front of Jeanne's house. René de la Roche went downstairs and opened the gate, and then went to the front door. He suddenly saw a shadow emerge from the wall and, a few moments later, he was doubled up with pain, his face burnt by sulphuric acid. Jeanne gave him first aid but did not call for the doctor until the following day. She stayed at his bedside for a month. Not only was René de la Roche disfigured, but he nearly lost his sight.

Jeanne's devotion was exemplary: she stayed with her disfigured lover night and day. After a search was carried out at Gaudry's house, some clothes were found that had been burnt with acid. When he was arrested, he admitted to the crime but exposed Jeanne as his accomplice. She was the instigator; he had only obeyed her orders: 'I went back to her house on January 11th. I told her that they were laying people off at the factory. It was three o'clock. Then and there she suggested the crime and swore on her daughter's tomb that she would marry me if I obeyed her.' The prosecution rejected the idea of a crime committed out of jealousy and chose to believe that Jeanne's motives had been vicious and diabolical, and that she had crippled her lover so as to make him her victim.

Jeanne's guilt was never physically proved. The most compromising object was the weapon used in the crime, that is vitriolic acid, a specifically female weapon which was very much in vogue at the end of the nineteenth century. (Out of 83 instances of these attacks which were recorded, 14 were committed by men and 69 by women. Between 1888 and 1890 there was a real wave of *vitriolage*.) This type of revenge, taken by deserted women on cavalier lovers or on their female rivals, was treated with a certain amount of tolerance by the law; this coincided with the feminist movement's struggle to challenge the civil status of women.

During the trial, the famous lawyer Maître Lachaud demolished the entire indictment; Jeanne's denials and the impossibility of establishing that she took part in this odious crime strengthened the case for her defence. After a brilliant speech for the defence which lasted several hours, Maître Lachaud turned to the members of the jury and said: 'Don't commit a crime; don't condemn this woman.' It was very late and the court adjourned until the following day. The fact that sulphuric acid was associated with crimes committed by women ruined Jeanne's chances of acquittal. After consultation, the court sentenced Mathieu Gaudry to ten years' imprisonment and Madame Gras to fifteen years' hard labour.

Throughout the trial, the law deliberately denied any sentimental motivation so as to support the argument that it was simply a heinous crime. Georges Macé, the head of the criminal investigation department, who had carried out the enquiry himself, refused to classify it as a crime of passion and wanted it to serve as 'a lesson to young men who, thirsting for pernicious pleasures, seek out old mistresses'. This was a theme much favoured by Barbey d'Aurevilly, as well as by Alphonse Daudet, whose book *Sapho* purports to be the account of his own experiences with a courtesan who was much older than himself and who prevented him from marrying a young girl from a good family.[29]

Ménages à Trois

The *ménage à trois* was a favourite theme in comedy and was endlessly portrayed on stage; but it also existed in real life. These rather vulgar situations prompted laughter and jeers, and their frequency and typical banality confirm their existence in the seamier side of life.

When transferred to the courtroom these *ménages à trois*, which were declared illegal, turn out to be rather different from the literary clichés. First of all, the third person is not always a schemer or a parasite who has wormed his way into the couple so as to share the favours of the master or mistress of the house. He was often a lodger who was either widowed or single and who had only a meagre income and shared his or her meals and sometimes the accommodation of a couple. This practice was very widespread among the working classes and offered considerable advantages. Apart from the income that they received from the board and sometimes lodging, the presence of a third person brought emotional rewards. The boarder forgot his or her loneliness, and bonds were established; sociability was strengthened and was considered more important than the couple's privacy. Working-class people were used to being outward-looking and were less concerned with conventional morality; they did not constantly try to conceal their behaviour.

Nevertheless, this way of life did not rule out privacy altogether. The limits to privacy depend greatly on the material conditions and the cultural background of each social group. Within each such group there are always conventions which establish areas of privacy. However narrow this space is, it can be allocated according to individual wishes – a chest of drawers or a small corner of a room can be a private space, a sort of invisibly partitioned-off area. In addition, the freedom of expression which was so typical of working-class relationships did not mean that a person was completely transparent; it is very likely that the notion of secrecy and the need to conceal one's thoughts were reinforced in a living space that was not very conducive to privacy.

Judges viewed this in a different light; each time they vehemently condemned the intrusion of a stranger into the intimate life of a couple. Since they considered overcrowding to be at the root of immorality, they viewed this way of life as an encouragement to debauchery, an open door to all vices.

This criticism reveals their desire to deny that there were certain forms of solidarity and sociability peculiar to the so-called lower classes, and which followed different rules from those that applied to the middle-class way of life. In the name of morality they discredited such relationships between workers and persisted in interpreting them as perverse. The bourgeoisie's voyeuristic attitude towards working-class mores revealed how they projected their fantasies on to these *ménages à trois*. In cases of adultery the judges gloated, since they thought they had concrete proof of the baseness and moral decay of the working-class milieu which daily wallowed in lewd and sinful behaviour. After having had their fill of smutty details and pouring out a stream of slander, they concluded that this suspect activity led straight to crime.

The judiciary's view of the working-class world reflected the social and cultural gap between the experience of the accused and that of the judges. This reality made any kind of dialogue impossible. Thus, Cosson, the husband who was accused of being an accomplice to the adulterous relations between his wife and their boarder, Jules Michel, preferred to bow his head and resign himself to a compromising silence, than to attempt to justify himself to men who blamed him without trying to understand him.

Monsieur Cosson, a metal fitter, left very early for work and did not concern himself with what his wife did all day. She divided her time between the wine merchant's shop and her lodgings at 21 rue de l'Orillon. In order to earn a little money, she cleaned for Jules Michel, who was a lodger in the same building. This former policeman, who had been dismissed for bad behaviour eight days before the incident took place, not only ate his meals in Madame Cosson's lodgings but was also having an affair with her; she was perfectly willing, as she was very attracted to men in uniform.

Her husband, far from being duped by his wife's behaviour, acknowledged that she 'failed in her duties as a wife': 'I know that my wife was leading a loose life; a while back, she even left me for eight days to go and live with a Republican Guard. But I didn't know she was having an affair with Jules Michel.'

The judges were appalled at this lack of perspicacity and accused him of complicity, criticizing him in the bill of indictment for being on such familiar terms with his wife's lover: 'Cosson must have been blind not to notice his wife's infidelity, but he didn't seem to mind and often went out drinking in taverns with the adulterous pair and got drunk in their company.'

During the preliminary investigation, Cosson, who was astonished by this accusation, remarked to the judge that it seemed perfectly natural to him to have a drink with the man who ate with him every day. But this commonplace situation in working-class milieux was sometimes unbearable for one of the protagonists.

After having accepted for a long time a triangular relationship out of weakness, complacency, self-interest or blindness, the husband might suddenly refuse to collude any longer. To his many failures another would have been added, one that touched his pride and his honour – his relationship with his wife.

Charles Bernaux, a vindictive husband who had been deceived, was also accused of having encouraged his wife's adultery. They had met in a licensed brothel in Valenciennes. After their wedding in 1869, the couple had moved to Paris. In 1870 Charles Bernaux was sentenced to six months in prison for theft. In 1871 he took part in the Commune uprising. After this episode, the couple appeared to lead an honest life. Elisabeth Bernaux took care of a concierge's office in the rue Marcadet, and Charles Bernaux worked as a metal worker for an omnibus company. In 1877 he met Carpentier, a compatriot, who was a gardener at the Jardin des plantes; he invited him to his home on a number of occasions. After a while Elisabeth Bernaux offered her services to him as a charwoman:

Since I had become a widower I had been living alone and no one did my house-work. Madame Bernaux offered to look after me; her husband was present at the time and gave his permission. It was arranged that she would mend my linen and clean for me.

She kept the key to my flat in her bodice. Bernaux seemed to have some affection for his wife, depending on his mood; but as for her, she openly said that she didn't love her husband any more after all the ill treatment she had suffered at his hands for so long. One day she told me that people thought I was her lover, and she added that her husband was very jealous but that that mustn't stop me from coming to see her. We became lovers at the end of March. When they moved to the rue Saint-Louis (to a two-room flat), they suggested I become their lodger. I continued to have the same intimate relations with her which had begun in the rue Marcadet, and all the while still without her husband's knowledge – at any rate, I think so, for although she flaunted herself with me, he didn't seem to pay much attention to it. I never gave her any money other than for board and lodging (75 francs a month).

It seems likely that when Elisabeth suggested taking care of Carpentier's housework, she had an ulterior motive, since she had been fed up with her life with Bernaux for a long time. One day she confided to the concierge at the rue Saint-Louis-en-l'Ile: 'He has always made me unhappy; at the rue Marcadet he used to ride all over me; he destroyed three or four pieces of my furniture and he threw my wallet into the fire when there were two 1,000 franc notes inside.' Bernaux's mother confirmed that the couple were discontented: 'As soon as I said something to his wife about her frequently going out late, she got angry and told me that she didn't love her husband any more and that she no longer wanted to stay with him.'

Her affair with Carpentier made her forget her conjugal disappointments. Every day she had lunch with her lover, and a neighbour who could see everything that was going on in the flat, noticed that Carpentier sometimes brought her large bunches of flowers.

According to the bill of indictment, Charles Bernaux was the only one who was responsible for this situation, since he had not only admitted Carpentier as their lodger but 'had accepted him on most intimate terms'. He was criticized for his complacency, for 'everyone knew about Carpentier's affair' and Bernaux 'seemed to encourage it'.

These statements are at variance with Bernaux's revenge. He had his suspicions and planned a diabolical and perverse trap so as to catch the two lovers *in flagrante delicto*, and shortly afterwards he avenged himself on his wife.

The complicity of the betrayed husband can be interpreted as a form of pimping, an accusation that was implied in the Coste case. This story of a *ménage à trois*, which was derided by a journalist from the *Petit journal*, revealed the bourgeoisie's contempt for working-class practices. The sarcastic tone and the unkind remarks in the press reflect a malicious representation of working-class customs. Shamelessly distorting the truth, this journalist refused to believe that the husband was unaware of his wife's infidelities and relentlessly accused him of profiting from it. Complicity gives adultery a more perverse and titillating dimension! He criticized the shameful depravation of the working class and ridiculed the lack of virility of the man who shared his wife. By intentionally ignoring the motive of passion in this crime, he reduced it simply to a sordid story of money.

Here was a man who wanted to reclaim his rights as a husband.[30]

An easy-going husband, that's what Coste was. It's true we don't know how

152

kind this fellow was. His idea of conjugal bliss was just about as far removed as you can possibly imagine from Othello's demands. As a builder, he may have been hard-working, but as a husband . . .

Well, it was Laforêt who was doing all the work – Laforêt was a work companion. He had made himself quite at home in Coste's house and was well ensconced there. He behaved as though he were the master. This intrusion took place while Coste was in prison for six months, in 1875, on a charge of theft.

When he was released, Coste found that Madame Coste had become, on her left hand, Madame Laforêt. He did not take exception any more than did the gentle zinc worker Coupeau, in *L'Assommoir*, when he discovered that the hatter Lantier was having an affair with his wife. You can see that novelists do not merely draw from their imagination, and that Monsieur Zola has positively written from life.

Where Coste's fortune differed slightly from Coupeau's was when, at the beginning of last April, Madame Coste asked the man whose name she bore for a small sum of money; it was to give the woman who looked after and kept their four-and-a-half-year-old child at her house. It was a paltry amount, thirty-six francs. But these thirty-six francs caused an incredible storm.

Up until then, the two builders had been like brothers together, drinking from the same bottle, carousing together – in short, they had shared everything. Only, generally speaking, it was Laforêt who paid for their revelry. The *ménage à trois* benefited from his generosity. Eating the money of your wife's nice man-friend in exchange for his tolerance was only logical as far as Coste was concerned. But to have to pay on top of it all! To have thirty-six francs removed from his pocket! Oh no! He would not tolerate that.

The mild husband suddenly became furious. He was angry with his companion, whom he suspected of having instigated this matter. One morning he bought a revolver and then loitered in the rue Geoffroy-Lasnier. In the afternoon, when Laforêt left work, Coste was waiting for him. He shot at him twice.

The bullets were lost in the victim's clothes. The only harm done was just a slight bruise. When the murderer was arrested, he said that 'he did not regret what he had done'.

His lawyer, Maître Nicolay, argued that it was jealousy, that his passion had been stirred, and he had suffered the fury of betrayal. He pleaded for an acquittal with tears in his eyes. However, this man could not be acquitted. The verdict was as generous as possible and showed considerable leniency. Three years' imprisonment was what Coste got away with.[31]

Hospitality was considered even more suspect if the third person slept in the married couple's bedroom. Overcrowding, which was then perceived as a form of debauchery, became notorious. Yet, when the lodgings consisted of only one room, it was rather difficult to arrange things in a different way. In the Moignon case, the neighbours were not at all surprised to see Pierre sharing the only room of their lodgings with his sister and her husband. Only the landlord, who had come to collect the rent, seemed uncomfortable:

The first time, a young man opened the door at eleven o'clock in the morning. The woman was lying on the bed between the sheets and was only wearing a draw-string nightshirt which left her shoulders uncovered. She seemed to be in the middle of the bed. There was a mattress on the floor and the person who had answered the door was sitting on it, smoking.

This visit did not perturb the brother and sister. They did not feel it necessary to stand up, and, wishing perhaps to be provocative, they displayed a certain amount of lasciviousness, which did not go unnoticed by the landlord.

The high cost of rents put a strain on household budgets, and families crowded into tiny lodgings; the neighbours showed understanding with regard to the mutual support that everyone needed. The Barbot couple, who already lived in a two-room flat with the young wife's step-parents, did not hesitate to have Amélie Lannoy as a lodger and to share their bedroom with her.

Madame Barbot had become friends with a certain Mademoiselle Amélie Lannoy, who was aged twenty-four, and in July 1875 had started work in the 'Compagnie française' shops where Madame Barbot worked. In July 1876, the Foulay couple [Madame Barbot's parents] asked the Lannoy girl who was ill at the time if she wanted to come and live with them; she accepted, and she stayed there until the end, in return for 25 francs a month for board and a contribution of 100 francs towards the cost of rent. Soon she was on the most peculiarly intimate terms with them. She shared the Barbot couple's room, and recently, when the accused stopped sleeping in his wife's bed, he lay on a mattress beside the Lannoy girl. Amélie Lannoy even got dressed in front of Barbot.

In the eyes of the law, this conviviality necessarily implied lechery. The judge was shocked by these people's immorality and lectured Amélie Lannoy:

'You must have been shocked by the situation in the household, that is, having to sleep beside the husband in the same room.'
'It was unimportant. I never had sexual relations with the accused. The Foulay couple and Barbot offered me hospitality and I accepted. I liked Pauline a lot. I have been blamed for many things, but I was only ever guilty of thoughtlessness.'
'Were you there when the husband and wife shared a bed?'
'I wasn't responsible for that situation.'
'Did you witness a terrible row in the night?'

'There had been an argument and he got up. Pauline got frightened but he didn't hit her.'

'It wasn't for you to be there. You should have left.'

'Events overtook my decision.'

Although the Smeyers case was similar to the cases discussed above, it was treated with far greater respect by judges and by the press. While the plot was still the same, the setting and the characters were rather different. The scene is no longer low-life. The case involves a respectable furniture dealer called Frédéric Smeyers who came from a good family. He was accused of attempting to murder his friend Pierre Leyniers on 19 February 1871. In this instance the prosecution reversed the roles: the husband was presented as being irresponsible and the friend and lodger was portrayed as a treacherous man who was guilty of having devised the plan to break up a marriage.

This is how the judge addressed Pierre Leyniers:

Here is a man who receives you in his home, obliges you, and whose friend you become. He has a young wife of twenty-two and he is twenty-five. He has been married for two years and he is happy. You who are thirty-five years old, you come and disturb the happy young couple.

At the time of the Commune Pierre was taken in by Smeyers, and then he rented a room at 36 rue des Ecoles (famous because of the Dubourg case) and continued to eat his meals at Julie and Frédéric Smeyers's house.

The article that appeared in *L'Evénement* attests to the court's desire not to confuse the mores of this honest bourgeois with those of depraved workers. Bourgeois hospitality is contrasted with working-class hospitality; the former is decent and friendly while the latter is calculating and immoral:

The husband stands in the dock; his appearance is agreeable, his attitude is excellent, his life, which is still a young one, is highly commendable. He is only twenty-six, which is exactly the same age as Monsieur Dubourg. The lover stands in the witness box. Is he aware of his position? We observe that he has taken great care in his dress. As for his attitude, we will not describe it; it will shortly be judged. We suppose that he hears, without properly understanding them, the harsh but deserved words spoken by the judge. The woman is relegated to a corner, at the back of the audience. The court did not wish to hear her: it rejected the adulterous woman's evidence as unreliable. She is crying, and, if truth be told, this is the best course for her. Perhaps her tears are sincere. We would like to believe it after reading certain passages in the letters which she sent to her husband when he was in prison; indeed, the poor man has been in prison for three-and-a-half months.

Coste, for a similar crime, was sentenced to three years' imprisonment, while Smeyers was acquitted.[32]

Husbands who have Grown too Old

In many couples there was a considerable age difference between the man and the woman. In a third of couples, this difference was greater than fourteen years. Like overcrowding, this disparity shocked judges, who never missed the opportunity to publicly criticize the unsuitability of these relationships. Their reaction stems more from an old social taboo than from a deep conviction that equality of age is a prerequisite for a successful relationship. In rural areas the village community expressed its disapproval *vis-à-vis* those who transgressed this social prohibition; a marriage that was considered unbalanced in this respect would provoke a hullaballoo. The ritualization of society's observation of private life does not occur as openly in urban areas. City life, which is more permissive, permits certain forms of unlawful sexual behaviour.[33]

The judiciary's observations on these age differences primarily met the demands of ethics. Faced with implied accusations, the replies varied according to the social group concerned. As the bourgeoisie internalized social taboos more emphatically, they felt guilty if they went against moral norms. Since they realized that their reputations would be at stake if they were discredited, they tried to justify themselves. Displaying unparalleled hypocrisy, François Duc, a doctor, explained that he had married a young girl twenty years his junior so as to protect her virtue, which was threatened by the immorality of the milieu in which she lived. These were the arguments he used to justify himself:

Madame Boulanger [his wife's mother] was separated from her husband and her life-style was not beyond reproach. Her daughter, who was then seventeen, was growing up in an environment that was very harmful for her virtue and for her future. I had just the cure for this patient. I saw a situation which upset me and which contributed to my feelings of affection towards her; these were soon to be expressed by a request for her hand in marriage. This was accepted, and in 1860 I married Mademoiselle Boulanger.

The assize judge was not convinced by this explanation and shrewdly replied:

The sentiments which you expressed with regard to the marriage are nothing if not honourable. I will, however, make one remark, and that is that your reason was somewhat fooled by your heart, for you were twenty-one years older than your wife, and this age difference should have made you think and question the marriage.

No doubt François Duc's fortune and his position made him more attractive to the young girl.

In another criminal case, Monsieur Carpentier, who was indirectly implicated, gave similar justifications in a respectful but more sincere tone:

Please permit me first to have the honour of thanking you for the kindness with which you questioned my wife yesterday about the odious remarks made by a vile woman; but you immediately emphasized the big age difference between her and me. You know that a few years back a mistake was made. As this mistake is just as much my responsibility as hers, let me explain this matter a little. When I met Marie, who had been an orphan since childhood, she was alone and terribly frightened, lost among the crowds of Paris, and in circumstances that could lead her even further astray. I can say with pride that, in spite of my age, I appeared to her as a man surrounded by the prestige of being very distinguished, something I had earnt from my work over the past twenty years.

Yes, I confess that a mistake was made, but in spite of the age difference, in this young girl's eyes I was still imbued with a sort of prestige which led to bewitchment, and after many long years of faultless behaviour on the part of Marie, and having become accustomed to her attentions and her devotion, I realized that it was necessary to make amends with a marriage which was approved by my family and of which my wife continued to show herself worthy. We are both terribly attached one to the other, and if there is any blame then, Sir, I accept my share of it. (Letter addressed to the counsel for the prosecution on 27 June 1877).

For working-class people, the problem was posed in different terms. The transgression of moral values was less important than the practical consequences of these marriages. The individual's friends and family, who were conscious of the risks involved, warned the future couple and made clear their disapproval. Aimée Mathurine's mother openly expressed her disapproval when her daughter told her that she planned to marry François Lebersorg: 'I was against this marriage because I thought my daughter was too young' (she was fifteen). Aimée's mother would have opposed the marriage, but she did not have the power to prevent it.[34] For young people from a working-class background could more easily go against the wishes of their parents, who were not in a position to pressurize them because of a dowry or by threatening to disinherit them. They were independent because they worked and could therefore do as they pleased – without taking any notice of the advice that they were given. They did not consider the age difference as an obstacle to their happiness. What did it matter to them if they reversed the order of things!

They did not feel the need to exonerate themselves in court. Pierre Gautré was not embarrassed to talk about the reasons for his choice of wife. He had been widowed young and was left with a child; despite the age difference of nineteen years, he married Marie Thein, a laundress who had worked for Gautré's deceased wife: 'Both of them were berated for the disparity in their ages, but they took no notice.' On the day of the trial, the judge asked Gautré for some explanations: 'When she worked for us she told us she was nineteen. When we went to advertise the employer said to her: "but you're only seventeen", and I was even unsure as she looked so young and had deceived me about her age.'

'Yet you still married her?'

'I don't know how it happened.'[35]

The fears voiced by one's social circle were sometimes well founded. As they were more vulnerable, these couples often found themselves faced with purely financial problems. At some time or other, the younger of the two will have to support the partner who can no longer work. The remarks made by the widow Lahaye, who became Pierre Féaux's victim because she refused to marry him, testify to her awareness of the difficulty of accepting this type of situation. Pierre Féaux, a sixty-year-old day-labourer, became the lover of the widow Lahaye, who was working for him as a charwoman. There was a gap of fourteen years between them. Pierre proposed to her; the widow Lahaye first consented and then changed her mind. To put an end to their affair, she moved out of her lover's home. He was furious and constantly pursued her; he refused to return some personal papers to her. Then his attitude suddenly changed, and, on the pretext of giving her back her birth certificate, he invited her to his house for the evening.

After they had eaten, Pierre Féaux had sexual intercourse with his ex-mistress. Thinking the moment was right, he proposed to her again, but naturally she still refused him. He then became very threatening, but the Lahaye widow did not give into his blackmail. Suddenly he got up, locked the door and uncovered the coal stove. Madame Lahaye managed to overpower him and to free herself; she opened the window and shouted for help. Féaux became wild, grabbed a knife and struck her in the stomach without wounding her; he finally struck her on the back of the neck with a razor. When the neighbours came into the room – after breaking open the door – they found Féaux lying beside his victim. He had just tried to commit suicide. When questioned by the judge as to her reasons for refusing to marry this man, Madame Lahaye replied: 'He was too old, and soon he wouldn't have been able to work and I would have had to support him.' He was sentenced to six years' imprisonment.[36]

The assize court was less lenient towards Louis Forestier, a former farrier, whose last job had been to feed cattle. He was sixty-three and had been out of work for the past four months and had lived from begging. His mistress, Anna Boudinot, who was thirty years younger than him, left her husband, who was a policeman and did not have regular work. In order to please her, Forestier spent all his savings (700 francs deposited in the Savings Bank at Saint-Germain). During the previous year they had lived together in a furnished flat at 12 rue

Alain-Chartier. This is how Louis Forestier was cross-examined on the day of the trial:

'When did you meet Anna?'

'I can't remember, but she was pregnant at the time. She was living in the lodgings rented out by Desplaces at the same time as me.'

'You had relations with her?'

'Yes.'

'How old was she?'

'I think she was thirty-five.'

'And you were sixty-three. Did you live with her?'

'I would be lying if I said no.'

'This woman was no more faithful to you than to her husband; in six days she stayed out overnight three times. Were you unhappy about this behaviour?'

'Yes, because she made me move and it wasn't worth making me leave my old lodgings just to leave me alone.'

'Did you say anything to her?'

'No, but I did say something to the landlord. I told him that this kind of life was wearing me out.'

'Did you want her to spend every night in your lodgings?'

'Yes.'

'On the night of 5-6th August, you went to bed at eight in the evening.'

'It was still light out.'

'She went upstairs with you.'

'Yes, I had lit the candle and she said to me: "There's no need for any light." I replied: "Not a word, I'll blow it out", which I did.'

'She had asked a neighbour to wake her early.'

'I don't know.'

'She had said she was leaving in the morning.'

'As she lied a bit, I didn't believe her. Perhaps she did want to leave me. At any rate I would have left her.'

'You woke up at four-thirty. Did you have an argument?'

'No, I got up twice to relieve myself.'

'Was she awake?'

'She wasn't sleeping because she could hear me getting up. I slept against the wall and she slept on the outside. At about one o'clock she did not consent and I said to her: "Don't worry, I won't pester you, I don't even care." Then when I got up I thought of how she rejected me and of all the misery which she made me endure. All this went through my head. I said to myself: she's made me squander 700 francs and she's created so much misery for me, and then when I want to go with her, she says: "It'll have to wait until tomorrow!" I became enraged.'

'When did you give her the 700 francs?'

'It wasn't in one go. It was before she got pregnant.'

'And you killed this woman because she refused to have sexual relations with you?'

'I was mad. I've never laid a finger on anybody. I took a thirteen or fourteen-centime knife which had a sharp point. It was in my waistcoat pocket.'

'When exactly did you get up?'

'It was about four-thirty. That's when I thought of it. I didn't know where I was hitting.'

'How did you hit her?'

'I dealt her a blow and she asked me to forgive her.'

'Did you hit her when she begged you for forgiveness?'

'Yes, I gave her a blow, she tried to kiss me. I pushed her away and I carried on hitting her.'

'There was blood.'

'I didn't see it.'

'You were looking at her face and hitting her in the ribs.'

'I didn't know where I was hitting her.'

Forestier had been out of work for three or four months and 'earnt his living' by begging (as he put it). His circumstances did not move the members of the jury, and he was sentenced to life imprisonment for the murder of his common-law wife; this was a harsh sentence, given his age.

This punishment is actually quite surprising, since the circumstances were far from being aggravating. Indeed, the total lack of premeditation, Anna Boudinot's bad behaviour (her refusal to have sexual intercourse with her lover), and Forestier's desire to commit suicide after the murder (when he was arrested he was found wandering around by the Seine, about to jump into the water) were all factors that should have been in the accused's favour. But he clearly looked very unpleasant. This, at any rate, is the impression you get when you read the introduction to the article that appeared in *Le Petit Journal*:

What a strange and loathsome case! To what depths must we descend? A more hideous brute has never stood before a jury! Forestier has fallen into that state of moral degradation where nothing remains of him as a human being. With him, feelings have been replaced by instincts – the instincts of wild beasts.

The counsel for the prosecution, Monsieur Chopin d'Arnouville, who was responsible for the indictment, painted a striking picture of the nocturnal drama which took place on the night of August 5th last, in a furnished building in the rue Alain-Chartier. It was a frightful scene, and the hero bore all the marks of vice on his face. Forestier is tall and bald; he has a narrow forehead, which bulges out at the temples, and small and deep-set eyes. He has a purple nose, a wide mouth, sunken cheek-bones and a receding forehead. He worked as a dairyman and his dress reflects this.

This description is as vivid as Emile Zola's descriptions of criminals in *La Bête humaine*, which illustrated Lombroso's theory of the born criminal. However, this journalist anticipated the theories of the famous criminologist to make the connection between biological degeneration and physical characteristics.[37]

*   *   *

When illness or old age disturbs the precarious financial balance of a relationship, the beginning of a break-up is in sight. The following story sums up in itself the difficulties experienced by workers when they reached retiring age. They were too old to continue in their trade and, since they could not live off their savings, they would seek out odd jobs which provided them with some income. The threat of the almshouse constantly weighed on the poor, tired after a lifetime of hard work.

The accused who appeared in court on 28 November 1874 was called Pierre Piplet. This 'little old man was thin, bald and toothless and looked about him with anxiety' (*La Gazette des tribunaux*).

In 1843, Pierre Piplet married a laundress who was twenty years his junior. Like the character of Coupeau in *L'Assommoir*, he worked as a roofer. Life followed its course, with children and work, until the day Piplet was unable to climb on to roofs because of his age. At the age of sixty-nine, in order to earn a bit of money, this man tried to re-adapt himself and worked as a shop assistant; then he delivered newspapers and later, by an irony of fate, he worked as a concierge in Versailles in 1873. Everything seemed to be working out all right when the tenants, annoyed by Madame Piplet's rudeness and by noisy domestic quarrels, complained to the landlord, who immediately dismissed them. As they did not know where to go, they agreed to separate. Madame Piplet moved in with her daughter in the rue du Rocher while waiting for her husband to be able to go into an old people's home. She refused to live in the same lodgings as he did and wanted to work as a laundress. Her children helped her to move out her bed and a few personal belongings. The new solitude threw Piplet into a state of utter distress. He suddenly realized the irreversibility of his circumstances and so he tried to make his wife change her mind. This was his version of events:

'On August 30th, I went to my daughter's house and asked her to come back. I said to her: "Adèle, come on, won't you come back?" She replied: "I'm my own mistress, I'm in my son-in-law's house." "But you can't leave me alone like this." "I don't care." She wouldn't budge, oh no! she's not kind!'

'And were you so kind?'

'Yes, it's true this time. Up until then I wouldn't have harmed a fly. I had never harmed my wife. Maybe I was wrong to be like that. They say you shouldn't beat your wife, but I think that if I had made her respect me more then all this wouldn't have happened.'

'Were you angry about being deserted?'

'Certainly.'

161

'Did you love your wife?'

'I adored her; I loved my children but I adored my wife. I have always lavished attentions on her. I was the one who, even since I became frail, always got up first to light the stove and to make her coffee. She went out to work and I would stay, as I could no longer do anything, but I took good care of the concierge's office. When she came in, her lunch was ready. I did what I could. I couldn't do much, I'm old and I have my aches and pains.'

That day, when Madame Piplet categorically refused to go back and live with her husband, he threatened to get the police to force her back.

'You were getting more and more angry?'

'A bit, to be honest. I then said to myself, this has got to stop, I'll kill her and then I'll kill myself.'

On 13 September he bought a pistol from a gunsmith and, as he did not know how to use it, he asked for it to be loaded.

'Why did you buy this pistol?'

'What could I do? At my age I was being thrown out like a dog! After supporting my family for thirty years, I was forced to beg for a crust of bread just like a dog! I've always worked, I've earnt my living, I had nothing to be ashamed of! Nothing, until the age of seventy-one – I've always been respectable.'

'That's true, and I have personally commented to the members of the jury about your good record. You bought a two-shot pistol?'

'Yes, one shot was for my wife and one was for me. I was at the end of my tether and I said to myself: no, it's no good, this must stop. She was in the middle of making a bed and I pleaded with her. I tried everything. She refused to come back to me . . . So . . . '

The old man broke off and covered his face with a large blue check handkerchief. He was sobbing loudly.

It took place on 19 September. He went up to her and, aiming at her head, fired at her at point-blank range. Then he aimed the weapon at himself and fired again.

To their great surprise, neither was wounded: the gunsmith had thought the old man was very suspicious-looking and so had replaced the bullets with powder, thereby saving two lives and transforming this tragedy into a comedy.

'Piplet, do you regret what you did?'

'Yes sir, yes I am very sorry for what I did. I love my poor wife terribly and I should never have thought of doing such a thing. What do you expect, I'm so unhappy. I regret what I did.'

'You meant to kill her, didn't you? And you had planned the murder?'

'Yes, yes, I was at my wits' end, I wished I was dead.'

The accused started to cry. The judge said: 'Don't cry, the members of the jury have heard all your explanations and have listened to them attentively.'

Here is the victim's testimony:

'I married him in 1843. I was a laundress and he was a roofer. Our marriage was a happy one. I have nothing to complain about. Recently, as he had grown old and slightly infirm, I had had to support him, and you know when you're hard up, you don't always get on well together and then happiness goes.'

'Didn't he drink a bit?'

'Yes, a little, not much, as he got excited quickly and he became lively.'

'He says that he told you off for not bringing up your children strictly enough and, in particular, for not teaching them respect.'

'He never had anything to complain about with the children; they never showed any disrespect towards him.'

'Did you also reproach him about this?'

'I respected my husband, perhaps less than I should have, but I was very fond of my children and so I defended them.'

'You were a concierge; why were you dismissed?'

'Because of our domestic quarrels.'

The witness explained that it was through necessity alone that she was forced to part from her husband. While he was waiting for a place in the old people's home, they decided that the accused would stay at his sister's. The witness would have liked to continue living with him, but she could not carry out her work as a laundress if she stayed with her husband.

'You spoke the language of reason, perhaps, but you should have let your heart speak. When one is married, and disaster strikes, then one should suffer it together.'

'I have always loved my husband; he has never been unkind to me. It is very unfortunate that we had to part and that after so many years together, we can't live together.'

After a brief consultation, the members of the jury acquitted Monsieur Piplet and, astonishingly, gave him 70 francs which had been collected for him. The case was closed and the jury had done its duty.

This incredible story is worthy of a serialized novel, yet its overtones are far too realistic for it to be a subject of derision or for one to ignore the social misery that it evokes.

Part III

Society's Attitude towards Crimes of Passion

6

To Kill for Passion

Under the absolute monarchy, indictment resided as a rule in the person of the judge, who had the power to discipline all the misdemeanants he considered deserved it. The law therefore offered no protection or legal safeguard for the accused. Nevertheless, jurisprudence imposed theoretical limits on the discretionary powers of the judge, by providing a relatively brief classification of the different types of crime. Specialists in criminal law under the *Ancien Régime* defined homicide according to how it was committed, and recognized four categories: homicide out of necessity (for example self-defence), death by misadventure, manslaughter through negligence, and wilful homicide or murder. In the last category a distinction is made between homicide that is termed 'intentional' and homicide that is committed 'without wilful misrepresentation and unpremeditated'. The charge of wilful homicide emphasizes the spontaneity of the offence where there was neither premeditation nor felonious intent, and this characterizes what is today called murder. The punishments therefore varied according to the circumstances of the crime. Among the different reasons for reducing the penalty were madness, love, adultery and a lack of premeditation, as well as impulsive behaviour, anger and especially remorse.

At that time, the term 'crime of passion' did not exist, even though it was implicit in the definition of extenuating circumstances and of homicide committed out of passion: 'The fourteenth reason that can contribute to a reduction in the sentence of a crime is love, especially if the offence is prompted by a sudden and unforeseen passion, of which one is not, in a certain sense, in control.'[1] This frenzy cannot, however, justify rape. Anger and impulsiveness 'also contribute to a reduction in the sentence of a crime, above all when this anger is occasioned by a legitimate cause. It is as a consequence of this rule that homicide committed on impulse is excusable. But this impulsive behaviour and this anger must be such that they make one lose control and do not give one time to think.'[2] Depending on the circumstances, the accused could thus receive a pardon, which only the sovereign could grant by means of a reprieve or a remission. During the nineteenth century, there was a return to this view of the crime of passion as 'excusable' because of extenuating circumstances.

The recognition of the specific character of the passions, which excused a criminal's behaviour, disappeared from jurisprudence with the reform of criminal law after the French Revolution. The drawing up of the Penal Code of 1791, which was the successor of *De l'Esprit des lois* and *Des délits et des peines*,[3] put an end to the discretionary power of judges and that of the king. Thereafter, sentences and sanctions were governed by the law which regulated justice. The keystone of this reform was the introduction of a jury, which had to be present both during the preliminary investigation and during the trial.

Although they were less arbitrary and inhuman, the new penalties were more severe because of the principle of equality in criminal law. Indeed, the 1791 legislation rests on the assumption of the free will of the individual, who is theoretically in control of his or her actions and responsible for them; people are equally to blame if they have done the same deed. The Code does not, therefore, distinguish between different types of murder. Whatever the motives and the circumstances, nothing can reduce the sentence.

Strangely enough, precisely at the time when the concept of 'crime of passion' was disappearing from legal texts, the public began to be aware of it. Joseph Gras was accused of killing his mistress by stabbing her twenty-two times, because she was reluctant to marry him and misbehaved. At the trial on 20 September 1791, the lawyer argued for the right to differentiate between crimes:

One should, I believe, distinguish considerably between crimes. Some are base and reveal a soul profoundly corrupted by wickedness. Others reveal a lively and passionate soul: these are the people who are driven to act on the spur of the moment, as did Monsieur Gras. . . . Who is rash enough to believe that he himself would never, in a fit of anger or despair or in a transport of love, sully his hands with blood?'

The lawyer requested a sentence of life imprisonment, which was granted.[+]

Using this sort of reasoning, criminal law gradually took into account the personality of the criminal and concentrated on the quality, rather than the intention, of his action. Public opinion, convinced of the individuality of each of the criminals and of the singularity of each of the crimes, played an active role in shaping legislation as it evolved into repressive measures.

The Penal Code of 1810 does not mention crimes of passion, since the term does not refer to any legal concept. While criminal law makes a distinction between manslaughter and murder, depending on whether the homicide has been committed with or without premeditation, and takes into consideration the criminal's mental state, it does not differentiate between the crime committed out of greed and the crime committed out of passion – with the sole exception of homicide that is provoked by adultery *in flagrante delicto*.

Nevertheless, in the early part of the nineteenth century the 'crime of passion' became accepted because of the refusal of the public – represented in court by judges and members of the jury – to include crimes committed out of passion with heinous crimes.

The criteria for this distinction were moral; they reflected the ethics of a society that was anxious to defend material possessions and private property of any kind. The utilitarian and mercenary aspect of crimes committed out of greed created this distinction by discrediting them through severe social censure. This is the inevitable consequence of a society that values the acquisition of possessions. Theft was, in fact, perceived by nineteenth-century society as being a serious threat to social order.

In contrast, the almost disinterested nature of the motives behind crimes of passion makes them somewhat special. The criminal who kills out of love, out of jealousy or out of resentment, far from being dishonoured, sometimes comes across as a hero. Furthermore, it is often difficult to establish the motives with any degree of certainty, and the domestic aspect of the crime, together with the low rate of recurrence, sets it apart from other crimes.

Thus, crimes of passion appear to be responses to situations of personal conflict, whose consequences affect a small group of individuals, united by family, sexual or simply love ties. This crime belongs to domestic life – to the family life, love life and daily life of individuals – which is the scene of so much emotional tension, and where violence exists without being subject to state control. Physical violence, which was theoretically an offence, seemed to be tolerated; the public feared neither the risk of disorder, nor the threat of outbursts that other forms of violence could cause. In certain respects, crimes of passion came just within the limit of social tolerance, and, far from provoking fear and anxiety, they served as a diversion for a society that was avid to hear tales of criminals and was very receptive to this image of love and death.

Another favourable factor is the similarity between crimes of passion and suicide, that individual act which signifies the assertion of the right to live or to die which one exercises over oneself. The criminal claims the right to kill in order to take revenge for a personal slight (which sometimes ends in a suicide attempt). At times, crime and suicide appear to be two facets of one single act. Suffering, exasperation and violent feelings which are common to crime and suicide justify the resulting outbreak of violence by legitimizing it. Nevertheless, even if behaviour during the early stages of these two acts is similar, they are in fact very distinct: suicide means being subjected to suffering and directing violence against oneself, and crime means revolt and aggression towards the woman or man held responsible for this suffering.

Furthermore, as perpetrators of crimes of passion know their victim intimately, they are able to justify their reasons for wanting to kill; these reasons are always personal and make the crime look like a settling of accounts, revenge for casting doubt on the accused's honour. This is an essential part of the defence of perpetrators of crimes of passion who, according to their way of thinking, claim the right to take the law into their own hands to re-establish the status quo.

The motives behind crimes of passion do not instil the same disapproval, and when members of the jury acquit this type of criminal, they are legitimizing the crime that has been committed because they implicitly recognize themselves in this person who has not become different, monstrous or abnormal owing to his behaviour. According to R. Saleilles, writing towards the end of the nineteenth century,

The emotion that prompted him to commit the crime is an emotion that anybody might have felt and that everybody can admit to. He was perhaps a little more violent than he needed to be, but it is only a question of degree. This man is not an individual who is apart from the rest, someone to be cast out of society; his crime would seem to be an accident, and not the manifestation of a dangerous personality who should be scorned and rejected.[5]

The perpetrator of the crime of passion is an amateur criminal and is unaccountable for his or her crime – the offence will never be repeated. Sentences are calculated on the basis of the risk of a crime recurring; this risk underlies a whole series of measures which form part of the penal system. In the public's mind, murder poses less of a threat than minor crimes which are repeated and the perpetrator of which is perceived as a public enemy. It is, in fact, highly unlikely that the circumstances in which a crime of passion was committed will ever occur again in the criminal's lifetime. The jury is more inclined to be lenient towards such crimes, since, not only is it rare for them to be repeated, but also, it is difficult to establish and measure the criminal's responsibility in such cases.

'I had to put an end to everything'; 'it could not go on any longer' – this is how the accused express themselves when they reach the climax of their despair. The crime of passion demonstrates the difficulty experienced in exercising control over one's actions; the impulsiveness of the act is revealed in the lack of preparation (although this does not preclude premeditation). Public opinion is prepared to recognize that men and women are not always capable of controlling their impulses where intense emotions are concerned. The possibility of failure and of broken relationships is not only plausible, but almost excusable, since it is human. During the nineteenth century, passion was regarded in a completely negative light, but this view did not go beyond warning the men and women who were not capable of overcoming their emotions to be on their guard. Far from being totally discredited, emotions were prized as useful sources of energy for human beings.

Once this passion has prompted criminal behaviour, it frightens the public because of its tragic and bloody dimension, and because it reveals the existential truth of humanity with its impulses and basic desires. The perpetrator of a crime of passion demonstrates the uttermost limit of passion and shows that the strength of these emotions can lead to murder and make the criminal unaccountable for his action.

Sentencing According to the Individual

The crime of passion is a 'different' crime, and as such it is punished differently, Through the decision of the judiciary, public opinion plays an active part in defining it. Throughout the judicial procedure, the power of the law is caught in a public relations game with public opinion which, according to the case, reinforces legal power, or limits it by opposition. This 'balance of power' serves as an indicator of the threshold of tolerance of criminal violence, and makes it possible to define acceptable forms of violence.

Thus, in the nineteenth century there emerged a gap between the law and its application. What emerged as well was the role of public opinion, which, by acquitting a certain type of criminal, distorted the law and put into practice the notion of sentencing according to the characteristics of the offender, before this was stipulated in legal texts. This concern to consider each sentence individually was part of the legal reform movement during the eighteenth century. Apart from the need to have a code that classified each criminal offence, it was also imperative that this code should be adapted to the individual character of each criminal; this was thought necessary less out of a 'sense of justice' than out of a desire to put to better use the system of penalties which were intended to rehabilitate and improve the accused. Nevertheless, the Penal Code of 1791, in an attempt not to re-establish the arbitrary nature of the *Ancien Régime*'s judicial system, allotted fixed and equal penalties for all perpetrators of the same type of offence. The Penal Code of 1810, while maintaining the legalistic and egalitarian concept which was based on the moral responsibility of the offender, made the penalties more flexible by introducing extenuating circumstances for minor offences. In criminal cases, when a jury was not able to appeal to extenuating circumstances and did not have a range of penalties to choose from, it refused to ask for the death penalty, either for fear of judicial error or because of the disparity between the severity of the penalty and the crime committed. When faced with the choice between the death penalty/life imprisonment and acquittal, the jury preferred to be lenient.

The number of acquittals is an indication of the conflict between public opinion and the power of the judiciary. In response to this opposition, the first reform of the Penal Code allowed for extenuating circumstances, with the right of judgement being reserved for the judges and not for the members of the jury, who continued to give acquittals.

171

The Act of 18 April 1832 put an end to this conflict by granting the jury the right to reach a verdict on extenuating circumstances. This established the balance of power struggle between popular opinion and the law and resulted directly in a reduction in the number of acquittals. The law became more flexible and the exercise of legal power more acceptable. One should not, however, interpret this as meaning that the power of the jury supplanted that of the judges. This information has been presented simply to highlight the pioneering role that the jury played in the movement for sentencing according to the characteristics of the offender, which was demanded by jurists and criminologists at the end of the nineteenth century. This role was emphasized by R. Saleilles, a well-known supporter of this movement:

The jury was the first to start taking into account the characteristics of the offender. It has been the instigator of this movement. The law only looked at the crime and applied an abstract penalty without concerning itself with the criminal. The jury had before it a man whose life and honour were in its hands. How could it then remain indifferent to what he was thinking, to his past record and to his previous existence? Finally, the jury was so absorbed with the sight of the individual that, unlike the law, it forgot his crime, and every day we continue to see examples of this. Eventually, crimes were classified according to whether or not they enjoyed the sympathy of the jury; there is an entire category where the jury always forgets the crime which has been committed and sees only the feeling, the passionate instinct, which was perhaps impossible to resist, which provoked the crime. Such crimes were finally given the name of 'crimes of passion', and the law applies the same legal penalty to them as to others, for the law is unaware of their existence. The jury goes over the head of the law and acquits. By doing this, it is sentencing according to the characteristics of the offender, since it takes into account only the individual.[6]

Saleilles justified the role of the jury by defining the penalty as the reaction of the public and the expression of social reprobation. Nevertheless, he became indignant at some improper acquittals and revolted against the fact that penal law should suffer 'the backlash of popular feeling and public opinion'.[7]

The judge was the sole interpreter of collective justice, and he had to sentence according to the characteristics of the offender, basing his judgement on scientific criteria, thereby eliminating the purely practical approach of some judgements. In order to adjust the penalty according to the social responsibility of the criminal, it was necessary to diagnose the perverted nature of the individual and the risk of recurrence after the criminal's personality has been subjected to clinical observation.

To adapt the punishment to fit the criminal's character meant that the offender had to participate in this game of introspection: tell us who you are, and then we'll know how to punish you. The perpetrator of a crime of passion was better suited than any other criminal to this experimentation, since he did not conceal his thoughts or try to justify himself.

In judicial practice, sentencing according to the characteristics of the offender meant a desire not only to distinguish categories of crimes, but especially to define them better by contrasting them with each other. A benevolent approach to crimes of passion tends to emphasize the outlawed character of the individual who kills out of greed. This extract from a speech by the famous lawyer Maître Lachaud, who was appealing for the specific character of the crime of passion to be recognized, illustrates this process:

And when you have before you a Tropmann, a Lapommeraye, or a Dumollard, what will your decision be? And what will ordinary people say when they see that you deal as severely with the man who kills his mistress in a moment of anger as with the man who has murdered five people in cold blood? Tomorrow, when you are reaching your judgement, you will look into the heart of this man, you will think of his children and you will do your duty – you will state that this man is innocent and not guilty.[8]

This practice of sentencing according to the characteristics of the offender normally applies to crimes of passion. Whatever the crime, members of the jury were more or less lenient depending on the personality of the offender and the circumstances. Acquittal was therefore not automatic, even in cases of adultery. While the first principle of criminal punishment is to restore social cohesion destroyed by the horror of the crime, this view was not necessarily shared by everyone. The sentence could divide public opinion and provoke reactions with untold repercussions. This is what happened in the Leroy-Dubourg trial, which, like many sensational cases, was on the front page of the newspapers in June 1872:

Matters of higher importance concerning the internal situation of the country and its relations with our German victors have suddenly been replaced by concerns of a different order, and we have received news of the murder of Madame Dubourg which has been published, peddled and commented upon with as much passion as if it had been political news of the utmost importance.[9]

Yet it was only an ordinary story of adultery. But the protagonists differed from other accused individuals in that they belonged to the aristocracy, a rare occurrence. It was very unusual to see a member of high society appear in the assize court, obliged to expose his private life. The newspapers willingly satisfied a public that was eager to read every detail of this tragedy, which was more like a farce. Immediately the 'rue des Ecoles case' ceased to appear as a trivial news item and became the subject of various manipulations. Yet only the unusual social status of the protagonists justified the stir that was caused. Here are the facts according to the version given in the bill of indictment which was read out in court on 14 June 1872:

In 1869 Arthur Dubourg married Denise MacLëod, who was nineteen, at Villiers, near Vendôme. They both came from respectable families. The young woman had an affectionate nature, but an uneven temper and a capricious, even violent, character; her imagination was passionate and unruly, and she would have needed gentle, but firm guidance. Her husband, unfortunately, was easy-going and had a frank and kind character, albeit a somewhat coarse one; he was thus unable to exert a salutary influence on her. He did not have a sound educational background, was lacking in tact, and did not always know the rules of social decorum. Furthermore, he had no occupation and did not know how to employ his time, and was therefore often a burden on those around him.

The young couple first lived in Normandy. They seemed to be close and very fond of each other. Then they spent a winter in Paris. Several deplorable scenes then took place. Madame Dubourg made some unfortunate comments; she said that she did not like her husband. He showed great affection towards her, however.

One evening, at the house of a family friend, Doctor Davet de Benery, she saw Monsieur de Précorbin (an employee at the Seine prefecture), whom she had met there before her marriage. This young man had shown interest in her and marriage had been talked about, but the plan was abandoned almost immediately since Monsieur de Précorbin had no private means.

Before long they started to have close relations. Précorbin asked one of his friends, Monsieur Dutertre, also employed by the local authority, and residing at 14 rue des Ecoles, to lend him his room so that he could receive his mistress there. Since last December, Précorbin and Madame Dubourg met at least once a week in this room. She concealed herself carefully behind a veil and so the concierge could not distinguish her features.

But Dubourg's suspicions had long been aroused. The last time he had shared his wife's bed she had told him that she thought she was pregnant. He had replied that this was impossible, or at any rate, if it were true, he could not be responsible for it.

On April 21st he left early on the pretext of going to Nogent to hunt, having previously told his wife about this trip. He has admitted that he hoped to catch his wife *in flagrante delicto*. After leaving, at seven o'clock, he immediately went and sat in a café in the rue Amsterdam, from where he could easily watch the entrance to the Hôtel d'Angleterre. He spent the day there, and a number of times he questioned a hotel waiter, to whom he had given some money, to find out whether a young man whom he had described, was with his wife. He also asked two messenger-boys in the place du Havre, the Ramys brothers, to follow her if she went out, and to inform him immediately of her moves. So that they would recognize her, he made sure that they delivered a letter to her personally.

Précorbin should have spent the day of the twenty-first in the hotel with Madame Dubourg, but he had reflected that this step might be imprudent and so had not come. On the following day, the twenty-second, she sent him a note to arrange to meet that very day in the room in the rue des Ecoles. Dubourg, after spending part of the night keeping watch at the Hôtel d'Angleterre, had returned to the café in the rue d'Amsterdam to keep watch there. At one o'clock, he was notified that his wife had left the hotel, and that after paying a brief visit to Madame de Boos she had gone off in the direction of the boulevard Saint-Michel. He immediately went to the vicinity of the Hôtel de Cluny where he had arranged to meet the two messenger-boys. At about three o'clock, he learned that she had entered the house at number 14 rue des Ecoles. He hurried there and asked the concierge if one of his friends had arrived with his mistress, saying that he too was waiting for his mistress.

The concierge told him that he had not seen Madame Dubourg go upstairs to her lover. Dubourg left and, after receiving further information, returned and hurried up the stairs. The concierge followed him. When he reached the sixth floor, and stood before the room lent to Précorbin by his friend, Dutertre, Dubourg told the concierge that he could hear his wife's voice; he said that he was a married man and offered the concierge 20 francs to open the door. The concierge refused and, as Dubourg was threatening to break down the door, also threatened to have him arrested.

Finally, Dubourg decided to knock on the door. There was a long silence; then Madame Dubourg heard her husband say: 'Denise, you mustn't hide. I have just received a telegram saying your child is seriously ill.'

Précorbin opened the window. He claimed that Madame Dubourg told him to escape and that he had thought that she would not be in any danger if her husband found her alone in the room. Whatever the truth of this allegation, he climbed out of the window and, by crawling on to the roof, managed to get to the next-door house and to get away. Madame Dubourg then opened the door. Her clothes were scattered around the room. She had been inside with Précorbin for an hour and was only wearing her shift, her petticoats and her bootees. Dubourg rushed into the room, shut the door, and shouted: 'Where is the wretch?'

'Arthur,' his wife replied, 'I beg you, don't call the police. People would talk! I would be dishonoured!' But he punched her violently in her left eye, then he beat her repeatedly with his sword-cane with such force that the weapon broke in his hands. He then pulled out a dagger and started to strike her again, despite the poor woman's supplications; she asked him to have mercy on her and to go and fetch a priest before she died. He finally went out, after locking the door. During this horrific scene, the concierge had gone downstairs. He had had neither the courage to try to protect the victim, nor the presence of mind to go and get help.

After fainting, Madame Dubourg dragged herself to the window, and signalled her distress; a neighbour came to her rescue. Meanwhile, Dubourg had notified a priest that a woman was dying at 14 rue des Ecoles. The doctors ascertained that Madame Dubourg had been hit fifteen times, eight times with a sharp instrument and seven times with a cutting instrument.

Three days later, on 25 April, Madame Dubourg died in hospital. She was just twenty-two years old.[10] Arthur Leroy-Dubourg was sentenced to five years in prison; the jury had allowed extenuating circumstances by rejecting the accusation of premeditated murder. People were expecting an acquittal, and the sentence was regarded as scandalous by the public, who considered that this man's action had been justified. This was also the opinion of the public prosecutor, who made the following statement: 'A husband may be a bad husband and not show his wife the tenderness he should, but if his wife lapses then he must defend his honour.' Such arguments merely served to corroborate article 324 of the Penal Code.

In the wake of the trial, Alexandre Dumas *fils* wrote a satirical tract called *L'Homme–Femme* which ended with these provocative words: 'Kill her!' This naturally prompted a big debate among the intelligentsia of Paris. The author, a real demagogue, inveighed against unfaithful women whom he considered to be the cause of moral decadence. This lampoon was written in a tone that was as ridiculous as it was misogynous; 50,000 copies were sold, and it prompted dozens of replies in the form of booklets, articles and open letters.

The controversy that this case caused touches on the area of women's rights and of a revision of the Civil Code which stated that a man owned his wife. The non-acquittal of the murderer gave rise to a fresh dispute on the rights of women. *L'Homme–Femme* belonged to the spirit of Thiers's new republic, which, in order to encourage moral order and restore internal security, set out to control the family. The conservative Republic could not therefore tolerate the insubordination of women in the face of social conventions; nor could it conceive of granting them even the most fundamental freedoms. Those who had crushed the uprising of the Commune had certainly not forgotten the *pétroleuses*, or incendiaries, to whom Alexandre Dumas *fils* was referring. The first years of the Third Republic coincided with the emergence of the women's movement. Among their demands were civil equality, in particular the right to divorce and education.[11] Far from being firmly established, the Republican government had to contend with internal struggles and to consolidate the political and social order. This political climate was not at all receptive to entering into a dialogue with women such as Maria Deraisme or André Léo who, through international feminist congresses (the first was held in 1878), demanded the suppression of legislation in favour of men in cases of adultery.

The enormous protest that Dumas's lampoon gave rise to was perhaps the reason for its success. Nevertheless, this reaction, and the sentence given to Madame Dubourg's murderer, testify to a modification in attitudes, but it was still too early to talk of change. It was not until 1884 that the divorce law was passed, which officially and legally allowed women to get a separation from their husbands in circumstances of adultery *in flagrante delicto*.

Did the severity of juries only reflect the political evolution of liberal Republicans, who were convinced of the flagrant injustice of laws concerning women? It also expressed social reaction to violence. This man, who had received an excellent moral and civic education, should have appealed to the law to establish adultery *in flagrante delicto*, or else should have put his wife in a nursing home, instead of resorting to criminal revenge. Crimes of passion started to be viewed with a new sensitivity and were considered a sign of barbarism and an insult to the law. Although the motives remained justifiable, the crime itself no longer was. The debate surrounding this case did not confront the question of the illicit taking of the law into one's own hands; it was not until the end of the century that the legal authorities and public opinion began to concern themselves with this aspect.

The Beginnings of Criminology

Throughout the nineteenth century, the problem of crime aroused great interest in many doctors and jurists. Towards the 1870s, a new science was born: criminal anthropology. Its theories were to completely change the traditional conceptions of crime on which the Penal Code was based. The emergence of scientific discourses and the accumulation of knowledge about crime responded to the need that was then felt to set up a more appropriate policy of repression. The Third Republic quickly responded. Indeed, the new Republic, which promised peace and moral order, seemed determined to reassure public opinion, which was particularly susceptible to widespread alarmist talk about increased violence. (It is worth remembering that the background of criminal anthropology lay in the strong demand for social protection, which had already resulted, during the Second Empire, in the reinforcement of police control of urban areas, the setting up of criminal records, and the Act of 30 May 1854, which established the transportation of convicts to the Colonies.)

The second half of the nineteenth century was marked by a change in forms of crime and by the increase in repeated offences against property. (According to the 1880 *Compte général de l'administration de la justice criminelle*, their number rose to 70 per cent.) The expansion of commercial practices encouraged the development of new, far more subtle techniques of theft, such as forged documents, misappropriation of funds and breaches of trust, all of which were added to the conventional thefts on which so many fears and so much hatred was focused: 'It is not the big, noisy and fierce crimes which threaten society the most; it is this currency of crime which is everywhere, and which everywhere is encouraging and increasing immorality: theft – a never-ending crime.'[12]

The laxity of criminal law was held responsible for the increase in crime: the new forms of crime, caused by economic and urban change, worried those in power who were unable to ignore the failure of attempts to reform the prison system. The disciplinary strategies of imprisonment should allow social control to rehabilitate the offender; but, far from bringing about any improvement, imprisonment encourages the strengthening of the criminal environment. The solution was to be a legal and medical one. Indeed, the period of criminology's high prestige coincided with a period when lawyers and governments were striving to reform penal codes.

By dismantling the mechanisms and the causes of offences and crimes, and by suggesting the classification of different types of criminals according to scientific criteria, criminal anthropology offered the authorities some means of making repression more effective. The variety of innovating research in human sciences, in medicine, in psychiatry and in biology facilitated the expansion of criminology. The aim of criminology was to subject each offender to clinical observation in order to determine a differential diagnostic in degrees of criminality. The criminal – metaphorically associated with a germ – was classified, labelled and catalogued, and became a part of science. This classification, which was, in fact, a process of categorizing criminals according to their individual characteristics, involved a fine division into categories that ranged, according to the traditional divisions, from the normal to the abnormal, the dangerous to the harmless, and whose aim was to deal with unlawful acts in a more satisfactory manner.

By committing murder or violating property, the criminal, that rebel who is resistant to the discipline of the social order, was described by criminologists as a dangerous threat, one that could be controlled only if the criminal, and not the crime, were made the subject of study. In many respects, these views belong to the extension of the social protection movement, which, ever since the seventeenth century, gave birth to new practices of confinement (to a mental hospital) and punishment, through the hospitalization or imprisonment of all those people it was considered necessary to exclude, whether they were beggars, tramps, madmen or delinquents.

Moreover, social intolerance towards crime increased as the propertied classes grew more concerned about the working-class movements which attempted to assert themselves as a force that the authorities would be obliged to enter into negotiations with. For a while the working class was silent, undermined and isolated after the bloody repression of 1871; but then it gradually reorganized itself so as to gain rights and to engage in the class struggle. It was therefore not a coincidence that the theory of the born criminal emerged several years after the Commune, for the typology of this criminal focused most of the fears and fantasies of the bourgeoisie, who were always prepared to put the criminal in the same category as the proletarian.[13] Behind the image of the born criminal there emerged the image of the 'bad worker', that degenerate, immoral and dangerous individual.[14]

178

It would be pointless to try to look for the origins of criminal anthropology. At the beginning of the nineteenth century, Lavater and Gall[15] were the precursors of a new discipline: phrenology. They believed that, by examining the protuberances and depressions of the cranium, they could perceive the degree of intelligence and different individual tendencies, including morality. This led to the idea that crime, just like madness, was the result of certain irregularities in the development of different regions of the brain and the skull. Criminal anthropology owes much to the work carried out by Cabanis[16] and, later, by Despine,[17] who, using different approaches, reasserted the connection between madness and crime. The influence of the work of Prosper Lucas should also be noted, as well as B. A. Morel's work, which demonstrated that degeneracy and crime were closely linked.[18]

In 1885 Paul Broca founded the Anthropological Society, and eleven years later criminal anthropology was established by Cesare Lombroso.[19] Lombroso was not, therefore, unaware of this previous scientific movement, and his work reflects the trends of a period that was influenced by Darwinism and Comtism. His theory was based on the observation that there was a criminal type which could be distinguished by deforming marks or particular signs, a survival in our developed societies of the primitive savage. This conception reflects the bourgeoisie's obsession with a diseased society threatened by the venereal danger, which was a source of degeneracy, alcoholism and crime.

As a military doctor, Lombroso made a detailed study of the anatomy of soldiers and claimed to be able to distinguish a normal man from a criminal. He was appointed professor at the University of Turin where he pursued his research, and made observations on the skulls of 383 criminals; in one of them he discovered an abnormally developed occipital cavity which was similar to that found in the higher vertebrates closest to man: anthropoid apes.

By making an anthropometric, biological, medical and psychological study of 5,907 living offenders, Lombroso isolated a criminal type which he initially believed to be common to the majority of criminals – the born criminal. This man, whose nature is different from the rest of humanity, is regressing towards an atavistic stage. His anti-social behaviour can be explained by his mental deficiency and the influence of heredity; he is, in a sense, destined for crime. Thus, at the end of the nineteenth century, after laborious anthropometric studies, there emerged a new portrait of the criminal which was more precise than ever before. It was now justified by a theory, expounded for the first time in 1876 in a book entitled L'Uomo delinquente. The born criminal was successively regarded as a savage, a pathological degenerate and a neuro-psychopath of an epileptic disposition. He thus appeared as a socially dangerous monster who was beyond redemption. Furthermore, Lombroso allowed for the existence of other types of criminals: the insane criminal, the criminal motivated by passion, the habitual criminal, and the chance criminal. He soon had a small following of young doctors and lawyers, a group that included Enrico Ferri and Raffaello

Garofalo,[20] who helped found the new school of positivism and also started up a review, *Gli Archivi della psichiatria e dell'antropologia criminale.*

Apart from a few differences, they embraced most of Lombroso's doctrine, that is to say the major role of hereditary factors in criminal behaviour, the existence of criminal morphological features, and the belief that factors such as atavism, degeneracy, epilepsy and mental deficiency influence criminal constitution. However, Enrico Ferri did not neglect the study of social factors and their influence on the development of criminality, a social phenomenon that was distinct from crime, and was the action of an individual. Before long, he had established himself as the founder of criminal sociology.

The positivist school did not simply give a scientific account of criminality; it also set out to take part in drawing up a policy of repression and in the implementation of a plan for the protection of society. To this end, Lombroso and his colleagues campaigned against classical criminal law and prevailing legal practices. According to Ferri, the classical school resulted in the breakdown of repression:

Classical doctrine failed in practical terms. In seeking to grade sentences, both according to the severity of the offence and according to the moral responsibility of the offender, it led to an abuse of extenuating circumstances. Judges were generous with short prison sentences which had neither an intimidating effect nor an effect of moral reformation.[21]

Henceforth, the determinism underlying Lombroso's theory of the criminal excluded the notions of free will and moral responsibility on which classical criminal law was founded.

Unlike the classical school, the positivists were no longer concerned with knowing whether the accused was morally responsible; instead, they tried to determine whether he was inherently criminal, in other words whether he was beyond redemption or not. The Penal Code should not merely punish a transgression, it should also ensure that society is protected by preventing a repetition of the crime. The penalty should, therefore, no longer be calculated on the basis of how serious a crime is, but rather of how dangerous the criminal is. The punishment varies according to the degree of social harm that he may cause, and this in turn varies according to the category to which the criminal belongs. Finally, the personality of the accused overshadows the criminal act.

The positivists criticized prison reformists by challenging the theory of improved conduct because of the sentence. The effect of a prison sentence is completely useless on degenerate criminals; it will never prevent crime, since these individuals cannot be rehabilitated.

In this climate of reform, criminal anthropology had the advantage of offering a coherent and revolutionary scientific programme to combat criminality. The positivist school gave rise to a great many hopes, particularly among certain politicians such as Taine, who went as far as proposing a straightforward death sentence for born criminals since one can be certain that for the rest of their lives they will remain 'orang-outangs':

If I were a lawyer or a legislator or a member of the jury, I would not show any leniency towards murderers and thieves, or the 'born criminal', and the 'morally insane'. When, in the entire life, in the intellectual, moral and emotional life, of the offender, the criminal impulse is isolated, accidental and probably temporary, one can, and in fact one should, pardon; but the greater the link there is between this impulse and the web of ideas and feelings, the more the man is guilty and should be punished. You have shown us lecherous and fierce orang-outangs with human faces; indeed, as such they cannot behave differently from the way they do; if they rob, if they rape and if they kill, it is because of their nature and their past, and it is inevitable. This is another reason to kill them as soon as one has established that they are, and will always remain, orang-outangs. In their case, I have no objection to the death penalty, if society stands to gain from it. (Extract from a letter written to Lombroso on 12 April 1887 and published at the beginning of the French version of *L'Uomo delinquente*.)

Ferri, who was less radical, suggested the mass deportation of these monsters. The legislators of the Third Republic, who were receptive to the ideas of the positivists, passed two laws which were aimed at reinforcing repression and which applied to habitual offenders. The first law was the Act of 25 May 1885, which introduced banishment for professional criminals and habitual criminals, so as to rid the country of dangerous men; and the second law was the Bérenger Act of 26 March 1891, which granted first offenders the benefit of a suspended sentence and which, conversely, enacted new, harsher penalties for habitual offenders.

Although the social and political climate of the day was suitable for this type of speculation, Lombroso's thesis prompted some spirited reactions and paved the way for a series of confrontations. As a reaction against the determinism of the Italian school, the Franco-Belgian school of the social milieu was formed, represented by Laccassagne, Tarde, Manouvrier, Durkheim, Joly, etc. It criticized the positivists for overemphasizing morphological abnormalities, for rejecting the notion of the perfectibility of human beings and, finally, for ignoring the influence of the social milieu on the development of crime.

The first congresses on criminal anthropology produced some heated debates between the two schools. During the first congress, which took place in Rome in 1885, Laccassagne made a speech that attracted considerable attention. He rejected the fatalist theory of the born criminal and presented a sociological analysis of criminality, stressing the primary importance of environment. The school of the social milieu rejected the notions of degeneracy and atavism, without however denying the influence of individual factors. It attributed a decisive role to society in the development of criminal behaviour, either because some criminals are subject to the influence of a corrupting environment from an early age, or because, by rejecting certain individuals, society encourages their progressive downgrading. The Paris congress of 1889 marked a significant decline in the influence of the positivists, caused in part by the attacks made by Tarde, Laccassagne and Manouvrier. Manouvrier criticized Lombroso's method by pointing out his lack of rigour and analysis. Thus, in order to be convincing, the statistics on the specific abnormalities of criminals should have facilitated a comparison with a sample from the so-called 'normal' population.

This opposition movement stimulated the development of the sociological analysis of criminality. Though they were united in their fight against the positivists, the criminologists of the 'school of the social milieu' did not always agree on certain ideological aspects, and there were many different views within the group.

Although criminal sociology during the period 1885–1900 may appear to be fairly elementary, the rejection of the dangerous and mistaken theory of the born criminal and the assertion of social responsibility represented, at that time, a fundamental step forward in the social sciences. When Laccassagne wrote that society has the criminals it deserves, he was expressing a sentiment shared by all the supporters of the school of the social milieu; he was emphasizing the radical perspectives of the movement, which were often lacking in contemporary interpretations of crime. Furthermore, the school of the social milieu directed its fight against crime towards social aid and the rehabilitation of offenders in the hope of saving them, something that the pessimism inherent in Italian positivist theories did not make possible.

Criminal Men and Women

Faced with the threatening spectre of the born criminal, that human monster who was prepared to kill in order to rob an honest man, the perpetrator of a crime of passion appeared to be a harmless individual. This was why, at the end of the nineteenth century, he was ignored by criminologists, who were more concerned with defining the concept of 'dangerous state' than with studying this kind of criminality – which was, however, responsible for more deaths. He was perceived as a normal, respectable human being and was thus disconcerting, because of the difficulty these experts had in explaining his behaviour and in finding a solution to his violence. Contrary to the theory of the born criminal, which had given rise to numerous pseudo-scientific demonstrations, criminologists restricted themselves to a very brief definition, which was more a product of subjectivity and the collective imagination than a serious analysis. The typology of perpetrators of crimes of passion was very oversimplified and was presented as being the reverse

182

of the image of the born criminal. Where the born criminal was described as ugly, degenerate and cruel, positivists painted the opposite picture of the perpetrator of a crime of passion; the born criminal was characterized by a lethargic temperament, the perpetrator of a crime of passion by a fiery, nervous and sensitive temperament. Unlike the born criminal, the perpetrator of a crime of passion is not distinguished by any degenerative and/or pathological abnormalities: 'In this individual one rarely, if at all, observes the organic abnormalities which produce the criminal type. The psychological characteristics are also greatly reduced in the areas where some crimes of passion are endemic and almost belong to daily life.'[22]

Lombroso regarded external appearance as the expression of an individual's real self; he described the physiognomy of the perpetrator of a crime of passion as appealing, even attractive. In short, this was a normal individual, an ordinary person, since 'his past was spotless' and nothing distinguished him from other people. He did not come across as mentally disturbed, either. In agreement with the positivists, Georges Tarde,[23] who represented the positivist school, reinforced this position by asserting that this type of crime was never caused by a pathological passion, a view shared by nineteenth-century judges and members of the jury. This concept of normality is a fundamental prerequisite in understanding the evolution of social reaction towards the perpetrator of a crime of passion who, in the following century, was regarded as suspect.

In order to justify their leniency towards him, the positivists relied heavily on this concept of normality, to which were added certain factors that were specifically revealing of the harmlessness of this type of criminal, such as the low rate of repeated offences, the lack of premeditiation, and the attitude of the accused before, during and after the crime, and especially his explicit repentance.

Unlike the professional criminal, the perpetrator of a crime of passion does not prepare his crime, which he often commits with ill-chosen weapons, without using cunning and, above all, without concealing himself. Ferri wrote that 'he acts in broad daylight.'

The fact that he commits his crime for all to see, without acting in an underhand way, implies that the criminal considers his behaviour to be justified and that he does not fear either social censure or dishonour. After carrying out the crime, the criminal does not even attempt to run away, and in certain cases hands himself over to the police. When he is arrested, he does not seek to deny the facts but immediately confesses to them, often firmly defending them. To the lack of depravity, and to the spontaneity of the act, can be added the signs of remorse expressed by the criminal, who condemns the slightest degree of perniciousness in his human nature. Without questioning the genuineness of the signs of repentance, Enrico Ferri wrote: 'These individuals confess their crime immediately with a sincere repentance, which is often so intense that they kill themselves or try to kill themselves immediately after the crime.'[24] The suicide can therefore be interpreted as an act of self-punishment, whose materiality expresses the will to make one's amends to society, and which often inspires the indulgence of public opinion.

In a reform plan for the Italian Penal code, Enrico Ferri suggested the acquittal of the perpetrator of a crime of passion with compensation for the harm inflicted on the victim, but only in cases when the accused corresponded in every detail with the typology of the 'ideal' perpetrator of a crime of passion (Penal Code of 1921, article 28, paragraphs 3 and 4):

The last category is that of criminals who act on the impulse of a passion which is not anti-social and which is excusable, such as love, honour, etc. For these individuals any sentence is clearly useless, in so far as it is intended to counter the psychological impulse, for the very circumstances of psychological upheaval in which they commit their crime negate any deterrent effect of the legislative threat. I think, therefore, that in typical cases of crimes of passion when there is no psychopathic disorder which requires confinement in an asylum for insane criminals, prison sentences serve no purpose. The precise compensation for the harm inflicted should be sufficient to punish these individuals, when they are already punished after the criminal release of their justifiable passion, by true and sincere remorse. One could also add to the compensation temporary banishment from the scene of the crime and the home of the victim's family.[25]

The notion of paying an indemnity, a sort of compensation, was not a new one, since it was accepted in societies that practice personal revenge as the norm, and made it possible to put an end to a dispute between two families or two groups while saving the honour of each.

The reforms sought by the positivists addressed a policy of social protection which was based on the effectiveness of sentences, whose usefulness depended on the practice of sentencing according to the characteristics of the offender. With a view to adapting the sentence in accordance with the personality of the offender, the positivist school created the notion of a dangerous state, which, together with potential for rehabilitation, formed the criteria for penal repression. The dangerous state meant the risk of a relapse, which depended on the potential criminal energy, and varied according to each offender; the maximum degree was reached by the born criminal and the mad criminal, and decreased until it reached nil with the perpetrator of a crime of passion; hence the leniency with which this criminal was treated.

The social protection movement, headed in France by R. Saleilles, marked the eclipse of the positivist school, whose over-radical views prevented any practical efficiency in the form of penal legislation and in judicial practice. But one fundamental element was retained: the notion of the dangerous state which made it necessary to judge the offender on the basis of his or her character, and not on the basis of what they had done, thereby concealing in a certain sense penal responsibility. This movement also sanctioned psychiatric power side by side with the power of the judiciary. Under the rational appearance of this approach, one can, however, imagine the danger inherent in the law which no longer intervenes to punish the crime but rather the possible risk of crime.

Lombroso and Ferri became aware that they had oversimplified their theory on perpetrators of crimes of passion and so they qualified certain assertions, but the lack of rigour in their method often made their theory confused and contradictory. They both realized the difficulty in defining the normality of perpetrators of crimes of passion. Thus, wanting to demonstrate the impulsiveness of the crime of passion, Lombroso suddenly associated perpetrators of such crimes with epileptics: 'Far more than ordinary criminals, they resemble impulsive madmen because of the impetuosity, the instantaneousness and the wildness of their crimes.'[26] The dividing line between madness and passion became blurred. Using Lombroso's classification of five types of criminal, Ferri found it difficult to determine to which category a criminal belonged, and so he recognized the existence of intermediary categories. Thus, the perpetrator of a crime of passion resembled the insane criminal or the casual criminal in certain respects:

One moves from the casual criminal to the perpetrator of a crime of passion who is in effect a more distinct variety of the casual criminal, while by his neurotic or hysterical or epileptic or mattoid temperament, the perpetrator of a crime of passion is often similar to the mad criminal, even to the point of becoming almost identical with him.[27]

The positivists give the impression that they felt trapped by the theory of the born criminal. Their mistake is that they wanted to justify the impunity with which they dealt with the perpetrator of a crime of passion by contrasting him with the born criminal, as can be seen for example in the question of premeditation, one of the criteria used to distinguish the two types of criminal. The crime of passion was at first presented as an impulsive, and hence unpremeditated, act. But, faced with the reality of the assize court, Ferri was forced to challenge this postulate:

Sometimes, however, there are perpetrators of crimes of passion who also premeditate their crime and carry it out insidiously, either because of their particular temperament, which is less impulsive, or under the influence of prejudices and collective feeling, as in the case of endemic crime. And this is why, according to criminal psychology, the criterion of premeditation does not have an absolute value to define the born criminal by comparison with the perpetrator of a crime of passion, since premeditation depends on the individual's temperament more than on anything else and is also found in crime committed by either of the anthropological categories of offender.[28]

The recognition that the crime of passion could be committed with premeditation, a sign of considerable depravity, weakened the notion of a crime committed on the impulse of a passion and paved the way towards a definition that was closer to reality.

The theorists ignored women's crimes for a long time, as the gender of the perpetrators disqualified their crimes from serious attention. Female crime was less frequent and yet more 'sensational', but it occupied a marginal position. Nevertheless, in the movement of this discursive overstatement on crime, Lombroso tackled the problem and displayed a real talent for misogyny and obscurantism. Instead of being relegated to conventional criminal categories, female crime was associated with prostitution, which was to women what crime was to men. This comparison evinced a desire to discredit and to give an inferior status to female offenders compared with male offenders. According to Lombroso, crime is a sort of perversion of genius, and the degeneracy of women is different because women are different.

The female criminal's abnormality displays far more serious characteristics than that of the male criminal since it represents a double exception: 'The born female criminal is, so to speak, a double exception, as a criminal and as a woman . . . , and she is therefore more monstrous.'[29]

In order to establish different types of female criminal, Lombroso adopted a similar approach to the one he had used to study the male population; he relied on anthropometric examination, physiology and psychology to demonstrate the marks of degeneracy that make female criminals similar to female savages who are characterized by their male features. He observed skulls, scrutinized facial expressions, counted hairs, measured and weighed them, and concluded that female criminals have many male features (a deep voice, hairiness, etc.): 'If one compares them to normal women, one can see that female criminals and prostitutes are more similar to men, whether they are normal or criminal, than to normal women.'[30] The view that crime was a destructive act, and therefore a virile act, explains this somewhat simplistic analogy.

The portrait of the born female criminal, in its physical and moral ugliness, was the product of horror stories. Since she was an exceptional criminal, a woman committed her crime with a cruel and diabolical sophistication which revealed a profoundly sadistic nature: 'She tends to make her victim suffer, to make him die gradually. Men are more savage, they kill and massacre without mercy; but they are less adept than women at prolonging suffering and making men endure the maximum pain of which a human being is capable.'[31] This opinion, which was asserted in reference to the stereotyped image of the female criminal as poisoner, shows the limits of this theory, which was not only reductive, but also discredited female crime by associating its depravity with that of children.

This image of the female criminal is not peculiar to Lombroso's theory; it is also found, expressed identically, throughout the literature of criminology: 'It is true, as so many moralists have said, that women are nearly always better or worse than men. When they are worse, they are so especially when they distance themselves markedly and in every aspect from their nature; in that case neither their cruelty nor their corruption knows any limits.'[32] Being depraved, she is also more dangerous because she commits her crime covertly, using men to carry out her unspeakable plan. She is the Eve of evil, the instigator – these were the images that criminologists inevitably exploited. Lombroso's theory of the female criminal synthesizes the far from innovative debate on the female character which states that her physical and intellectual inferiority stems from her physiological peculiarity: her sexual, emotional and intellectual passivity in the face of the conquering and active male is caused by the respective roles of the ovum and the sperm.

In conclusion, women do not seek pleasure in the sexual act; indeed, they do not experience the need or the sensation, since they are organically frigid. This negation of female sexuality fits in with the idealized image of the protector of the home, the mother who is both nurturer and teacher. She is the ideal woman whom men wish to reduce to sexual silence so that she can fulfil noble family roles, sheltered from carnal pleasures which are a dangerous source of disorder.

The definition of different categories of criminals does not apply to the female model. Whereas the perpetrator of a crime of passion is characterized by honesty, beauty and normality, the female criminal embodies evil and depravity. The great master criminologist associates her with the born female criminal and shows no leniency towards her since she is depraved, plans her crime and does not show any signs of repentance. All the elements that enabled Lombroso to be benevolent towards the perpetrator of a crime of passion are lacking in his female counter-part, who does not commit the crime under the irresistible impulse of the violence of a passion but, on the contrary, premeditates it with coldness and skill: 'We are not, therefore, dealing here with those outbursts of passion which blind even decent men and turn them, for a moment, into murderers, but rather with a slower passion which is more deep-seated and which makes evil instincts ferment, and which gives time to calculate and to prepare the crime.'[33]

Such a dissimilarity between female and male perpetrators of crimes of passion can be explained by the complete lack of a sense of morality in women, who embody the forces of evil. A more intense excitability and serious provocations are enough for criminal tendencies, which are physiologically latent, to get the better of them: 'Women do not become criminals because of the intensity of their passions, for in them these are colder, but because provocation has made this latent criminality emerge.'[34] Women have an innate propensity towards evil which makes them potential criminals.

As she is cruel by nature, passion leads her to crime 'because she has been able to make that latent streak of wickedness emerge'.[35] This apparent gentleness can thus prove to be fearsome 'if a morbid excitation of the psychic centres awaken her evil characteristics; . . . it is obvious that from the harmless semi-criminal which the ordinary woman is, a born female criminal who is far more terrible than any male criminal will emerge.'[36]

The woman who acts with passion can also demonstrate a far greater capacity for feeling than the majority of other women and can behave sexually like a man. Her amorous nature is then liable to lead her to dangerous outbursts. Hungry for sensual pleasure, she does not hesitate to have casual relationships; her attitude towards her sexuality then forms a criterion for abnormality: 'Virginity and marriage are social institutions which are suitable, as are all customs and institutions, for the average woman, that is to say for the sexual coldness of the normal woman; these women are too passionate not to infringe these rules.'[37]

The reality of the assize courts reflected this statement. Indeed, the law displayed great interest in the sexual behaviour of female criminals and female victims. Repression was based on the gap between their behaviour and the norm. The woman who was 'mad about her body' was punished more severely than a virtuous woman; even when she was a victim, a woman's sexual behaviour had to obey morality; otherwise the accused would be exonerated for having killed a licentious woman.

Ten years later, Camille Granier carried out a study of female criminality from a more sociological point of view, and tried to find the reason for the numerical difference between female and male crime. He asserted, without proving it, that women could repeat offences as much as, if not more than, men. This research was a reworked version, which was perhaps more accessible, of Lombroso's theory. The author wanted to prove, above all, that female criminals represented a dangerous threat to society and that it was necessary to combat the inequality of repression, since women enjoyed the leniency of the jury far too often. In effect, the majority of criminologists, judges and members of the jury were benevolent towards certain forms of female crime (for example, infanticide and vitriol-throwing), defending those women whom they regarded as victims of a patriarchal society. For other women, physiological and psychic inferiority was an excuse in itself: in the eyes of the law, women, being inferiors and minors, were not considered responsible for their behaviour.

The Desire for Criminal Suppression

Criminal suppression was a very fashionable topic in the first decade of the twentieth century and was of great interest to doctors and lawyers, who discussed the moral responsibility of the perpetrator of a crime of passion and a suitable punishment. Between 1900 and 1910, there were about a dozen works on this subject. Out of this body of work there emerges the desire to understand the personality and the behaviour of the criminal by giving greater importance to psychological analysis than to a sociological explanation. This approach entailed the refusal to give this crime the tenor of a social fact by presenting it as an individual, timeless and universal act with no connections to a social, economic and political reality. Psychiatrists and psychologists, called upon by the legal authorities, took hold of the individual who had become the target of legal and medical knowledge. This appeal, coloured by a degree of suspicion, formed part of the continuation of the movement to sentence according to the characteristics of the offender and of the influence of criminal anthropology. The effectiveness and the meaning of the punishment were to be found in the knowledge of the intimate self of the accused.

To this end, the accused were increasingly subject to medical and legal investigation. At the beginning of the nineteenth century, only monstrous crimes against nature were the subject of medical reports, and this marked the limits of the influence of psychiatrists.[38] In the 1880s a new direction was initiated; people were surprised to see judges demanding a medical report in the criminal preliminary investigation of a case such as the Marie Brière case, a commonplace story of a crime of passion.[39] Twenty years later, lawyers and doctors were still referring to this case study to justify the use of a psychiatric approach.

Marie Brière, known in the world of entertainment under the name of Maria Béraldi, was born in Bordeaux in December 1848 of respectable but not very well-off parents. She came to Paris in 1867 and entered the conservatoire the following year; she left in 1873 and started her career as an opera singer. According to witnesses, she had an impetuous and romantic nature. This ambitious and fiery young woman remained a virgin, despite the temptations to which her position exposed her. In September 1877, accompanied by her mother who went everywhere with her, Marie went to Biarritz. During her stay there she met Monsieur Robert Gentien, a rich landowner from the Bordeaux area, who lived mostly in Paris where he 'led the easy existence of the idle [rich]'. This young man, who was then thirty, courted Marie without receiving her favours. But on her return to Paris, she agreed to meet him and became his mistress. 'On the accused's own admission, her downfall cannot be blamed on misleading promises of marriage. She admits that she was carried away by an intense passion.'[40]

The two lovers used to meet in the rue de Hanovre, in a furnished flat which Gentien rented especially. Marie Brière was caught one day by her parents' concierge and was thus forced to confess to her liaison. Her mother immediately went to see Gentien and created a fuss, demanding that he marry Marie. Gentien was greatly irritated by this dispute and started to distance himself from Marie, who, as she was afraid of losing him, chose to break with her parents. In January 1878, he went off on a trip and persuaded his mistress to accept a contract to work in Brussels. On her arrival, she discovered that she was pregnant and suddenly lost her voice.

When Gentien returned she told him that she was pregnant. He was very angry and advised her to have an abortion, but she refused and a daughter was born to her on 2 October 1878. Gentien refused to accept paternity and displayed an intense repulsion towards her. So as to be able to continue seeing her lover, Marie placed her daughter with a wet nurse in Saint-Denis. But Gentien came to see her only infrequently and was very cold towards her. Suddenly, in April

1879, the child died after getting bronchitis. Marie was in despair; she blamed her lover and was convinced that the child would not have died had it been with her. Gentien took advantage of this to reduce the allowance which he gave her every month and made it clear that he wanted to part from her. Marie Brière was very distressed by her daughter's death and tried to commit suicide in front of her lover, who naturally prevented her from doing so.

When she learnt that she had been replaced by another woman, she devised a plan for revenge, and, from July, she committed her thoughts to a small diary which reveals how she progressed along the path to crime.

In November, after receiving a letter from Gentien in which he demanded that she disappear completely from his life (Marie still went to his house to make scenes and wrote him blackmail letters; he continued, however, to pay her allowance), she acquired a revolver, but had not yet decided to take action. A portrait of Gentien was found in her jewellery box next to a portrait of her daughter; on the back of the photograph of her lover was written: 'I give my life and the life of her father to my dead daughter.' On 1 January she wrote these words on another photograph of Gentien: 'Sentenced to death by me, Marie.' On 7 January, as Robert Gentien came out into the rue Auber, accompanied by a young actress, Marie Brière fired and wounded her lover in the back and on his leg. She had been following him and keeping watch over him for the previous two months.

Was this a tragedy of jealousy, or the act of a neurotic woman, the doctors asked. Here is the statement made by the famous psychiatrist, Doctor Blanche:

I had several interviews with Mademoiselle Brière. This young woman comes from a family of insane people. Her mother has, on several occasions, suffered from madness. One of her uncles, she told me, died in the Pau asylum. I won't mention her brother who has a wild and unruly character. He left his parents and went off to South America; I have been informed that he is now a herdsman in the pampas of Argentina. As for the accused, she was brought up by a wild mother who one day threatened to throw her out of the window; she inherited this pathological predisposition from her. From an early age she displayed signs of being wild. She told me that at the age of twelve, when she was at boarding school, she had an intense feeling of affection for one of her companions; this young girl appeared to be indifferent to her, and so Marie tried twice to commit suicide. This tendency to be easily excited continued throughout the accused's adolescence, and now Marie Brière is dominated more than ever by her passions and her feelings. She said, and even wrote, that on the day her child died, she resolved to kill her lover. Yes, when she shot at Monsieur Gentien, she knew what she was doing. But at that moment she was under the influence of passions which stemmed from such morbid over-excitement that it was very difficult for her to resist the feelings, which dominated her and obliterated all sense of morality in her.

She was indeed responsible for her behaviour, but her mental state at the time of the crime was not that of a normal person – such was the judicious conclusion given by Doctor Blanche, whose analysis of the accused was taken into consideration.

Marie Brière, defended by Maître Lachaud, was acquitted. This verdict did not surprise anyone; the medical report did not influence the members of the jury in the slightest, for the sight of the seduced and abandoned woman was sufficiently moving in itself. Her story was not new, but, henceforth, this type of accused woman was subject to psychiatric examination.

Legal experts, aware of the difficulty of establishing the responsibility of the perpetrator of a crime of passion, looked to science to justify and rationalize their judgements. First, they examined the role of the passions. For the first time, a lawyer tried to define the notion of a crime of passion: 'We believe that by crimes of passion are meant those crimes caused by love, which also have a disinterested character and where the violence of the passion alone has provoked a man who normally behaves properly.'[41] As they were utterly convinced of the coercive power of love throughout the criminal's development, criminologists gave absolute priority to the psychological description of amorous behaviour in analysing the causes of crimes of passion. How was it possible for love, that noble sentiment, to be transformed into murderous hatred?

The question of sexuality, which was tackled with diffidence, first appeared in the form of moral criticism in the same way as alcoholism and laziness. The intention was to show that freedom of behaviour, characterized by sexual precociousness, free love and adultery, not only resulted in licentiousness, but also created criminal tendencies. Criminologists, who were not familiar with sexual psychology, did not devote much time to this rather delicate area; instead, they preferred to study more common psychological phenomena such as jealousy, hatred and revenge. This was the approach adopted by Louis Proal,[42] who analyzed the causes and the consequences of jealous behaviour on suicide and on crimes of passion.

Female jealousy, in particular, was focused on, and was the subject of much comment. Proal described the jealous woman in a less obsessive tone than Lombroso but with equal misogyny; it was simply a caricatured portrait. As a potential criminal, the jealous woman came across as an emotional tyrant who greatly relished the pleasure of revenge. The emotion of jealousy was not even worthy of great love and was the vulgar product of a proud nature: 'Female jealousy contains far more selfishness and pride than love.'[43] It was only the seduced and deserted woman who received Proal's pity, because she was more likely to choose suicide than revenge. Was it not, after all, in women's nature to know how to suffer and to sacrifice themselves?

Another cause of crimes of passion was female adultery. In order to avert this danger, Louis Proal urged husbands to be vigilant: 'Above all, in sexual matters men should not exercise violence towards a young wife, for that would soon shut her door only to open it to a more gentle lover.'[44] He must not be in a position of inferiority, either: 'Vanity plays an important part in a woman's love. In order to love her husband, she must be proud of him.'[45] Furthermore, men should be wary of adulterous women, who are past masters in the art of disssembling and whose hypocritical character was compared to that of the feline species. They should also be on their guard against women who rebel against the patriarchal order, for the woman 'who before her marriage has deceived her family, will later deceive her husband.'[46] He naturally strongly advised men against having relationships with younger women.

More dangerous still was the sensual woman: 'If a husband is ever incapable of satisfying the passions of a dissolute woman, he runs the risk not only of being replaced, but also of being killed.' But men could rest assured that these licentious women were rare, since, in women, 'the sexual need is not as powerful as in men', whose sexual passion is characterized by violence and brutality. 'It is men who attack and provoke, and their choice is determined by physical attraction, rather than by moral qualities.' In women, however, it is the reverse; flirtatiousness and vanity get the better of sensuality. Women are susceptible to tenderness, attention, and compliments; they are repelled by brutal passion: 'Her love is more psychological than physical.'[47] In conclusion, Louis Proal condemns the adulterous woman who, given the peculiarity of her nature, is 'more guilty than men because her sexual makeup makes it easier for her to be virtuous'.

Proal's conception of female sexuality was directly influenced by the work of Lombroso and Krafft-Ebing. The latter's theories are merely a reflection of all the clichés articulated in bourgeois ideology; for the bourgeoisie was anxious to protect the institution of the family from the excesses and disturbances that could result from the unleashing of uncontrolled female sexuality: 'If a woman's mind is normally developed and if she has been brought up properly, then her sexuality is not very well developed. If this were otherwise, the entire world would just be one vast brothel, and marriage and family life would be impossible.'[48]

This intelligible act, the crime of passion, which was still in the domain of reason, raised a serious problem for criminologists – the problem of punishment. The impunity that these crimes enjoyed was considered scandalous, and provoked censure from lawyers whose stance was to mark the first change in the development of the social acceptability of this type of crime. They strongly criticized the pernicious role of the jury, which was held responsible for lack of authority in the implementation of the law; by acquitting perpetrators of crimes of passion, it was legitimizing the right to take the law into one's own hands. The jury was criticized for allowing itself to be influenced, for turning the court-room proceedings into a spectacle, for being too gentlemanly and acting with too much propriety, and for showing pity towards the murderer instead of the victim. Some lawyers expressed their fears about this lenient attitude, and they proposed limiting civic society's right to examine judicial practice by drawing attention to the incompetence of juries in legal matters.

While this new debate was directed at punishing perpetrators of crimes of passion, there was however a refusal to sentence them in the same way as criminals whose offence was based on greed. They should be punished, but in a different way. Criminologists were convinced that, from the legal point of view, perpetrators of crimes of passion were like any other murderers; yet they disputed the effectiveness of a long prison sentence, as far as rehabilitation and prevention of this type of crime were concerned:

If the criminal has acted under the influence of passion and if there is no risk of a repeated offence, then the sentence should frighten him or rather frighten others, but it does not need to correct him, to improve him like the common law criminal. It is not necessary to recreate an honest soul in the individual who has always retained it.[49]

Doctors and lawyers, who were torn between their desire to punish and the view they held of the personality and the behaviour of the perpetrator of a crime of passion, continued to distinguish him from other criminals: 'All of us, including the members of the jury, and against our better judgement, find that the perpetrator of a crime of passion is as likeable as other criminals are odious. He appears to us as a poor wretch far more than as a guilty man.'[50]

The image is clear: he is a man worthy of pity, who has been spiritually persecuted; he is a decent man whose suffering transforms his character and who has been turned into a murderer because of the victim's provocations. From society's point of view, he is far less dangerous; morally, his responsibility, although difficult to establish, is minimal. At the beginning of the twentieth century, criminologists were still explaining the decision to carry out the crime by appealing to the dominating power of the impulsiveness of the passion, which undermines the will and draws the individual into crime. Not only does the amorous passion remain fascinating, but it also explains in itself the criminal process and is the basis for the lack of responsibility of the perpetrator of a crime of passion. This theory is the legacy of canon law and ancient law, which was forgiving towards those who behaved violently because of the pain and the anger of jealousy or lost honour. Such an act does not bear the stain of dishonour because of its motive and its impulsive character, in the face of which the decent man is powerless. Is not the fury with which the act is committed proof of the frenzied state of the criminal? The same applies to premeditation, which, far from making the crime seem well thought-out and intentional, endows it with an even greater degree of irresponsibility. This is Saleilles's contention:

If one takes people who are obsessed with an idea, those who are heading towards a so-called crime of passion, then the more compelling and blind the obsession, the more it overpowers the individual until it possesses him entirely, and the more his will appears cold, calculating, patient and well thought-out.

There is nothing more patient, or more premeditated, than the criminal obsession of certain murders.[51]

Premeditation does not, however, mean that one can conclude that the crime has been committed with complete free will; it provides an additional excuse for the crime of passion.

When Louis Holtz wrote, in connection with perpetrators of crimes of passion, 'It is imprudent to sentence them, and it is unjust to acquit them,'[52] he was echoing, on the one hand, the embarrassment of lawyers, and, on the other hand, the new sensibility that was starting to emerge. The complaints about excessive acquittals expressed the need there was to stop allowing men to settle their disputes by crime, which was a sign of barbarism, and reflected the will to give the punishment a civilizing function. The civilized man displays complete self-control, and should leave it up to the judiciary to settle his personal disputes. The problem presented by the punishment of criminals shows the awareness of the legal profession that it was necessary to curb personal justice, an outmoded social practice. Public opinion largely supported this view, as can be seen from the following article, which appeared in *La Revue des deux mondes*.

Crimes of passion are the crimes which our juries and which public opinion treat the most leniently or with the most false pity, and yet, when one examines them, they are the most heinous, the most dangerous, and above all the most antisocial crimes. If Monsieur Proal had better demonstrated this, in a work whose objective was 'to study and to evaluate the principles underlying the penal system using the most modern theories', I do not think he would have deviated from his plan; and he would no doubt have had the opportunity to make a number of useful remarks.

What is, indeed, inexcusable and profoundly evil in the crime of passion is that the criminal does not for one moment weigh up the right or even the life of others against satisfying his base appetite. That is what today, unfortunately, we refuse to see. 'She was resisting me, so I murdered her', or 'He wouldn't marry me, that's why I threw vitriol at him.' Not only do we no longer feel what is bestial in these cries of female vanity or in the pride of frustrated instincts, but, if truth be told, we come close to admiring those who utter these cries, and almost envy them. And as for their victims, we feel sorry for them, no doubt, but deep down we are not far from believing that they have deserved their fate! . . . Neither love nor hatred that is responsible for death is any less guilty than greed which is responsible for robbing; and I will add that, despite appearances, there is something more dangerous in the former, for there is something more antisocial in these motives . . .

If the social order does, indeed, have no other more fundamental aim than to allow others to judge personal animosities or disputes, then whoever sets himself up as a judge of these grievances is going against the aim of the very institution which he claims to continue to enjoy. The crime of passion is, simply, a negation of the law, of which all other crimes are but a violation, a return to barbarism, and a regression towards bestiality.[53]

It is possible to detect in this statement – which it would be simplistic to interpret as expressing a reactionary point of view – the existence within the social order of thresholds of tolerance towards certain forms of violence and crime which are dependent on changes in mentality.

Personal justice, a relic from primitive societies, is perceived as a negation of the law, of authority and of discipline. At a certain stage in its development, a society can no longer tolerate that individuals should supplant the state: 'It is a distinctive feature of a civilized society that it places the law in the hands of the state because no one among its citizens can be a judge and a party to his own case.'[54] The state must, therefore, strengthen the legal apparatus so as to increase its monopoly on violence and force men to control their urges by allowing everyone to be a judge of how to settle personal animosities and disputes. Did Tocqueville not hope that the progress of democracy would bring about lawful behaviour and that disorder and crimes of passion would increasingly diminish?

The problem of how to punish, and the attendant difficulty in establishing criminal responsibility, introduced a series of questions as regards the mental stability of the perpetrator of a crime of passion, which had already been challenged in judicial practice by means of medical and legal investigations. The temptation to employ psychiatry started to appear among lawyers such as Louis Holtz, who could not ignore certain ideological trends: 'The progress of medicine and psychology has taught us that perfect mental health is as rare in human beings as is perfect physical health'.[55] This inevitably made it necessary to examine the personality of the perpetrator of a crime of passion. Is the individual who allows himself to be carried away by passion sane, and are all his mental faculties intact? These diffident questions, to which no answer was provided, did nonetheless cause the criminal to be viewed as someone outside the norm. As this shifting view started to emerge, psychiatry appeared and offered criminologists a clinical definition of this phenomenon; henceforth, the criminal appeared as a pathologically unsound individual.

The first book on this subject was written by the psychiatric doctor, Hélie Courtis, in 1910, and was entitled *Etude médico-légale des crimes passionnels*. It was a genuine plea for making each perpetrator of a crime of passion undergo psychiatric analysis so that both the criminal's personality and the circumstances of the crime could be taken into account in order to evaluate the degree of responsibility. With the involvement of psychiatry and anthropology, responsibility, which was previously linked to the idea of free will and to the healthy mental state of the individual, started to depend on psychological determinism, which was reflected in the intelligibility of the crime, in the criminal's behaviour, and in the social danger that he represented. It was in the name of this danger and of social protection that psychiatry became influential in the judicial process. Doctors were considered experts who were empowered to discover and to evaluate the treatment that the criminal should receive, since he was ill and was a threat to society's health. 'While lawyers continue to ignore the psychological analysis of the mental state of the criminal, one must question the ethical and legal legitimacy of certain sentences.'[56] The decision as to the validity of medico-legal reports should not, however, be left up to the investigating magistrate.

Furthermore, Hélie Courtis, drawing on the works of Krafft-Ebing, challenged the concept of normality and demystified the notion that passion over-powers. He made a distinction between two types of states conducive to a crime of passion. As to the first of these, the physiological state pertaining to the passions, it is perfectly natural for a normal man to feel the effects of passion, and one should bear in mind 'temporary disorders which emotion introduces into the psychological mechanism and the new state in which the capacity for psychological resistance, in so far as it is formed by ethical and legal constraints, is a degree lower than in the normal state'. Nevertheless, Courtis believed that the individual could learn to correct and to control the manifestations and effects of passion – it was simply a matter of training. This assertion that it was possible to fight the impulsiveness of passion insidiously re-introduced the notion of free will.

Finally, the source of the crime of passion could be described as a long struggle between impulse and mind. Indeed, passion and thought are not in contradiction: 'In passionate natures, passion grows under its own influence despite being combated for a long time by moral and intellectual resistance. But if a trivial event, a purely accidental cause, destroys the last grains of thought and self-control, then passion is transformed into crime.'[57] Courtis wondered if this abrupt change might be a sign of mental illness. He suggested that the responsibility of the offender should be judged in accordance with his ability to control his impulses and no longer on the basis of his previous history, a factor that had always influenced juries. The criminal's reputation should be disregarded, and only his personality and the precise circumstances of the crime should be taken into account.

As to the second state of mind, the pathological state pertaining to the passions, Courtis defined it as a state of temporary madness, with loss of consciousness, and explained this process by taking up Krafft-Ebing's description: 'Passion causes circulatory troubles (spasms or dilation) in the brain; then they become independent, cannot be spontaneously obliterated, and create a temporary mental disorder.'[58] These changes in circulation will be short-lived in the physiological states; they will last longer in the pathological states and will result in a deterioration in the brain cells, which reduces the capacity for psychological resistance. Emotion causes an outburst of passion of such intensity only in cases that are pathologically predisposed. These states of brain deficiency are either congenital or the consequence of degeneration. Courtis attributed this loss of cerebral energy to a wild, debauched life of sexual excess. Like the moralists, doctors contributed greatly to increasing the public's anxiety that licentiousness causes degeneration.

1930: A Dangerous Madman

During the 1930s, perpetrators of crimes of passion no longer had any of the reassuring features that previously characterized them. They were presented as mentally ill and, paradoxically, as responsible for their behaviour. In 1931, Louis Rabinowicz's *Crimes of Passion: A Study in Social Psychology* was published; it was the first critical analysis of positivist theory. Eleven years later, E. de Greeff, the great Belgian theorist, wrote the last work on this subject, *Amour et crimes d'amour*, which was a psychological study of the personality and behaviour of 120 perpetrators of crimes of passion. Both Rabinowicz and de Greeff initiated a debate that was radically opposed to that of the positivists and which turned the 'decent perpetrator of a crime of passion' into a degenerate who was virtually a savage. He was insidiously similar to the born criminal: 'He's a poor devil, burdened with a history of mental illness, a victim of an unstable temperament, sometimes infantile, often illiterate and, on the whole, inferior.'[59] This, according to de Greeff, is his true portrait.

Rabinowicz's description reinforces this negative image: 'He has a violent, bloodthirsty character . . . . The motives that guide him are no more interesting, or less dangerous for society, than those that drive the murderer motivated by greed.'[60] Rabinowicz's intention was to destroy the exalted character with which crimes of passion are endowed and to remove 'the mask of idealism which people try to give them by exploiting the sentimentality that is in all of us. The crime motivated by love is proof not of a sublime heart, but of a base and perverse heart. Suicide, alone, is a sign of love.'[61]

Far from being a source of energy, the passions have a harmful influence on men who do not resist them. Indeed, Rabinowicz relentlessly tried to discredit the passion of love and compared it to a state of madness. It is lost energy, a debilitating waste, a form of intoxication which was just as pernicious as morphine. Passion is an abnormal state, 'if not pathological, an excrescence, a parasitism. The passions are morbid and come close to, or else culminate in, madness. The moment they lead to crime, these passions cease to be social and become criminal.'[62]

Rabinowicz attacked sexual love, which tends to be the main motive for crimes of passion: 'Sexual love is behind the vast majority of crimes of passion, if not all of them.'[63] He criticized sensualism, which poisons the life of individuals:

We are declaring a merciless war on crimes of passion, but we are not attacking that sublime and truly superior form of love which is emotional love, a magnificent synthesis of sexuality and tenderness; we are, however, criticizing quite openly that violent, primitive and animal form of love, that is to say, sensual love that leads to murder.[64]

He was later criticized for devaluing love, reducing sexuality to a simple need for release, and for portraying them as harmful forces which lead to crime.

De Greef was more radical and rejected any connection between crimes of passion and amorous relationships: 'Experience teaches us that suicides and murders for love, in fact, have nothing in common with the intensity of love, or with the extraordinary depth of passion, but only with serious inadequacies in the personality of the criminal.'[65]

Crimes of passion are associated with a simple psychological process of revaluation:

One should bear in mind that at the root of crimes of passion there is always an acute process of revaluation, either of a living person or of some thing. And this revaluation exists only in the emotional tension of the individual, a tension in which many feelings, generally of a fairly base and often contradictory nature, concur, but whose outcome is perceived as a whole and is qualified depending on the circumstances: love, one's rights, and justice. These are words which in such situations only have a purely subjective value.[66]

What criminals and the general public, including some judges, mistake for love is thus simply a process of revaluation. In order to prove the lack of true amorous feelings, one only has to point to the indifference shown by criminals towards their loved ones in times of illness. This negation of amorous feelings considerably debased the criminal, and challenged the association that criminologists had made, for many decades, between crimes of passion and crimes of love.

Nevertheless, this process subjects the individual's mind to such enormous stress that it then produces a genuine state of suffering which has the effect of ennobling some of these crimes and of making them legitimate in the eyes of the general public. De Greef takes into account this suffering, which, when it reaches a certain degree, pushes the individual towards despair and gives rise to suicidal tendencies. Nevertheless, the acuteness of this state should not excuse the criminal. To give way to suffering is proof of an individual's inferiority and baseness:

The normal man, who is reasonably honest and reasonably careful in his moral behaviour, takes care up to a certain point not to give way to despair or to resentment, and not to release in himself those processes of degeneration whose consequences he can see; the criminal, in most commonplace situations, also arrives at this point.[67]

Although revaluation of the loved one, jealousy and suffering are normal elements of human psychology, these states are murderous only in cases of mental degeneration: 'In individuals who are mentally damaged, instincts that are exacerbated by jealousy find, therefore, an existing mental state which is particularly suited to giving it a dangerous and lasting form.'[68] Compared with this dangerous madman, the perpetrator of a crime of passion, as described by Ferri and Lombroso, is all but forgotten. Nevertheless, de Greeff acknowledged that in other societies, and at other periods, this crime might have been committed by sane individuals. 'At a certain moment in history, some crimes are suspected of being pathological.'[69] From the time when moral censure came into force, acts that were committed by everyone in primitive ages tended increasingly to be carried out only by a certain section of the population, namely those who were mentally inferior and those who had little self-control over their psychological stability.

It is interesting to examine this relationship between criminality and pathology. How and by what right does social intolerance towards one form of criminality turn a criminal into an individual who is necessarily mentally ill? This new debate belonged to a period of significant decline in the crime rate, but it is generally accepted that a reduction in criminal aggression makes any remaining crime intolerable. In the preface to a new edition of de Greeff's work, published in 1973, C. Debuyst refers to this evolution: 'Another question is whether crimes of passion are of interest to the modern reader. It should be noted that, compared with other types of murder, they have diminished in number and renown, and that, as ways of life have changed, this "violent solution is almost an anachronism".'

De Greeff never portrays the perpetrator of a crime of passion as a madman who acts in a state of dementia; otherwise the criminal could benefit from article 64 of the Penal Code, and de Greeff's aim is to show that the criminal is responsible at the moment when he commits the crime. According to him, the criminal is completely conscious of what he is doing when he acts: 'Even during the most intense emotional paroxysm, the individual always knows the moment when he lost control.'[70] According to him, the individual freely chooses to give way to the emotional impulse. Although the part played by free will is substantially reduced, 'the crime is still a voluntary act, in the sense that it cannot be carried out unless the voluntary centres remove the inhibition which hitherto was preventing the crime'.[71]

The theory of the impulsive murder committed against the individual's will is wrong, and allowed the criminal to justify himself and sometimes to escape punishment; but crime is an act of free will committed with the consent of the accused. Before killing, he works out a scenario so as to overcome the inner resistance he experiences, for example by consuming a large quantity of alcohol 'to fortify himself', and giving way 'to dramatizing and hysteriform symptoms aimed at autosuggestion, so as to work himself up into a rage'.[72] In order to justify the punishment of perpetrators of crimes of passion, and to make them appear more odious to the public, one simply had to endow such crimes with the character of well thought-out and voluntary acts, and to assert that each criminal could have controlled his urges.

De Greeff did not believe in the repentance of perpetrators of crimes of passion; they might admit that they had committed an offence, but not that they had been in the wrong. In this case, the improvement in the conduct of perpetrators of crimes of passion would be only an illusion. As regards punishing crimes of passion, de Greeff maintained that it was necessary to sentence according to the characteristics of the offender, but there was no longer any question of his being acquitted.

For psychiatrists, the relationship between madness and passion, which had long been established, did not work, since diagnosing pathological passion presented some difficulties. Doctors such as Capgras and Lévy Valensi recognized that psychiatric investigations were needed, since all crimes of passion could be delirious crimes. But these investigations did not always succeed in distinguishing between pathological delirium caused by the passions and the physiological state caused by the passions, since in both cases the emotional state was the same.

The second problem concerned criminal responsibility; in fact, the basic meaning of article 64 of the Penal Code[73] did not admit that an individual could be mad and guilty at the same time. But psychiatrists, while asserting that madness lay behind every criminal act, refused, like criminologists, to accept the adequacy of equating a delirium caused by passion with a lack of criminal responsibility. In order to defend their point of view, they stated that the perpetrator of a crime of passion was mentally ill and that, whether he was emotionally unbalanced or paranoid, he was not strictly speaking in a state of dementia at the time of the crime. In these contentious cases, bordering on passion and psychopathology, it was better to choose a penal solution rather than a medical one: 'Each time that the protection of society cannot be guaranteed by medical measures, and that there is a risk that leniency might increase the individual's harmfulness, one should allow penal repression to be fully enforced, even if the criminal appears to be more or less mentally deficient.'[74] The insistence that perpetrators of a crime of passion should be subject to penal repression reflected the medical profession's compliance with law and order. This self-effacement before the power of the judiciary was merely a temporary strategy. Doctors were waiting for the moment when the judge would ask for advice from the psychiatric expert, no longer in order to establish the guilt of the accused, but to ascertain whether it was preferable to punish or to treat him. This hope was expressed in 1932 by G. Heuyer in an article called 'Psychoses and Crimes of Passion':

When the Penal code allows for sentencing according to the characteristics of the offender and for an unspecified sentence, when the accused can be assessed in special units for mental examination, and when it is possible to place people who are emotionally and effectively unstable in psychiatric wards of prisons, then the expert will be able to give an opinion in which the rigour of his medical diagnosis does not compromise the protection of society. He will then be able to replace the insoluble notion of responsibility with that of curability and susceptibility to persuasion, which should be the by-words of psychiatric investigation.[75]

It was not until some time later that psychiatry, without encroaching on legal territory, asserted itself as the second authority for the protection of society. The offender now faced the double threat of prison or the asylum.

7

The Reality of the Assize Courts

The Victim

What are the actual criteria used to differentiate criminals? An examination of court records provides a definition of the archetypal crime of passion which was considered 'ideal' both by the public and the judiciary, and explains how different sentences were applied. Curiously enough, elements that are extraneous to the criminal act, such as the personality of the victim, play a key role.

The victim's role, personality and life-style are fundamental in the process of evaluating the criminal responsibility of the accused. This approach can be justified in so far as the two protagonists of the drama take part in the development of the conflict. In order to understand the chain of events that has ended in murder, it is necessary to analyse the role of both the accused and the victim. This apparently justifiable and necessary approach raises a number of problems. Indeed, judges do not merely explain, they pass judgement on the victim and criticize him or her in appropriate situations. In theory, the judicial authorities have the role of protecting the moral interests of victims. But it is common for judges to collude with the accused in making the victim bear the responsibility of the criminal act if the victim's behaviour is regarded as immoral. This is even more likely since criminals use, as part of their defence, the strategy of accusing the victim, following two typical patterns: either they describe the real or imagined suffering and the feeling of injustice which they have endured, and which made them change from victims to aggressors, from oppressed to oppressors; or else they justify their crime by presenting themselves as upholders of justice, redressing wrongs, and accuse the victims of committing such misdeeds that they felt obliged to punish them.

During the preparation for the crime, all criminals-to-be undergo this process of self-justification in order to persuade themselves of the need for retribution against their future victim – a woman, usually – who is deemed to be the only one responsible for the tragedy. Indeed, the criminal act can be carried out only if the criminal-to-be is at one with his conscience; this situation obtains when he has the approval of all those around him and when his circumstances fit in with the tragic decision of having a duty to fulfil. At that moment, he stops seeing his case as unique, and the path towards the final crisis seems inevitable since it is no longer possible to be forgiving. The criminal invests himself with the heroic role of dispenser of justice in order to defend important principles.

Driven to the brink of despair because their companions have rejected them, such men assume the right to take the law into their own hands so as to punish these 'wicked women'. The accused Shenk explicitly asserted this right: 'My wife can confirm that she gave me every reason to do what I did, and I can even say with certainty that, since these orgies were taking place before my very eyes, if I hadn't acted she would have considered it cowardly of me to tolerate her debauchery.'[1]

Another man spoke in similar terms: 'I have always forgiven her and treated her gently, sometimes even severely, without managing to get any results. In a word, her misbehaviour led me, on that fatal day, to . . . .'[2]

Since the victims have been guilty of licentiousness and have gone off the straight and narrow, they must be punished in retaliation. The Civil Code of 1804 invested men with the role of head of the family and gave them full, or nearly full, rights over their wives, who were regarded as minors. Men were in charge of family order. If a woman did not conform to her role of wife and mother in accordance with generally accepted norms, then her behaviour would lead to a breakdown in family order. Emile Zola, among others, was absolutely convinced of this:

Destitution and shame attack a family only when vice takes root. Often, the fault belongs to the husband, but sometimes the wife is responsible. Anyway, this is unimportant since the result is the same. The man drinks, the woman runs around, the pair of them drag themselves into the mud, and they both incite one another. This is what happens most commonly. Sometimes, one of them finds the strength to stop before their ruin is complete. He or she then suffers and their life is shattered anyway. This sad outcome of the life of immoral working-class families is perhaps more dependent on the wife than on the husband. It is an almost inevitable outcome if the woman has led a dissolute life before getting married, which is a very common occurrence.[3]

In order to justify their authority to act, the accused naturally blamed the misbehaviour of their victim by appealing to the ethical standards dictated by prevailing codes of conduct and adopted by most people. Thus, men who had always lived outside conventional morality, and whose behaviour could be described as licentious by the very people who were judging them, appropriated certain values which they claimed to hold dear, such as proper conduct, faithfulness, the good upbringing of children, honour, etc. The majority asserted the legitimacy of their crime in the name of these principles. The example of Jean Marié is one of many:

My wife left me three months ago after I reproached her for her behaviour in her parents' presence. She had been coming home late, at about two in the morning, and I demanded to know where she was spending her time . . . . She would shout loudly, on purpose so as to wake the child, and so that I wouldn't say anything else, for she knew I didn't want to upset our child . . . . One day when I had told her to come back early so as to fetch the child from school, as I had an errand to do after work, well! she came home at one-thirty in the morning and said that she wouldn't bother herself any more. So I hit her. I think I had the right to do so.[+]

In a statement written by Médard Savary, aged forty-three, from prison at Mazas, he described his attempt to murder his wife, who was ten years his junior. This provides a rich source of information and makes it possible to put into perspective the many causes of a crime of passion committed after a legal separation, and also to analyse the actual charge brought against him. The accused's self-justification clearly emerges. Apart from his genuine suffering, he portrayed himself as the persecuted victim of a treacherous wife; but as far as the judges were concerned, this cabinet maker attempted to kill his wife because she refused to support him while he was idle. Not only did he not work, but he also used to beat her up. The prosecution described him as a man 'accustomed to satisfying his taste for idleness and debauchery at his wife's expense. When she left, he found that he had only himself to rely on, and he tried to get his victim back.' The prosecution avoided mentioning the accused's state of health (he suffered from rheumatism), which prevented him from working. This disability was confirmed by the welfare office, which gave him a certificate authorizing his name to be removed from the list of taxpayers.

Savary's wife left him because of his threats and his violence; however, this should not disguise the fact that he felt affection for her, an affection that was clearly mutual since the couple had lived together for over ten years. The reductive process employed by the prosecution suppressed and denied the emotional factors that might have made it easier to understand this tragedy. This statement, far from presenting 'a wild beast', revealed this man's weaknesses and his feelings of love. But this was an aspect which the prosecution deliberately ignored, since they refused to hear certain explanations. Savary came across as a bad worker, and his idleness was enough to reinforce his moral guilt.

Furthermore, he neglected to relate that he had hit his wife so much that he had caused her to have a miscarriage, and that on another occasion he had tried to murder her by sticking a pair of compasses into her stomach. What is important in the following statement is not so much the omissions of the accused about his own behaviour, but his expression of jealousy and his affection towards his wife.

However, the main interest of this defence lies in the portrait of Elisabeth Savary, who was presented as being unstable and a bad housewife, as well as taking advantage of her husband's generosity and wanting to be free. She was a working-class woman and was determined to be mistress of her destiny; none the less, she yielded to her husband's possessive character and to his desire to have a happy home.

In order to convince the judges, Savary peppered his speech with practical and private details which tell us a great deal about different aspects of the daily life of the working class. His very picturesque account of how they met in a wine merchant's illustrates the simplicity and spontaneity of amorous relationships which were not without their charm. In criticizing Elisabeth's misbehaviour, he was describing violence among women, but also their complicity against men and their resourcefulness in earning their living or in getting a separation from their husbands.

On this issue, it is worth noting that both Elisabeth and Médard had recourse to the legal authorities to settle their marital disputes, on the one hand for a legal separation, and on the other for the letter written to the public prosecutor to ask him to sort out their marriage (a fruitless move). Moreover, one can see once again the consequences of a judicial decision on the development of the criminal. Savary was deeply wounded by the separation, which forced him to face up to the reality of his situation; on returning home, he also noticed that his wife had stripped their conjugal bed, leaving him with only the mattress – an irreversible slight which provoked criminal anger.

This is his story:

I met my wife in May 1867, when she started work at the wine merchant's where I usually ate my meals. She was holding two small sausages in her hand. She started the conversation by saying that the sausages seemed to be a bit 'off' and so I smelt them and agreed, then I threw them out into the street. Her tired face and her clothes made me feel so sorry for her that I invited her to share my meal. She willingly accepted. So she told me her problems. She had just given birth to a still-born baby son and had stayed in hospital for four months.

After the meal, she said that she wanted to thank me and gave me her address in the rue Saulnier, then we parted. When I went back to the workshop in the Passage Saulnier, where I was employed by Monsieur Philippe the cabinet-maker, I thought about her, since I was single at that time. I decided to try and start up a relationship with her, so I wrote to her and arranged to meet her the following day in the Passage Delorme near where she lived. She came and walked for a while but it started to rain and she said she wanted to go home. I accompanied her.

She became my mistress on that day. I helped her as much as I could afford to. It was at least four months before she found herself a job. She fell ill and I saw to it that she was treated. She soon recovered.

From that period, we had relations more regularly. She started working for a laundress in the Saint-Honoré market and delivered laundry. During that time, I had already noticed that she was bad-tempered, but I had grown fond of her and I didn't have the heart to break off with her. She left the place where she was living and came to live with me in the rue du Faubourg-Saint-Antoine.

One fine day, she disappeared for no reason. I didn't hear a word from her for six weeks, and then I received a letter saying we should meet. I did so.

I thought the house where she was living was a bit suspect and so I asked around and found out that her employer was a prostitute. I wrote to my mistress and said that if she stayed in that house she could forget about me. After a while, she left there and came to live with me. It was a while before she found herself a situation. Then she found a job working for a hosier in the rue des Petites-Ecuries; she didn't stay there long and came back to my house for a month, then she found a job in the employ of an usher in the rue des Acacias and stayed there for about three months.

I was fed up with seeing her constantly changing jobs, and so we combined our savings and she opened a small greengrocer's in the rue d'Oran. After eight days she left this shop and came back to my house in the Faubourg-Saint-Antoine. She remained for a while, thinking of what she could do to earn her living, and she decided to sell fine foods from a basket, that is to say to go door-to-door selling.

At that time I noticed that she wasn't leading a very regular life-style; sometimes she didn't come home at night, and I warned her that if she carried on like that we would fall out. One day she announced that she was leaving me. I asked her why and she said that she wanted to be free. She went to get a cab and left.

Shortly afterwards, she loitered around the workshop and asked for me. She asked me to go back with her. She came to my house sometimes. I asked around and found out that she was living with the Béguignon couple in the rue Saint-André-des-Arts. Béguignon was a policeman. His wife was reputed, with good reason, to be a woman of easy virtue. I told Elisabeth that I didn't like her living in that house. She answered me rather unpleasantly. So, as I could see that there was no way of reaching a solution, I broke off with her. At that time she was pregnant.

The war broke out and I joined the national guard. One day I received a letter from her saying she wanted to see me. I met her as she had asked and then our relationship started again. Her situation forced me to, for she was in an advanced stage of pregnancy. She moved in with me on the same day. After several days, on her request I introduced her to the battalion and she was given a job as canteen woman.

In October of that year, she gave birth to a still-born child – it was premature. During the time I spent with her when she worked as canteen woman I discovered her bad temper. When she recovered, I told her that I didn't want to work in the canteen any longer and I joined the company. Then she started to sell coffee and spirits to the troops along the ramparts. She was leading a very irregular life, and was away from home sometimes for two or three days. I let her know that if she continued to behave like this we wouldn't be friends for much longer.

One fine day when I came home I found that she had moved out. Eight days later she came to see me and told me that she was renting the room she had had when I met her.

The Commune uprising broke out and I left the national guard. One morning, out of the blue, she came to see me and promised me that she would be good in future. At the same time she suggested I become involved in her trade and I agreed. She was selling butter and eggs in the Faubourg Saint-Denis, and I stayed with her for the entire period of the uprising.

After the uprising, I thought of working in my trade of cabinet-maker. I looked for work and I got a job with Monsieur Sapy in the rue Saint-Louis en-l'Ile, where I remained until 1874. Our relationship was often broken off. At that time we lived in the rue de Reuilly, where she gave birth to a boy. Our banns had been announced, but then another rift between us made me give up the idea of marriage.

She got it into her head that her mother, who lived, and still lives, in Bordeaux, should come and stay. I waited for her mother to come, and then on the day she was arriving I went out on to the path to wait with my wife. I accompanied her home and left them together and went to sleep at the house of one of my brothers. We stopped living together during that period. In spite of that, we continued to have relations; I had rented a little room in the hôtel d'Indre-et-Loire and she used to come and see me. She would come and eat with me. Sometimes she brought her mother with her.

Every Sunday we spent the day together. She made me spend all the money I earned. One fine day she came to see me in the workshop and asked me if I would agree to live with her again. I accepted as I was very much in love with her. . . . Then it was definitely settled that we would get married three weeks later. On 16 January 1875 we were married in the town hall of the XIIth *arrondissement*.

After the wedding I continued to work for Monsieur Sapy. After four months, she suggested I become her assistant and help her in her business. It went well for a while, but the war started up again, and then she admitted that she had got married to give herself a name and to wash away the past, but that she had thought I wouldn't live long. I had such bad rheumatism I was in a pretty sorry state and, in fact, I could barely stand up when I got married. She started to quarrel with her mother and forced her to go home. Once this good woman had left, she took her bad moods out on me. Life was becoming unbearable. At that time, she had decided to get a separation. She spoke to some women who were separated and asked them for advice on what to do.

From that period on, she put all her energy into passing me off as an idler and a drunkard. . . . Because my rheumatism had become gouty, I could no longer work in my trade which meant I had to put up with her ill treatment . . . .

At around the beginning of December, she gave birth to a son who lived for only four days. A month before her confinement, she had had a fight with one of her neighbours in the market. She was sentenced for this by the court; the market police inspector was present and can testify to it.

I forgot to say that she got friendly with the concierges by giving them fine food, and she used to tell all sorts of stories about me. One point I should mention is that she wouldn't let me go to our child's funeral on the pretext that it was more important to sell the butter. Only the child's wet nurse accompanied the funeral procession. This is proof of her feelings.

In the market, she scorned me because I got tired and she always wanted to draw attention to my absence to discredit me. . . . [He claimed, moreover, that she had pounced on him when he was cleaning his tools and had injured herself in the stomach with a pair of compasses. She obtained a medical certificate from a doctor.] . . . She seemed very happy, as at last she had a reason for a separation. She went to a public letter-writer to get a request for legal aid drawn up.

She stopped doing any household chores and I had no more clean clothes. She also neglected her personal hygiene. And all this – she said so herself – was to make me feel disgusted with her.

She left our lodgings in the most dreadful state. She went for two months without sweeping our bedroom. She refused to have sexual intercourse. It was hell. . . . [On 23 June 1876 they appeared before the judge, and Savary agreed to make a request for separation.] . . . Imagine my surprise when I went home that very day and saw that my wife had taken with her everything she could carry. She left me without money or property . . . . She had stripped me of everything, and I was left with no job, almost an invalid. She hadn't even left any sheets on the bed. . . . [On the day a legal separation was granted, Savary did not appear before the judge.] . . . The sentence was passed, and I was sentenced in my absence as I didn't have the money to pay a solicitor.

As for me, I had gone back to my former employer, Monsieur Sapy. I was fed up with my life and as I couldn't see an end to it all, I decided to put an end to this miserable existence.

Nevertheless, he approached his wife on a number of occasions to ask her to live with him again, and was constantly hanging around the places where she worked and lived, armed with a revolver. He was arrested, and on 20 November was sentenced to a fortnight's imprisonment for carrying an illegal weapon and for making death threats. His wife went to see him and he begged her to live with him again. She agreed and interceded on his behalf.

Throughout my detention, she made sure I had everything I needed to make my time in prison more pleasant, and in one of her letters she expressed the desire to live with me again. On the day the sentence was passed, she told the judges that I was very good and that she regretted what had happened. It was obvious to everybody that we were going to start living together again. The day I came out of prison, she was waiting for me at the Mazas gate. She helped me into her cab . . . , and we spent the day together. In the evening she had ordered our supper. After eating, she asked me if I wanted to spend the night with her and she took me to a furnished flat.

That night, Savary was apparently very jealous and threatened his wife, and said to her: 'If I ever catch you talking to a man, I'll do him in – and you as well.' On the following day, since his wife wanted nothing to do with him, he tried to explain to her that, since had spent the night with her, she had given him back 'all his marital rights'; but she would not give in.

I wrote a letter to the Public Prosecutor and explained my situation to him as regards my wife, and I asked him how to make my wife comply with her duty. After this letter, the police inspector said to me: 'You wrote to the public prosecutor which is why I sent for you.' Then he said to me: 'Your wife showed great weakness in sleeping with you. I have reproached her on this subject, but what do you expect, she does not want anything more to do with you.' I thought it was funny that a magistrate should tell me that, just because my wife wouldn't have me any more, that was enough, but he wouldn't listen to me any more and dismissed me.

A separation can prompt a revaluation of the partner who has been lost. For Médard Savary, Elisabeth's departure meant an emotional rejection whose practical consequences were aggravated by his illness. This revaluation can be clearly seen in a letter which he wrote to her during his first prison sentence:

> I have tried everything to forget you, but nothing works. Today I am resigned to die or to live with you; one of us must die. I never would have thought it possible to love you so much. Time has not healed anything; on the contrary, my affection for you has grown. I beg of you, dear wife, let us forget the past and live together again; otherwise, either death or hard labour await us.

It is most likely that the domestic quarrels and beatings were caused by Savary; but violence was definitely not the main reason for the break-up, which happened when the accused fell ill and started to work irregularly. Elisabeth had no intention of 'running the household' all by herself and being mistreated. During a confrontation between herself and Savary, she criticized him for not doing his duty:

You deceived me. When I gave myself to you I thought you were a good person and that we could get married, but it wasn't long before I saw what you were really like and I wanted to leave you. You pursued me relentlessly, and didn't give me a moment's peace and quiet. You used to hit me to get money out of me. I managed to leave you several times, but you always knew where to find me, and because of your death threats I used to agree to go back with you. Finally, I decided to marry you in the belief that the Good Lord would perhaps bless our marriage. Despite your faults, I loved you a lot and I thought you could mend your ways, but no sooner were we married than you started to treat me twice as badly. All I ever got from you was beatings, drunkenness, insults, dead children and three murder attempts. What had I done to deserve this? Had you ever seen me with a man?

Savary instantly retorted:

You threw me out because you didn't like me any more and wanted someone stronger. If I ill-treated you as you say, then why did you wait for me outside the gate at Mazas when I came out last December? You went round telling everybody that I was a decent man and that you had been wrong to have me sent to prison. You spent a night with me in a hotel, and the next day you no longer wanted to see me. It made me lose heart.

Savary did not succeed in convincing the judges that his behaviour was justifiable, despite skilfully exposing his wife's faults. This time the bad mother, who neglected her home and was spendthrift and capricious, gained the court's favour. She was not guilty of provoking the revenge of an offended husband, for he himself could not claim to have been exemplary in his behaviour. Had it been the opposite, he would easily have convinced the judges of his victim's guilt.[5]

Criminologists confirm this notion that the victims take part in the development of the crime; they say the victims are responsible for triggering off the decision to actually commit the crime by their provocations, insults and challenges to the accused. The mere refusal to go home when asked to do so can justify murder. When he was questioned, Louis Jouault asserted:

I went to the wine merchant's across the street from her boss and drank a glass of wine. That's when I saw her. I said to her: 'Go home', and she said: 'No, I won't go home.' I was irritated and I didn't know what I was doing and that's when I fired my pistol at her. It made me lose my head.[6]

The following challenge issued to Jacques Michel by his wife was rather more spectacular. At six o'clock in the evening on 24 October 1870, he came home, and, according to his daughter, the couple quarrelled:

He was a bit drunk, but only slightly; he said he wanted to eat, and then he told my mother off. He took his gun and fired it into the air. Then he went to reload his gun and said to us: 'Kiss your mother now, because I'm going to kill her.' My mother replied: 'Don't be afraid, children, your father is far too lazy to kill me', and she turned towards him and then he released the trigger.[7]

If the behaviour of the victim drives the future criminal into a fit of anger and despair, public opinion considers that the victim deserves to be punished. The victim's personality and behaviour towards the accused provide an excuse for the crime, as is evident from a comparative study of criminal cases such as the Moyaux case and the Guillot case, which shows how this type of process works.

On the day of Victor Moyaux's trial,[8] the counsel for the prosecution stated: 'Forgery was Moyaux's first crime, and forgery led him to commit murder.' The accused did not share this view: 'My wife's misbehaviour was the cause of my misfortune.' We know that Adrienne Moyaux left the marital home, abandoning her daughter to go off to the United States with her lover. On her return to France, she tried to see her child, but Victor bitterly opposed this. His feelings of affection for his daughter were beyond doubt, and the idea that his wife might take her back was unbearable. He apparently said to the child's wet nurse: 'I'd rather see her dead than with her mother.'

In this case, both the jury and the judges colluded with this dispenser of justice so as to criticize this 'loose woman', whose behaviour was judged by society and formed the basis of the accusation. During the cross-examination, the presiding judge placed the blame on the unfaithful wife: 'I must point out here that, after that period, your life changed completely. Up until then you were hard-working, you led a regular life, and your behaviour was almost beyond reproach. Ever since your wife left you, your life-style has completely changed.

Witnesses confirmed this judgement. Madame Bergot said: 'As far as I'm concerned, nothing would have happened without Madame Moyaux'; and Madame Penchot heard the child 'often complaining that her mother beat her'.

The speech for the defence was based entirely on Adrienne's character, and her absence from court that day was considered an admission of guilt: 'Madame Moyaux is not here; she was told that her presence would not be fitting in a court-room where, shortly, the representative of the prosecution will sentence her with some harsh words, and she decided to withdraw.'

The blame was laid at Adrienne's door, and she was held responsible for her husband's despair by public opinion, which accused her of having failed to fulfil her role of guardian angel of the home. Her duty, in a trying and difficult period, was to lead her husband back on to the straight and narrow, and to help him face setbacks by providing him with a peaceful family home. Instead of this, she deserted him and her child to indulge in adultery. Victor Moyaux came across as a dispenser of justice, and because of his wife's misbehaviour he escaped the death penalty and was given a life sentence of hard labour.

In the Guillot case, the accused portrayed himself as a man who was oppressed by his wife and became the aggressor only so as to put an end to his suffering. His wife's behaviour acted as a catalyst and, as in the previous tragedy, male revenge was transferred to the child. Throughout the preliminary investigation, Modeste Guillot asserted that he had been badly treated by his wife and thus was no longer the master in his own home and had to put up with all sorts of harrassments. His wife would not, for example, give him the key to the bedroom so that he could go and lie down for an hour or two when he came back tired from the market. She refused to account for what she did and where she went. Whenever Modeste reproached her, she would reply: 'I don't give a damn about you; I'll go where I please and do as I please.' The couple's discord was evident, and, if the neighbours are to be believed, Madame Guillot was not very affectionate towards her husband. The following statements do not claim to be objective or impartial, but they do give an idea of the unhappiness which this man daily experienced.

First, the ironmonger from the rue de Vanves gave his account:

I was never present at one of their quarrels, but I heard people say that they often argued. This man was not master in his own home, and his wife put his employees above him. I can't really say which of the pair was in the right, but I think the mother-in-law had turned her daughter against her son-in-law. I often saw Guillot half-drunk. He didn't have a regular job.

The coalman from the same street added:

One day when Guillot had been thrown out by his employees, his mother-in-law and his wife, he came and asked me for hospitality. He said that they had told him off for being drunk and that they wanted to pass him off as a madman. I only ever saw him drunk once, with his employees.

A neighbour living further away, a clothier from the rue de l'Ouest, took his side:

His wife, his mother-in-law and his uncle treated him badly in all sorts of ways – they bullied him, they used to throw him out of his home, criticize him for his laziness and taunt him about his stay at Sainte-Anne's mental hospital. But he was very gentle and I never saw him drunk. On two occasions, he came to stay in our house for four days. He loved his child. They used to throw him out without any money and his employees used to beat him up. His mother-in-law and his wife are responsible for everything that happened.

Modeste Guillot's sister, a seamstress, added, perhaps out of loyalty:

His wife may have some very good points but she didn't know how to handle him. Instead of being gentle with him, she reproached him and ordered him about. She wore him out. He drank partly out of irritation and despair. He was afraid that he would lose the child if there was a legal separation.

Another neighbour prided herself that she knew both of them very well:

The two of them used to confide in me. The husband used to drink on an empty stomach; he was very gentle and polite, and when he drank he became excited. His wife complained about his laziness, his drunkenness and his threats. She threw him out on a number of occasions; I thought this behaviour rather extreme and let him stay with me.

It is very likely that, being irritated by everyone's hostility, and roused by alcohol, Modeste Guillot proved to be violent, even threatening, and that he neglected his business so much that he went bankrupt. What is certain is that his wife's family wanted to have him shut up in Sainte-Anne's. Zélie's uncle admitted it and gave Guillot's violence as an excuse: 'As we were convinced that danger was imminent, and as we wanted to get rid of him at any cost, at least temporarily, we decided to say that he was mad. By this means, we managed to get him arrested at least for a while, but since he wasn't mad they then released him.'

From the prison at Mazas, Modeste Guillot wrote to the examining magistrate to explain the torments he had to endure in his home, the constant criticism and his mother-in-law's hatred. He said that, not only did they want to get rid of him, but 'they had thrown him out of the house five times and he had even had to ask one of his neighbours for hospitality'. In addition, 'his wife refused to sleep with him because she didn't want to have any more children'. Modeste Guillot was very hurt at being rejected, and could not reconcile himself to his wife leaving, for she had threatened to get a separation. One witness gave the following account: 'One day, he got down on his hands and knees and kissed her hands, saying that he wouldn't drink any more.' Zélie was unmoved and made a request for a legal separation. To this end she made a statement at the police station so as to obtain an order preventing her husband from returning to the marital home. This separation and the selling of his business meant ruin and solitude for him.

He was unable to face up to this break psychologically and materially, and was confronted by the determined attitude of his wife, who provoked him by saying that he might just as well leave, as the house had been sold. After a quarrel he rushed upstairs into his daughter's room and strangled her. Later, when he described this moment, he exclaimed: 'I was completely beside myself and I don't know how I got to my daughter's bedroom; I couldn't believe I was there, I thought I was being pursued down a precipice by my wife, her uncle and her mother.'

The ill-treatment he received and the way he was imprisoned on occasion were not mentioned at all in the bill of indictment. The judges described him in the following way: 'Guillot has always been lazy and drunk and is a violent and coarse man; his wife, whom everyone describes as hardworking and with a gentle nature, behaves excellently.'

The indictment particularly stressed 'the degrading passion which dominated the accused': 'In order to satisfy his inclination for solitary drinking, he would secretly go down into the cellar and get so drunk that he would be laid out for hours on end. Under the influence of his drunkenness, he picked quarrels with his wife and neglected his business affairs.'

Although Modeste Guillot did drink, he was not an alcoholic; this was established by the medico-legal report:

Guillot's habits have not been fully established. He did not frequent taverns or cafés; he was thought to drink alone in his cellar. That, at any rate, was what the assistant greengrocers said, as they did not take part in his bouts of drinking. Nothing can be found either in the past or now to indicate alcoholic intoxication in the medical sense of the work; there is no trembling or insomnia. His mind has not been affected, and there are no symptoms either of the sluggish debility of chronic alcoholism or the deviations of acute or peracute cerebral states.

Medical opinion was omitted from the bill of indictment.

In contrast to Adrienne Moyaux, Zélie Guillot was portrayed as a respectable woman who, in order to look after her financial interests, rejected a husband, who was not only a 'drunkard' but, above all, a bad shopkeeper. Surely it was Modeste Guillot's duty to make a success of his shop and to pay his bills? Bankruptcy confirmed his incompetence and, in a certain sense, justified his wife's behaviour, for she wanted to save his property. Was it not up to the law to protect one's possessions? Furthermore, Zélie Guillot's moral conduct was beyond reproach. She had not had any lovers and was an exemplary mother; therefore she was not morally responsible. The accused was not granted any extenuating circumstances and was sentenced to death.

* * *

These two cases are very good examples of how judges manipulate details that are extraneous to the crime in order to highlight the criminal character or to excuse it, and also of how the victim's behaviour influences legal decisions. Sentences vary not only depending on the crime committed and on the murderer's personality, but also in relation to the role of the victim, whose behaviour is closely scrutinized by the law. The acquittal of a criminal can be interpreted as society's condemnation of the victim and as the legitimacy of the right to take the law into one's own hands.[9]

Committing the Crime

The second factor that is liable to influence the judgement of the accused's criminal guilt is the execution of the crime. In order to determine the intention to murder, the judicial authorities look for proof of premeditation, and then they concentrate on how the crime was carried out, on the number of blows and on the weapon used. All these elements play a not inconsiderable part in the classification of sentences. Since the aim of criminal law is to punish deliberate crimes as severely as possible, one can question the validity of this evaluation procedure. Judges thus regard premeditation as the most important of aggravating circumstances. (The jury is asked to comment on this point at the time of sentencing.)

In cases of crimes of passion, premeditation is, on the contrary, the mark of even less criminal responsibility. R. Saleilles was the first to challenge the value of this view. Premeditation was considered to be proof of an uncontrollable obsession, which reduced the freedom of action of the criminal-to-be. Another aggravating circumstance was the cruelty that the accused showed in carrying out the crime. Bloodshed and the number of blows inflicted are therefore taken into account. According to the judges, the facts themselves should show the degree of homicidal intention. This is a very arbitrary criterion, as one cannot say that the man who has attacked his victim with a knife is more of a criminal than the man who has used a fire-arm.

In the vast majority of crimes of passion, the accused, far from denying his intention to kill, claims responsibility for his act, and judges, therefore, have no need to prove his guilt. In cases of crimes committed after a violent argument, when a blow becomes fatal, violence and bloodshed are used to measure the degree of criminal intention.

Sébastien Billoir's trial illustrates the arbitrary nature of this practice. Billoir was a retired former soldier, accused of murdering his mistress, the Lemanach girl, and cutting her into pieces to get rid of the corpse. The accused admitted this last fact, but denied any homicidal intention. Here is his version of events:[10]

On November 2nd last, at about seven o'clock in the evening, Jeanne came in; it was later than usual. She had drunk a little and I told her off for staying out so long. I was rather sharp with her as she said that she had lingered on with a girlfriend, and I had told her not to talk to anyone when she was alone in the streets of Paris.

Meanwhile, she was getting dressed, and at one point she knocked a glass I was very fond of off a shelf. She was crouching down and picking up the pieces when I rushed at her in a mad fury and kicked her violently in the stomach. She collapsed. She went quiet all of a sudden. I hastened to look after her and threw water on her face, gave her some vinegar to inhale, and carried her to the bed;

from her contorted expression and her eyes, which were glazed over, I could see that it was all over.

I then fell beside her and stayed until eleven o'clock the next morning in a state of utter nervous exhaustion. When I finally recovered myself, I had only one thought and that was to get rid of the corpse. I was insane and thought of the dishonour to my family. When I went out for a moment I couldn't walk; it seemed to me that everyone was staring hard at me and that they could see from my face that I had just committed a guilty act.

I went home and that evening I laid the corpse out, near the fireplace, and then in my wretched state I found the courage to carry out the mutilation which you know about from the description which I gave in the preliminary investigation. The following evening I took the upper part of the body to the Seine embankment, looked for a deserted spot and threw the parcel in, after I had loaded it down with stones.

On the third day, I made a second journey with the lower part of the body. That evening, I saw a small boat with two men on the river and I was so frightened that I ran away without looking to see whether the new parcel that I had thrown in had sunk to the bottom.

The date of 2 November was disputed by the prosecution with the intention of proving premeditation and of accusing Billoir of having cut up the victim while she was still alive.

After this account had been given at the trial, the public prosecutor exhibited a wax reconstruction of the victim's mutilated body. This provoked great commotion, and at that very moment the public prosecutor cried out: 'Do you know what people are saying, Billoir? They are saying that you opened up Jeanne Lemanach alive, because the corpse was completely bloodless.'

THE ACCUSED: I know nothing about anatomy, but I swear that I never touched her alive.
THE PRESIDING JUDGE: You caught her in her sleep and you put your hand over her mouth so as to smother her cries. Your alleged kick is not admissible. There is no sign on the body that she was kicked, except that the stomach was cut open. You cut open her stomach and touched the aorta.

The doctor who was asked to give evidence admitted, however, that a violent kick in the stomach can cause death, but this is never immediate. One can imagine that Billoir waited for his mistress to die without going to get help.

Was this murder intentional, or unintentional? It is not for us to decide. What is important, though, is the enactment of the court-room scene which emphasized the monstrousness of the crime by stressing sordid details without trying to understand the accused's motivation.

Indeed, in the case of Sébastien Billoir, the judges made no attempt to explain the motives behind the crime. The lawyer was the only one to ask himself:

But every premeditated, planned crime has a reason, a motive. What was Billoir's? His crime has no cause whatsoever, and was thus the result of violence, a wholly understandable violence in a man whom people say has been in a constant state of drunkenness recently. If he had wanted to get rid of the Lemanach girl, all he had to do was to tell her to leave his house; it is not feasible that, between a domestic quarrel and the guillotine, this man should have chosen the latter.

In all trials, the detailed accounts of murder scenes, which are then further magnified by the press, do not merely fulfil the emotional need that sensationalism, cruelty and monstrosity create: they also reflect the conviction held by everyone that the degree of guilt can be calculated in relation to the blood shed.

On the day of the trial, if need be, judges call for the evidence of doctors to explain criminal barbarity: 'With what fury the inhuman wretch struck his victim. Doctor Languier's report testifies to this. The blade of the knife was nine centimetres long; some wounds in the corpse were much deeper than that, which proves that the murderer stuck the knife in as far as the handle.[11] In the case of Jean Pène, who was accused of attempted murder, 'the doctor noted that the Duprat girl's wounds were serious and inflicted with great force and real fury.'[12]

Washing and dressing a corpse was considered perverse and sadistic. Louis Perdriat was criticized for treating his mistress's body in this way: 'Perdriat, when you killed her the butcher's boy inside you came to the fore. You took the body, you carried it out onto the landing and you washed it like an animal which has just been bled at the slaughterhouse.'[13]

Attempted suicide served to dispose the jury favourably towards the accused, provided that the judges recognized this attempt as genuine. During a quarrel, Georges Solhart hit his wife very violently and threatened to kill her, and then he tried to throw her out of the window. His wife cried out for help, thereby alerting the neighbours who came running. Solhart had let go of his victim by now and, armed with a knife, tried to kill himself. The judge was of the opinion that Solhart's life had been sufficiently at risk for his suicide attempt to be regarded as genuine.[14]

The judges responded differently in the case of Louis Forestier, especially as the accused behaved particularly unpleasantly and insensitively throughout the preliminary investigation. This provided ammunition for the counsel for the prosecution, who, on the day of the trial, quoted an extract from the cross-examination of the accused by the examining magistrate: 'In describing to us the details of this gruesome scene, which happened barely twenty-four hours ago, have you no feelings?' 'What do you expect? What's done is done.'

In the face of this refusal to repent, the counsel for the prosecution concluded: 'We cannot help but be astounded by such coldblooded behaviour.' The judges did not succeed in discrediting the accused's desire to commit suicide, and members of the jury allowed themselves to be influenced by the evidence given by the policeman who arrested Forestier on the Quai de Grenelle: 'Does the witness believe that the accused intended to commit suicide?' 'Yes. He was rolling something in his hand. I asked him what it was and he replied that it was a tie with which he intended to tie his feet together before throwing himself into the water.'

According to the journalist writing in the *Petit Journal,* 'The jury took these considerations into account; it ruled out the death penalty.' Forestier was sentenced to life imprisonment.[15]

The slyest culprits quickly weigh up the consequences of their behaviour. They do their utmost to get the jury on their side. The nervousness they feel when they appear makes this court-room game easier. Others, who are utterly depressed, are resigned: 'What's done is done.' They do not understand the need to make amends. Faced with the risk of not recognizing themselves in the image that the judges have created, they give up and passively watch the enactment of their trial.

The Three Acts of the Court-Room Drama

Once a crime has been committed, it comes within the sphere of the judiciary. The accused must then take part in a very special performance. They are placed in a situation where they are performing and in confrontation, and their behaviour changes according to the three different stages of this drama – arrest, preliminary investigation and trial – during which a series of power relationships is set up between the accused and the judges.

Generally speaking, the time between the execution of the crime and the arrest is very short, at most a few hours. The criminal is taken to the police station, where he does not display any resistance and is very loquacious with both the policemen and the superintendent; he expresses himself freely and without thinking about the consequences of what he says.

With the emotional shock, the accused finds himself in a situation of extreme nervous tension and feels the need to communicate so that he can confide or justify himself. His statement is a continuation of the crime he has just committed. When the victim has escaped death, the accused loudly expresses his disappointment, and swears that he will try again; in the reverse situation, he can look downcast. But whatever the outcome of the crime, he always expresses his resentment towards the victim and very rarely shows any signs of remorse.

Another factor that encourages this spontaneous communication is familiarity with the police premises and with the policemen. The police station, which opens on to the street, is part of the daily life of the residents of a particular neighbourhood; the same applies to the police superintendent and his men, to whom people have gone to recount some trifle, to lodge a complaint or to ask for advice. Far from being intimidating, the superintendent's attitude prompts confidences; for he wants to obtain precise information so that he can write a report, and does not seek to judge the man who sits before him but simply asks questions which are neither orders nor especially accusations, for example 'How long have you known your wife?' 'What was your motive for acting?' 'Tell us how you committed the crime' 'Were you jealous of Madame B . . . ?' 'Do you regret carrying out this crime? Would you do it again under the same circumstances?'[16]

Every movement and every word spoken is to be recorded and used to prepare the bill of indictment. Only compromising details that could damage the accused's case will be withheld. For example, in the case of a heinous crime, committed by a despicable individual, the words or attitude of repentance will be passed over, with the exception of suicide attempts, which judges have sometimes shamelessly interpreted as vulgar play-acting. The statement serves as a guideline for the examining magistrate by providing him with the first details on which to base the charge. Since the perpetrator of a crime of passion does not try to deny his or her crime, the judge's task consists essentially of finding out what caused the criminal to act, and in particular of constructing the criminal personality of the accused and establishing his degree of responsibility.

The cross-examination of the accused takes place in court, the symbol of power, which is an unfamiliar setting and makes an impression on the accused, who is on his guard. He is faced with a man who questions him in order to obtain information, details with which to manipulate him. The judge belongs to the ruling class and embodies social order and political and economic power. Through his status and his language, he is in charge of the situation, and the accused who stands before him is on the defensive. The feelings of guilt and social inferiority that the accused harbours exacerbates the terseness of his replies, which display no tone of rebellion, aggressiveness or even cunning. It is rare for the accused to try to withdraw their statements; they nearly always admit to their intention to kill and take refuge in the inevitable system of defence which consists in persuading the judge that they are the victim of another victim. In order to be forgiven, and even shown approbation, the accused do their utmost to adapt their justifications to the norms that the judicial authorities recognize; this accounts for their sometimes exaggerated need to show themselves committed to prevailing values, such as the virtue of women. It is not always easy to understand the dividing-line between signs of wounded pride and the claims that are the product of manipulation. If one reads the cross-examinations, one can easily detect the feeling of general discomfort that the cultural and social gap creates. In order to be better understood, the accused choose to write to the examining magistrate: 'I wanted to say all this to you during the preliminary investigation, but I was too flustered by your severe manner.' This sentence, which comes from a letter written by Madame Dounou (1875), clearly indicates the difficulty that ordinary people experience in communicating with judges.

The need to write stems not only from a feeling of intimidation. During cross-examinations, judges set up a portrait and a scenario in which the accused do not recognize themselves, and so, in order to reclaim their crime and their image, some write a statement in which they claim responsibility for their crime and justify it. Although what they write is obviously biased since they are trying to be persuasive, it does display spontaneity and enormous freedom of expression.

This move often ends in failure, since their speech is ineffectual and is suppressed by judges who take no account whatsoever of these statements which are without legal value. They are simply evidence of the impotence of the individuals, who are listened to only when they adapt themselves to current thinking.

Witnesses for the prosecution or for the defence do not escape from this judicial performance and take part in the preliminary investigation. They too feel intimidated by the legal system, but they are more willing to be cross-examined.

The importance given to crime in nineteenth-century society endowed the individual who was to testify in a criminal case with an extraordinary status. The witness was no longer addressing his fellow men in a familiar place, such as the concierge's office or the tavern, but in the law courts, in the presence of a judge who could be considered a class enemy and, at any rate, as incapable of understanding what had taken place according to the accused's value system.

This unfamiliar situation of appearing in court was liable to encourage the witness to feel a certain solidarity with the accused, by deliberately restricting his statements and revealing only those details that were essential to the preliminary investigation. The witness's attitude was often characterized by mistrust and a sense of propriety. However, some witnesses, convinced as they were of the self-importance of their role and of the seriousness of the situation, were very verbose, giving a great many details and personal judgements.

The words of the accused were mutilated and manipulated and received even worse treatment on the day of the trial, which was above all a public performance. The public's passion for crime was reflected by a constant attendance at hearings in the assize courts. Indeed, the public was not content simply to read the report of the trial in the newspapers: it wanted to see and take part in the actual event. In the first place, the physical presence of the accused, who was the object of desires and violent repugnance, endowed the proceedings with a much-awaited intensity and caused a certain amount of agitation. Whether he was a monstrous or an insignificant character, for a few hours the accused was a hero in the eyes of the general public.

In certain particularly scandalous or spectacular cases, there were such crowds that people had to push their way into the court-room. There was a very select public in the courts in those days, upper-middle-class ladies and fashionable writers. Alexandre Dumas *fils* and Octave Feuillet attended Victor Moyaux's trial, as did Mademoiselle Schneider and many other ladies, who all vied with one another in the magnificence of their dress.[17] The trial of the widow Gras certainly drew in the crowds:

Although proceedings do not commence until about eleven o'clock, by nine o'clock in the morning the court-room, which was ten times too small for the liking of the inquisitive people who obstructed all the corridors, was swarming with a privileged public carrying cards issued in advance. For the last few days, the attempt to get hold of admission cards, particularly on the part of the ladies, has been somewhat frantic, as it is a great many years since a case has aroused such enormous interest in the public. . . . We observe, as in other proceedings, that the best places are occupied by the ladies in the most elegant dresses, among whom there is not, however, anybody famous. . . . We would point out in the court-room the presence of Monsieur Paul de Saint-Victor and Monsieur Ludovic Halévy . . . as well as Monsieur Coquelin and Monsieur Mounet-Sully from the Comédie-Française.[18]

Whatever their social position, people were not afraid to parade themselves in court; it was almost a society performance. While it was unadvisable for a young woman to go to the Opéra ball, she could, with complete ease of mind, attend trials, where talk was sometimes of a nature that would, on any other occasion, have been called scandalous.

The trial was the final event and a simple repetition of the preliminary investigation; it took place without any surprises or incidents. There was no new detail in the statements to disturb its smooth running. Only this time the stake was high, since the fate of the accused depended on the verdict of the twelve members of the jury who took part as spectators, invested with the supreme power of dispensing justice. For all those present, the essential facts would have been read out in the bill of indictment at the beginning of the proceedings. Very often, the tone and subject of what was said made the outcome of the trial seem predictable.

The role of the accused during the trial was part of the process of sentencing according to the characteristics of the offender; he also determined the definition of the 'ideal' perpetrator of a crime of passion. There was, therefore, an essential stage during which a power relationship was forged between the judge and the accused. Killing cleanly, without too much brutality, being able to justify oneself and placing the blame on the victim were not sufficient to legitimize the murder and assure the goodwill of the jury. On the day when the sentence was to be passed, the accused allowed himself to be divested of his crime and adopted an attitude that complied with the judges' expectations.

After the bill of indictment had been read out, the judge cross-examined the accused, asking him questions which were in a certain sense answers; the accused limited his replies to 'Yes' and 'No, your Honour'. As he was impressed by the judicial machinery, and anxious not to provoke the anger of the judges, the

221

accused resigned himself and submitted to this monologue of questions. The situation seemed to be under the control of the judge who, depending on circumstances, could at any moment deprive the accused of his role, so as better to mould him in the image that was prepared behind the scenes.

Some rejected this manipulation and demanded the right to be heard. Célestine Béal interrupted the presiding judge with the remark: 'There's no point in asking me questions if you've made up your mind and don't want to believe me.' The judge asked her to control herself and she answered back: 'But it's true, it's pointless you asking me questions.'[19]

It would be wrong to think that the accused is completely excluded from the judicial game and is taking part in his trial merely as a spectator, for he has the means of setting up a power relationship by refusing, for example, to take part in the cross-examination. Pierre Moignon was exasperated by the judge mocking his attempted suicide and said to him: 'If you're going to be like that, I don't want to say anything else.' The judge replied: 'Moignon, you know very well that I'm not preventing you from speaking.'

Besides, the accused's silence disturbed judges and jury. Victor Moyaux, who was guilty of killing his daughter, refused to speak at his trial. This is how the incident was described in *La Gazette des tribunaux*: 'Victor Moyaux collapsed onto a bench, as if exhausted. The judge questioned him in vain, for he would not utter a word. He bowed his head and wiped his tears with his hands. The judge continued to harass him: "Come now, Moyaux, I beseech you, tell us why you committed this abominable infamy."'[20]

This dialogue, or rather this monologue of questions, is somewhat surprising. Why this relentless attempt to obtain further information when the facts were established and the accused admitted them and accepted the sentence that he was about to receive? What more could the judicial apparatus ask for in order to judge this man? There was the accused's comments on himself. Apart from admission, what was required was self-examination, self-explanation. The machinery of the penal system cannot function with one law, one offence and one perpetrator responsible for events: it needs additional material, the intimate knowledge of the man who is going to be sentenced, otherwise the practice of sentencing according to the characteristics of the individual is meaningless.

By his silence, the accused prevents the judge from performing his role. How can one evaluate the personality of this criminal, how can one judge his crime, if he will not reveal his secret and say who he is? For it is not a crime, but a man, who is being judged. By refusing to take part in this production, the accused is expressing the desire to be sentenced, but not to be judged. By so doing, he risks incurring the hostility of members of the jury.

Conversely, his docility and his eargerness to conform to the role that everybody expects will be gratefully received. To this end, the accused must be seen to be humble and submissive; he should not defend himself, but make a confession. Admission is the first tangible sign of the desire to submit to the social order, and attests to the will of the accused not to escape the punishment which he owns up to deserving. The judiciary in turn notes this desire for reconciliation by accepting his confession as an extenuating circumstance.

The individual who is too arrogant, even insolent, is called to order and compromises his chances of receiving a pardon. Thus, Louis Féaux, who persisted in denying his intention to kill, was told by the judge: 'Come now Féaux, I am saying this in your interest. Do not destroy the goodwill that the jury may be disposed to show towards you.'[21] For the accused who attempts to escape justice exacerbates his situation. In the Billoir case, the journalist noted that 'Billoir committed a murder, and after this savage act, instead of repenting and giving himself up to the police, and thus deserving a degree of clemency, he coldbloodedly cut up his victim.'[22]

To be more cautious, the accused did their utmost to be self-effacing. As they stood in the court-room they looked down and displayed an air of contrition. They presented themselves looking clean, and workers never wore a black suit, the distinctive sign of belonging to the bourgeoisie. (At the end of the nineteenth century, clothes were still an indication of one's social and professional circumstances among the working classes.) The accused were very perturbed by the court-room drama. For the first time in their lives, these men and women were going to appear on the front page of the newspapers and be the object of society's attention. A sad fame! They were submissive and respectful as they listened to the accusations of the judge who paraded their private life which had been distorted and sullied by all kinds of sordid detail.

All forms of rebellion against the judicial order were penalized. For this reason, spectacular developments and bitter exchanges between the two parties were rare. On the day of her trial, Célestine Béal clearly did not understand the implications of her behaviour. This young woman, who was thirty-five, worked on a regular basis as an embroideress. She had been living with Antoine Becker, a butcher, for the previous six years – or rather, he had been living with her, without paying any rent. According to him, he grew tired of the violent behaviour of his common-law wife and decided to part from her. On 12 September 1872, despite the attempts that Célestine made to stop him, he had his furniture moved to Madame Cocher's house in the rue de Maistre. Madame Cocher was his sister-in-law, and Célestine suspected her of being his mistress. On the day of the move, Célestine had a knife sharpened and then hid on the corner of the avenue de Clichy and the rue de Carrrières and waited for Madame Cocher. When she appeared, Célestine leapt out at her, grabbed her by the throat and stabbed her; but no serious harm was done and her clothes were simply torn. Madame Cocher succeeded in disarming Célestine, and she was immediately arrested by the police who had been alerted.

As she stood before the judges, Célestine Béal was violent and jealous; she behaved in an extraordinary fashion, shouting rude remarks at her ex-lover and her victim. With her outspokenness, she attempted to defend herself, but her quick-tempered explanations and her insolent manner seriously damaged her case, for judges do not like to be divested of their role of accusers. Here are some extracts from this unusual trial:

'My lover was unemployed and came to live with me in the lodgings which I shared with my sister.'

'He complained about your violent behaviour?'

'I had good reason to be angry, for Becker used to go with this woman and I found out that she was having relations with him.'

'Madame Cocher?'

'Yes.'

'But isn't that his sister-in-law?'

'People said that they didn't know each other, but they knew each other all right . . . Do you understand?'

'He didn't tell you that he was going to Madame Cocher's, because he knew of your animosity towards her!'

'He told me that he was going to the rue Mercier; if he had told me that he was going to stay with Madame Cocher, then my pride would have been wounded and I would have said to him: "Go then!" He shouldn't have told me lies; it wouldn't have given me the shock it gave me afterwards. He deceived me. I helped him to move. Had I known where he was going, don't you think I would have done something? I would have broken every bone in his body. He lied to me, he said: "Don't worry, I'll be back; the flat doesn't suit us because of your sister." Then I heard him say to the carter: "Rue de Maistre." I knew for certain, then. I immediately ran after the cart, pulled off a chair and broke it into pieces. I went back upstairs, took a knife, and sharpened it. I went to the rue de Maistre, the door was shut . . . . I didn't ambush her; I was waiting but I wasn't hidden.'

'What did you do when you saw her?'

'She turned around when she saw me, proof that she felt guilty. She started to walk, I didn't want to take her off-guard, I'm not a coward. I went and stood face to face to her with my knife.'

'But you did deal her a knife blow?'

'I most certainly did.'

'Did you want to kill her?'

'No, and the proof is that I let the knife drop. When I heard her cry out and saw her fall to the ground, I stopped. I could have killed her ten times over, if I had wanted to. . . . '

Although she was vindictive, she felt no resentment but attacked her victim when the latter was being questioned. Madame Cocher stated: 'I have lived at Clichy for a long time in the same house as my brother-in-law.' (The presiding judge added that the information given to the police about the witness was very favourable.) 'My brother-in-law had warned me to be wary of her and told me that she had said she was going to kill me.'

At that point, Célestine Béal interrupted:

'Oh! That's too much! I can't listen to this. I could throttle her.'

'She said to me: "You strumpet, I'm going to kill you"; she wanted to strike me several times, but I fended her off with my arms, so that she couldn't get at me. The police came to my rescue; when they grabbed hold of her she dropped the knife.'

'This woman is getting on my nerves!'

The evidence given by Antoine Becker provoked another quarrel:

'Recently, I had gone to live with her. She lived with her sister in a small flat. I slept in the dining room.'

'Who was her sister?'

'She was a young lady, a kept woman. She had a flat in Paris and this one where she entertained. I only stayed there for six weeks. I didn't want to stay there any longer. The accused used to ill-treat me.'

'Why did she quarrel with you?'

'Out of jealousy, because she didn't want me to go to see my sister-in-law. So when I moved out I gave a false address, because I knew that she would smash all my furniture if I told her where I was going.'

Célestine interrupted:

'I most certainly would have smashed everything. I would have chucked everything out of the window, you would have moved out quicker that way. No need to spend 40 francs getting the furniture taken downstairs, it would have saved on costs. Oh hell!'

Becker, addressing the accused, said:

'I didn't think you were capable of killing, but then recently I was always afraid that you would give me a nasty blow, and I didn't dare sleep with you.'

'Oh, what a nerve! So you didn't dare sleep with me? And the day of your move were you scared when you spent the whole day in bed with me?'

'Aren't you ashamed to stand here and say such things? You wretch! You're still wearing one of my cardigans!'

'Yes, your cardigan and your waistcoat and your shirt – I gave you all of that.'

'You want people to think I'm someone else. I don't need to answer.'

'Half the time you didn't work. You owed money everywhere. Yes, I fed you, do you hear! This man is hiding under the mask of hypocrisy. He is making my life a misery.'

The presiding judge then said:

'No, you have made your own life a misery.'
'No, it's him, and that's why his son was convicted as a communard. He thought it was me who had had him convicted.'

In a provocative move, the accused referred to this political event which was likely to harm her lover's case, for any connection with a communard was enough to make someone suspect.

If Célestine had known how to control herself and to repent, the judges would certainly not have sentenced her to six years' hard labour. This was a severe punishment for a failed attempt to kill someone, carried out by a woman who was overwhelmed by jealousy and on the verge of being deserted – these circumstances are usually interpreted in favour of the accused woman.[23]

The trials of perpetrators of crimes of passion emphasize the confessional character of the judicial drama. After owning up to their crime, the accused must admit that they have committed an offence by showing deep regret. A suicide attempt made immediately after the crime is the most obvious sign of repentance. If such an attempt takes place when they are already in custody, it loses its credibility. On the day of the trial, the accused make a display of contrition before the all-powerful organ of justice which is capable of destroying their future; they verbally express their regret in a language that lacks eloquence and is often clumsy. Louis-François Forestier replied to the presiding judge who had asked him whether he regretted his crime: 'I would give my right hand for it not to have happened.'[24]

It is not for us to judge the degree of their sincerity, especially as these men experienced great difficulty in finding the right words to express their remorse and to convince others of it. Their verbal impotence was genuine; as they were conscious of cultural differences, they tried to adapt their language and their behaviour to that of the judges. The judges knew how to exploit this difference in order to shock members of the jury by proving the barbarity of these criminals who used odious, vulgar and violent language during the preliminary investigation or when they were arrested. In order to avoid this, defendants adapted their behaviour and censored their language; at this point physical gestures replaced the verbal expression of their repentance.

Tears, sobs and fainting always cause a surge of emotion among members of the jury and the public, who interpret them as a desire to repent and to beg for forgiveness. Every crime is an implicit form of accusation directed against society, which cannot but feel guilty towards these individuals whom it has failed to integrate. At the trial, the public expresses a certain gratitude towards the accused who confesses and repents. Society is thus relieved of its own feeling of guilt; it can then aspire to rehabilitate this man or woman who has so clearly expressed a desire to make amends.

Repentance must be manifest, as is testified to by this call to order by the presiding judge during the trial of the Lelong case: 'Instead of withdrawing into silence and pride, you would do better to ask the jury for pardon.' Furthermore, these physical manifestations are a continuation of the crime of passion, and recall the dramatic intensity of this act; they represent a sort of final dénouement, long awaited by the public and the press, which always respect those moments when the criminal sobs or faints:

Today the assize court has witnessed the dénouement of this personal tragedy where, it is believed, jealousy and passion played a major part. The accused, who after killing his mistress tried to kill himself, appeared before the jury on the charge of murder . . . . When he reached the dock, he was overcome with genuine shock. He was sobbing as he answered the questions put to him. Each time certain memories were conjured up before him, he could not control himself, his face became flushed and contorted; he was hiccuping convulsively and he twice collapsed and was given some vinegar to inhale. The poor wretch twitched his dry lips as if trying to quench a raging thirst. The guards at his side supported him.[25]

Coldness and insensitivity are perceived as blatant proof of the intrinsically criminal character of the accused. The impassive and indifferent individual excludes himself from the judicial drama. This lack of participation is then interpreted as proof of contempt and insolence, which judges do not forgive. The press is always waiting to seize on this type of detail about the accused's bad behaviour, which produces comments of the following variety:

There is constantly an evil smile on his thin, pursed lips. There is something false and shifty in his expression when the presiding judge questions him. He turns his head away and bends forward slightly, as if summoning up his patience to hear him through. Then, when the question has been asked, he suddenly straightens himself and arrogantly discusses the charges brought against him.

Louis Gassion's behaviour provoked the same criticism. *La Gazette des tribunaux* wrote:

At first, his sad and resigned attitude inspires sympathy, but as soon as he starts to talk, the feeling of pity which one had starts to fade somewhat. The accused speaks in a high and mighty tone, wears an expression of scorn on his face, and his gestures are theatrical; he sometimes emphasizes his protestations with a smile or rather a sardonic grin, which has an unfortunate effect.[26]

Those who know how to show evidence of repentance receive absolution from the judges and the jury on condition that the crime is admissible, that is to say excusable. The judicial drama should make it possible to determine whether the accused is similar to the 'ideal' criminal and to punish the individual who deviates from this ideal. Sentencing according to the characteristics of the offender not only serves to adapt the law to current opinion, it also makes it possible to establish the norms of criminal behaviour that coexist beside the law. During the nineteenth century, the law did not entirely proscribe criminal violence in domestic life and implicitly took part in it by dealing with certain crimes of passion with impunity; it thus allowed the existence in certain areas of gaps which could be filled by revenge.

Conclusion

If one had to conclude by briefly defining crimes of passion, it could be said that these tragedies of domestic life express little of the passions of love which our imagination likes to fantasize about in matters of love and death. On the one hand, there are accidental crimes which form a part of habitual violence: the man who is unable to control his aggressive urges goes beyond the limits of a domestic quarrel and turns into a murderer. This is a squalid crime, where the victim's provocations matter just as much as the murderer's alcoholism. On the other hand, one can point to desperate acts by lost men who avenge themselves on their companions whom they blame for their misfortune. Some confuse their private lives with social oppression and shout such slogans as, 'Down with the Versaillais, long live the Communards!' But the judiciary interprets their crime as an act of personal justice, which is simply a challenge issued by individuals with no hope.

People still kill for honour, that prized possession for those who have virtually nothing else left in life. It is an asset to be defended at great personal cost and, in spite of the law, on pain of unbearable ruin. This claim is often heard by judges who acquit many of the accused, as if there were in some sense a right to take the law into one's own hands in certain crimes.

Nowadays, perpetrators of crimes of passion are relegated to the category of 'insane' and fade into the dreariness of everyday poverty. They are regarded as failures, undeserving of any special attention unless they have committed sacrilegious acts, such as cutting up and eating the flesh of their beloved one. In the last century, lawyers presented them as decent individuals and 'gently' rebuked them. In the eyes of the law, they had one excuse: their passion, which affected their willpower. These wretched madmen made an impression on a public thirsting after powerful emotions and bloody thrills. This very real violence fuelled their imagination. Everyone regarded the defendant who was about to be judged not simply as a mentally sick person, but as a true criminal, and they enthusiastically waited outside the court-room to see this man who was said to look just like any other. The public, ever eager for something out of the ordinary, something sensational, perceived the criminal act with a great deal of genuine emotion, for its theatricality exacerbated the tragedy of life.

This intense feeling was widespread at the end of the nineteenth century. The significance of human destiny seemed to weigh very heavily on everyone's mind. Just as one could not escape one's fate, one could not escape death, which was painfully present in each story, marked by the early loss of a mother, a child or a wife. Exhausted by the ordeal of life, they cried out: 'I must end it all' – death was the sole outcome of their tragedy.

These crimes of passion were also tragedies, and they fascinated a society which was susceptible to the dramas of domestic life. The human dimension of this unlawful act endowed it with a very special status, and the anguished cries were better understood by individuals who were constantly faced with the adversity of fate. The force of so many struggles and the harshness of everyday life threatened each person's fragile stability and made murder easier to understand. Within this comprehension lay tolerance. Even more noteworthy was the allowance made for the right to take the law into one's own hands. For this was a private matter and a question of honour! Society became an accomplice by implicitly giving its approval to settling accounts in this manner. Finally, there is the word *passion*, a key word, which explains and justifies excesses of violence.

Judicial kindness was unexpected, and was an exception to the prevailing ritual of sentencing and imprisonment. At a time when lawyers and criminologists were trying to make penalties more effective by classifying different types of offenders, perpetrators of crimes of passion were slipping through the net. There was no term, just a brief definition of no particular interest which eradicated the complexity and irrationality of these crimes. From the legal point of view, they were classed alongside other crimes involving murder, but they were judged differently when it came to sentencing. This recognition of an alternative law was a sign that state power had not succeeded in asserting itself. But it was not long before society was punishing those who assumed the right to take the law into their own hands. The state now controlled all expressions of violence, whether public or private. The punitive reaction to crimes of passion was part of a process of democratization; the individual was no longer meant to act as a substitute for the judiciary, which was the new administrator of domestic conflict.

Away from institutions and society's watchful eye, individuals applied themselves to getting round the rules that had been imposed on them and to creating their own way of living. This imperceptible foray into the sphere of counter-culture suggests that social and political order did not always follow mechanisms of power defined in terms of 'dominant' and 'dominated'. It is important not to overlook the resources of those who wished to rebel; they skived off work on Mondays, they cohabited, they spent their wages in taverns, and they constantly wandered from job to job, thereby refusing to comply with the established order of things.

Between the crisis point in these explosive situations and the accounts of the lives of these bit-part players in history, there is clearly prolonged confusion. Whereas one might have expected to find the criminals taking centre-stage, it is the women, their victims, who through their individuality have gradually asserted themselves to such an extent that the personality of their murderers has been relegated to the background. If so much space has been devoted to these characters, it is because certain aspects of their lives have been completely ignored by those men and women – trade unionists, humanists and feminists – who have been so concerned to show the exploitation of women and their sexual inequality that they have neglected certain freedoms that such women had.

The constant exposure of the subservience of working-class women has concealed the fact that they were able to find different ways of doing things and to devise other roles for themselves. Women also knew how to trespass in the paths of disorder. But this freedom had its price. It crushed the man, who, in begging his companion not to abandon him, displayed a certain degree of weakness. The story of these murderers, who were very ordinary individuals with everyday worries and misfortunes, contrasts with the story of their women, whose experience was altogether different. This image was undoubtedly too difficult for such men to cope with; instead, they chose the untenable reality of women as victims and men as murderers.

The court-room records, although biased by the establishment viewpoint, expose the murderer, a commonplace man who one day plays the leading role in an extraordinary drama. Certain aspects of working-class life emerge from the cross-examinations, providing the opportunity to think about the behaviour of lovers in this milieu, to capture the differences, oppositions or similarities compared with the prevailing cultural models. Marital conflicts and their settings reveal the relationships between the sexes, and how they are expressed and experienced.

However, this is not a sociological study of couples and the relationship between working-class men and women at the end of the nineteenth century. That kind of survey all too often produces anonymous statistics, thereby running the risk once again of censoring the very people who were meant to be given the opportunity to speak. By entering into the domestic life of these households, by bringing them to life again through court-room scenes, we have seen images that run counter to those normally presented by literature and history. These images expose working-class opposition to certain moral values and reveal the gaps in state power over civic society.

Apart from the information that can be obtained from the legal archives, the press offers a rich variety of viewpoints. During the nineteenth century a lot of space was devoted to crimes of passion, which were placed on a par with political events by the contemporary press. Nowadays, these appear to be ignored by the so-called 'serious' newspapers, and yet they never cease to intrigue the public, who regard them with ambivalent feelings of attraction and cautious repugnance.

These tragedies of domestic life hold a certain fascination because of the heightened quality of the crime and because of the emotion generated and laid bare by the press; they awaken shameful fantasies in everyone's imagination. Furthermore, crimes of passion inspire fear of the individual who, although not a public enemy, disturbs the social order. They have long disappeared from the front page of newspapers and been relegated to the gutter press, but they have recently reappeared, discreetly, in the popular press. Even more noteworthy is the fact that the social sciences have begun to take account of the value of the news item in revealing social norms, crises and collective images.

The aim of this book has been to establish crimes of passion in the historical process. On this point, it is worth challenging their traditional exclusion, which shows the difficulty of understanding this type of crime intellectually; it has been normally despised or ignored, but now it is being given its due regard.

When we give crimes of passion an important place in history, we reject the idea that they are merely items of fossilized knowledge and allow them a prominence that avid readers of newspaper items have never granted them.

Notes

Prologue   The Moignon Case

1 *Translator's note*: La place de Grève is an open space on the banks of the Seine where dissatisfied workers used to assemble.

Chapter 1   Image and Reality

1 This figure refers to the 735 crimes of passion committed in France between 1871 and 1880; cf. Table 2.
2 *Translator's note*: the throwing of sulphuric acid at a victim. The usual victim in such cases appears to have been a successful female rival rather than the husband or lover of the accused. Although not a new phenomenon according to some writers, popular awareness of it was heightened in the 1870s and there was an increase in frequency. In *La Contagion du meurtre* (1894), the crime writer Paul Aubry devoted an entire chapter to the new *vitrioleuses*.
3 The 80 prisoners fall into the following occupational categories: 28 workers (mechanics, butchers, etc.), 15 day-labourers (odd-job men), 6 artisans (shoe-makers, cabinet-makers, etc.), 4 servants, 2 soldiers, 12 shopkeepers (wine merchants, costermongers, etc.), 6 shop assistants, 2 policemen, 2 procurers, 1 person of independent means and 2 doctors. Out of 9 female prisoners, there were 3 women who did not work, 2 prostitutes, 1 shop assistant, 1 parasol maker and 2 seamstresses.
4 Denis Poulot, *Le Sublime*.
5 Ibid., p. 180. 'Sublime' is slang for 'bad worker'.
6 From a report edited by Michel Chevalier, following the World Fair in London in 1862. Itinerant workers were a great handicap to French industry as they deprived it of a stable and experienced workforce.
7 The Moyaux Case, judgement of 14 May 1877.
8 The Gassion Case, judgement of 8 November 1877.
9 *Translator's note*: the Military Pensioners' Hospital in Paris.
10 The Parizot Case, judgement of 27 July 1877.
11 The Lecomte Case, judgement of 8 February 1879.
12 Norbert Elias, *La Dynamique de l'Occident*, p. 295.

13 J.-C. Chesnais, *Histoire de la violence*.

14 Ibid., p. 100.

15 *Translator's note*: from 1825 the Ministry of the Interior published an annual *Compte général de l'Administration de la justice criminelle*.

16 Yvernès, 'De la justice en France, de 1826 à 1880' in *Annales de démographie internationale*, 1882, p. 229.

17 In a study on legal separations ('Les Séparations de corps', in *Annales de démographie internationale*, 1882, p. 384), Jacques Bertillon noted: 'Divorce and separation are very frequently found among the middle-class professions, in particular business people.' The study for the period 1865–75 found that the annual average was as follows: landlords of independent means and professional people, 12.5%; traders and shopkeepers, 13.5%; farmers, 2%; workers, day-labourers and servants, 13.3%.

18 Louis Proal, *Le Crime et le suicide passionnel*, p. 283.

19 The Sthul Case, judgement of 13 June 1872.

20 The Marambat Case, judgement of 20 December 1875.

21 Article in *L'Evénement*, 21 December 1875.

22 The Poujet Case, judgement of 9 August 1876.

23 The Barreau Case, judgement of 13 May 1876.

24 P. Cère, *Les Populations dangereuses et les misères sociales*, p. 140.

25 The Monchanin Case, judgement of 5 December 1871.

26 The Tazé Case, judgement of 23 September 1872.

27 The Dubourg Case, judgement of 14 June 1872.

28 The Pourcher Case, judgement of 3 April 1879.

29 The Santin Case, judgement of 18 March 1873.

30 The Pierrelar Case, judgement of 8 March 1871.

31 The Lebersorg Case, judgement of 14 July 1871.

32 Archives départementales et dossiers d'instruction de la cour d'assises de la Seine, 1871–1880; serie D2 L18.

33 Cf. P. Ariès, *Historie des populations françaises*.

34 The Dupont Case, judgement of 26 August 1877.

35 The Billet Case, judgement of 28 September 1879.

36 Out of 89 individuals who were accused, 1 was aged between 16 and 20, 9 were 20–25, 14 were 25–30, 19 were 30–35, 16 were 35–40, 13 were 40–45, 6 were 45–50, 4 were 50–55, 3 were 55–60, 3 were 60–65, and 1 was 65–70.

37 Out of the same group of 89 accused individuals, 36 were single, 32 were married, 9 were married and separated (legal separation), 6 were remarried, 5 were widowed, and 1 was remarried and separated (legal separation).

38 Cf. M. Frey, 'Marriage et concubinage dans les classes populaires à Paris'.

39 The Gendarme Case, judgement of 28 May 1877.

40 Emile Zola, 'Types de femmes en France', in *La Femme au xixe siècle*, p. 30.

Chapter 2   The Cry of Rebellion

1 Parisians were familiar with this house, which was described by Xavier-Edouard Lejeune in his Memoirs of *Calicot*: 'The firm of Crespin senior was a hire purchase company where one could buy all manner of goods. A customer who was unable to pay 100, 500, 1,000 francs or more immediately to buy furniture, linen, material or jewellery, for example, would pay one-fifth of the amount and write out promissory notes for the rest, which were payable every week, every fortnight or every month.

After the first payment, one could go into one of the shops which were designated on a list, and collect one's purchase. This was a similar service to that provided by street-sellers, but on a larger scale. Each shop on the list received purchase coupons and paid a charge of 20% to Crespin in exchange. The customer was unaware of this and thought that he was paying the same price as everyone for the goods, especially since he only showed his purchase coupons at the till. In fact, he was paying 20% and even 30% more than people who paid for their purchases in cash, since the shopkeeper did not wish to lose any of his profit. The seller had to be fairly perceptive to recognize at first sight a person who subscribed to Crespin's scheme and to act accordingly. . . . Monsieur Crespin, born in Doudeauville in Normandy, had already made a fortune, by taking advantage of this enormous class of poor people.' (X.-E. Lejeune, *Calicot*, pp. 219, 220).

2 The Moyaux Case, judgement of 14 May 1877.
3 The Barbot Case, judgement of 11 October 1877.
4 The Dubien Case, judgement of 25 October 1878.
5 The Breffeil Case, judgement of 24 September 1874.

Chapter 3   The Path to Crime

1 The Savary Case, judgement of 28 June 1876.
2 E. de Greeff, *Amour et crimes d'amour*.
3 The Zich Case, the Trouvé Case and the Savary Case.
4 L.M. Despres's statement, the Tiétard Case, 1872.
5 The Michaud Case, judgement of 25 January 1875.
6 The Barreau Case, judgement of 13 May 1876.
7 P. Bouzat and J. Pinatel, *Traité de droit pénal et de criminologie*, p. 253.
8 The Pène Case, judgement of 30 November 1874.
9 The Billoir Case, judgement of 15 March 1877.
10 The Savary Case, judgement of 28 June 1876; the Marié Case, judgement of 7 October 1876.
11 The scene of the crime: home (42 cases), street (21 cases), tavern (10 cases), stairs (9 cases), workplace (7 cases).
12 Enrico Ferri, *La Sociologia criminale*.
13 The weapon used in the crime: firearms (30 cases), knives (35 cases) and tools (12 cases); crimes committed without the use of a weapon: physical violence, sulphuric acid, strangulation and poisoning (12 cases).

Chapter 4   The Break

1 The Jouault Case, judgement of 11 February 1873.
2 The Balade Case, judgement of 30 April 1879.
3 Cf. Arlette Farge, *Le Désordre des familles*.
4 The Monchanin Case, judgement of 5 December 1871.
5 The Solhart Case, judgement of 26 November 1873.
6 The Kemps Case, judgement of 14 June 1877.
7 The Descombes Case, judgement of 16 May 1873.
8 The Couturier Case, judgement of 16 April 1873.
9 The Breton Case, judgement of 13 January 1879.
10 The Gassion Case, judgement of 8 November 1877.

11 The Trouvé Case, judgement of 12 May 1876.
12 The Elisabeth Prévost Case, judgement of 12 October 1876.
13 Emile Zola, 'L'Adultère dans la bourgeoisie', in *La Femme au xixe siècle*, collected essays edited by Nicole Priollaud, p. 151.
14 The Tronché Case, judgement of 23 July 1872.
15 The Shenk Case, judgement of 21 November 1872.
16 The Dée Case, judgement of 21 February 1876.
17 The Duc Case, judgement of 28 September 1874.
18 Cf. A. Corbin, *Les Filles de noces*.
19 Maxime Du Camps, *Paris, ses organes, sa vie et ses fonctions, 1869–1875*, vol. III, p. 434.
20 The Pourcher Case, judgement of 3 April 1879.
21 The Brazier Case, judgement of 11 April 1876.
22 The Douard Case, judgement of 26 June 1877.
23 *L'Evénement*, 21 October 1875.
24 The Billet Case, judgement of 28 September 1879.
25 The Brossier Case, judgement of 7 October 1871.

Chapter 5   The World Upside Down

1 Alphonse Esquiros, *Les Vierges martyres*, Paris 1842.
2 The Pierrelar Case, judgement of 8 March 1871.
3 The Gautré Case, judgement of 23 February 1878.
4 The Parizot Case, judgement of 27 July 1877.
5 The Marié Case, judgement of 7 October 1876.
6 The Langlais Case, 1875.
7 The Gaudot Case, judgement of 10 May 1879.
8 The Perbos Case, judgement of 4 December 1879.
9 The Savary Case, judgement of 28 June 1876.
10 The Poujat Case, judgement of 9 August 1876.
11 The Breffeil Case, judgement of 24 September 1874.
12 The Shenk Case, previously mentioned.
13 The Gautré Case, judgement of 23 February 1878.
14 The Bessières Case, judgement of 10 March 1874.
15 The Gaudot Case, judgement of 10 May 1879.
16 Cf. above, the Pourcher Case (adultery).
17 The Lerondeau Case.
18 The Vallaud Case, judgement of 28 July 1824.
19 The Parizot Case, judgement of 27 July 1877.
20 The Bessières Case, judgement of 10 March 1874.
21 The Perbos Case, judgement of 4 December 1879.
22 The Barbot Case, judgement of 11 October 1877.
23 The Guillot Case, judgement of 25 November 1878.
24 The Kemps Case, previously mentioned.
25 The Dupont Case, judgement of 27 August 1877.
26 The Shenk Case, judgement of 21 December 1872.
27 The Duc Case, judgement of 28 September 1874.
28 *Translator's note*: This is a preparation made from the dried bodies of Spanish fly, once thought to be an aphrodisiac.
29 Alphonse Daudet, *Sapho*; Jules Barbey d'Aurevilly, *Une Vieille Maîtresse*.

30 The Coste Case, judgement of 10 July 1878.
31 *Le Petit Journal*, 11 July 1878.
32 The Smeyers Case, judgement of 6 June 1872.
33 Cf. E. Shorter, *Birth of the Family*, and J.-L. Flandrin, *Le Sexe et l'Occident*.
34 The Lebersorg Case, judgement of 14 July 1871.
35 The Gautré Case, judgement of 23 February 1878.
36 The Féaux Case, judgement of 15 May 1875.
37 The Forestier Case, judgement of 27 October 1874.

Chapter 6   To Kill for Passion

1 M. Jousse, *Traité de la justice criminelle*, p. 629.
2 Ibid., p. 615.
3 Montesquieu, *De l'esprit des lois* and Beccaria, *Des délits et des peines*.
4 Bellart, *Annales du barreau moderne*, 'Affaire Gras', vol. III, p. 34.
5 R. Saleilles, *L'Individualisation de la peine*, p. 87.
6 Ibid., pp. 14 and 15.
7 Ibid., p. 90.
8 Assize Court of Aisne, 24 April 1875.
9 *La Gazette des tribunaux*, 15 June 1872.
10 This episode was never explained; the accused and his family refused to give the reasons why they covered up the fact that Madame Dubourg was sent to a rest home. She seems to have been pregnant at the time and, according to the evidence given by a female friend, was suspected of adultery.
11 The Association for Women's Rights was founded in 1870 by Léon Richer and was chaired by Maria Deraisme. See L. Klejman and F. Rocherfort, *Le féminisme en France 1868–1914*.
12 H. Joly, *Le Crime, étude sociale*, p. 51.
13 Cf. L. Chevallier, *Classes laborieuses et classes dangereuses*.
14 D. Poulot, *Le Sublime*.
15 J. K. Lavater (1781–1803), *Essai sur la physionomie*, and F. J. Gall, *Fonction du cerveau*, 1808.
16 P. J. Cabanis, *Rapport du physique et du moral*.
17 P. Despine, *La Psychologie naturelle*, 1868.
18 P. Lucas, *Traité physiologique de l'hérédité naturelle*, 1847, and B. A. Morel, *Traité des dégénérescences de l'espèce humaine*, 1857.
19 C. Lombroso (1836–1909), army doctor, then psychiatrist and later expert in forensic medicine at the University of Turin and the University of Pavia.
20 E. Ferri (professor of criminal law in Rome), *La Sociologia criminale*, 1881; Garofalo (presiding judge in the Naples Court of Appeal), *La Criminologia*, 1885.
21 Ferri, *La Sociologia criminale*, p. 32.
22 Lombroso, *L'Homme criminel*, p. 114.
23 G. Tarde, 'L'Amour morbide', in *Archives de l'anthropologie criminelle*, 1890, vol. 5, p. 592.
24 Ferri, *La Sociologie criminelle*, p. 113.
25 Ibid., p. 573.
26 Lombroso, p. 114.
27 E. Ferri, *La Sociologie criminelle*, p. 134.
28 Ibid., p. 113.
29 Lombroso, *La Femme criminelle et la prostituée*, p. 429.

30 Ibid., p. 270.
31 Ibid., p. 69.
32 H. Joly, 'Les Femmes, criminelles passionnelles', in *Archives de l'anthropologie criminelle et des sciences pénales*, p. 275.
33 Lombroso, *La Femme criminelle*, p. 506.
34 Ibid., p. 507.
35 Ibid., p. 517.
36 Ibid., p. 428.
37 Ibid., p. 498.
38 Cf. M. Foucault, *Moi, Pierre Rivière ayant égorgé ma mère, ma soeur et mon frère*.
39 The Brière Case, judgement of 7 January 1880.
40 *Le Figaro*, 8 January 1880.
41 L. Holtz, *Les Crimes passionnels*, p. 11.
42 L. Proal, *Le Crime et le suicide passionnel*.
43 Ibid., p. 159.
44 Ibid., p. 166.
45 Ibid., p. 185.
46 Ibid., p. 184.
47 Ibid., p. 196.
48 R. Krafft-Ebing, *Psychology of Sex*, p. 17.
49 H. Courtis, *Etude médico-légale des crimes passionnels*, p. 57.
50 J. Sur, *Le Jury et les crimes passionnels*, p. 27.
51 Saleilles, *L'Individualisation de la peine*, p. 65.
52 Holtz, *Les Crimes passionnels*, p. 63.
53 F. Brunetières, 'Le Crime passionnel', in *La Revue des deux mondes*, pp. 211 and 212.
54 Sur, *Le Jury et les crimes passionnels*, p. 34.
55 Holtz, *Les Crimes passionnels*, p. 20.
56 Courtis, *Etude medico-légale des crimes passionnels*, p. 54.
57 Ibid., pp. 75 and 102.
58 Ibid., p. 106.
59 de Greeff, *Amour et crimes d'amour*, p. 20.
60 Louis Rabinowicz, *Crimes of Passion, A Study in Social Psychology*, p. 4.
61 Ibid., p. 2.
62 Ibid., p. 242.
63 Ibid., p. 59.
64 Ibid., p. 145.
65 de Greeff, *Amour et crimes d'amour*, p. 101.
66 Ibid., p. 19.
67 Ibid., p. 95.
68 Ibid., p. 127.
69 Ibid., p. 306.
70 Ibid., p. 243.
71 Ibid., p. 244.
72 Ibid., p. 247.
73 Article 64 of the Penal Code: 'No crime or criminal offence has been committed if the person breaking the law was in a state of mental disorder at the time of the crime.' If madness is established, then the crime is eliminated since there is no ground for prosecution.
74 E. Capgras, 'Crimes et délires passionnels', *Annales médico-psychologiques*, p. 47.
75 G. Heuyer, 'Psychoses et crimes passionnels', *Revue d'hygiène mentale*, July–August 1932, p. 211.

Chapter 7 The Reality of the Assize Courts

1 The Shenk Case, judgement of 21 November 1872.
2 The Dée Case, judgement of 21 February 1876.
3 Emile Zola, 'Types de femmes en France', in *La Femme au xix' siècle*, p. 33.
4 The Marié Case, judgement of 7 October 1876.
5 The Savary Case, judgement of 28 June 1876.
6 The Jouault Case, judgement of 11 February 1873.
7 The Michel Case, judgement of 13 October 1876.
8 The Moyaux Case, judgement of 14 May 1877.
9 The Guillot Case, judgement of 25 November 1878.
10 The Billoir Case, judgement of 15 March 1877.
11 The Helfrich Case, judgement of 26 October 1874; *Le Petit Journal*, 27 October 1874.
12 The Pène Case, judgement of 30 November 1874; *La Gazette des tribunaux*, 1 December 1874.
13 The Perdriat Case, judgement of 28 April 1877.
14 The Solhart Case, judgement of 26 November 1873.
15 The Forestier Case, judgement of 27 October 1874.
16 The Forestier Case.
17 The Moyaux Case, judgement of 14 May 1877.
18 The Gras Case, *Le Petit Parisien*, 24 July 1877.
19 The Béal Case, judgement of 7 December 1872.
20 The Moyaux Case, judgement of 14 May 1877.
21 The Féaux Case, judgement of 15 May 1875.
22 The Billoir Case, judgement of 15 March 1877.
23 The Béal Case, judgement of 7 December 1872.
24 The Forestier Case, judgement of 27 October 1874.
25 The Michaud Case, judgement of 25 January 1875; *La Gazette des tribunaux*, 28 January 1875.
26 The Woeblen Case, judgement of 28 June 1877.

Sources and Bibliography

I. Archive Sources

Ministerial records and preliminary investigation dossiers for the Seine assize courts; D2 U8 series.

Balade, Charles, judgement of 30 April 1879.
Barbot, Louis, judgement of 11 October 1877.
Barreau, Pierre, judgement of 13 May 1876.
Béale, Célestine, judgement of 7 December 1872.
Bessières, Pierre, judgement of 10 March 1874.
Bernaux, Charles, judgement of 30 August 1878.
Bernou, Jean-Baptiste, judgement of 25 November 1875.
Billet, Jacques, judgement of 28 September 1879.
Billoir, Sébastien, judgement of 15 March 1877.
Brazier, Jean-Claude, judgement of 11 April 1876.
Breffeil, Léon, judgement of 24 September 1874.
Breton, Eugène, judgement of 28 June 1876.
Breton, Gustave, judgement of 13 January 1879.
Brière, Marie, judgement of 7 January 1880.
Brossier, François, judgement of 7 October 1871.
Charrier, Marie, judgement of 20 October 1875.
Coste, Guillaume, judgement of 10 July 1878.
Couturier, Antoine, judgement of 16 April 1873.
Couzimier, Jean, judgement of 5 August 1876.
Dée, Antoine, judgement of 21 February 1876.
Degrange, Jean-Louis, judgement of 13 March 1875.
Descombes, Claude, judgement of 16 May 1873.
Douard, Aréna, judgement of 26 June 1877.
Dréville, Antoine, judgement of 13 September 1872.
Dubien, Jean-Baptiste, judgement of 25 October 1878.
Dubourg, Arthur, judgement of 14 June 1872.
Duc, François, judgement of 28 September 1874.
Dupont, Alphonse, judgement of 27 August 1877.

Eon, Adolphe, judgement of 21 April 1876.
Fassin, François, judgement of 7 October 1871.
Féaux, Louis, judgement of 15 May 1875.
Feuillerade, René, judgement of 3 April 1876.
Forestier, Louis, judgement of 27 October 1874.
Gassion, Léopold, judgement of 8 November 1877.
Gaudot, Charles, judgement of 10 May 1879.
Gautré, Pierre, judgement of 23 February 1878.
Gras, Eugénie, judgement of 26 July 1877.
Grimm, André, judgement of 18 November 1876.
Grossi, Charles, judgement of 24 December 1875.
Guignot, Jean-Jacques, judgement of 24 December 1878.
Guillot, Modeste, judgement of 25 November 1878.
Helfrich, Adam, judgement of 26 October 1874.
Jouault, Louis, judgement of 11 February 1873.
Kemps, Alexis, judgement of 14 June 1877.
Labe, Jean, judgement of 26 October 1871.
Lebersorg, François, judgement of 14 July 1871.
Lecomte, Charles, judgement of 8 February 1879.
Ledoux, Adélaïde, judgement of 7 January 1879.
Lelong, Victorine, judgement of 10 July 1875.
Marambat, Auguste, judgement of 20 December 1875.
Marié, Jean, judgement of 7 October 1876.
Meilander, Jacques, judgement of 10 December 1875.
Michaud, Emile, judgement of 25 January 1875.
Michel, Jules, judgement of 13 October 1876.
Michel, Jacques, judgement of 12 March 1871.
Moignon, Pierre, judgement of 24 January 1874.
Monchanin, Etiennette, judgement of 5 December 1871.
Mordret, Jacques, judgement of 5 December 1874.
Moyaux, Pierre, judgement of 14 May 1877.
Paris, Antoine, judgement of 13 September 1871.
Parizot, Victor, judgement of 27 July 1877.
Paulmier, Philippe, judgement of 24 January 1877.
Pène, Jean, judgement of 30 November 1874.
Perbos, Barbe, judgement of 4 December 1879.
Perdriat, Louis, judgement of 28 April 1877.
Perney, Pierre, judgement of 29 December 1872.
Pierrelar, Eugène, judgement of 8 March 1871.
Piplet, Pierre, judgement of 28 November 1874.
Ponsart, Adolphe, judgement of 11 September 1877.
Poujet, Auguste, judgement of 9 August 1876.
Pourcher, Marie, judgement of 3 April 1879.
Prévost, Elisabeth, judgement of 12 October 1876.
Prévost, Victor, judgement of 21 November 1879.
Santin, Jean-Baptiste, judgement of 18 March 1873.
Savary, Médard, judgement of 28 June 1876.
Schaeffer, Xavier, judgement of 14 June 1878.
Servet, Baptiste, judgement of 5 December 1874.
Shenk, François, judgement of 21 November 1872.
Smeyers, Frédéric, judgement of 6 June 1872.

Solhart, Georges, judgement of 26 November 1873.
Sthul, Catherine, judgement of 13 June 1872.
Tazé, Jean-Baptiste, judgement of 23 September 1872.
Tiétard, Godefroid, judgement of 7 November 1872.
Tronché, Pierre, judgement of 23 July 1872.
Trouvé, Isidore, judgement of 12 May 1876.
Ulrich, Jean, judgement of 14 December 1875.
Vallaud, Auguste, judgement of 28 July 1874.
Viallard, Jeane, judgement of 17 March 1873.
Woeblen, Emile, judgement of 28 June 1877.
Zich, Marguerite, judgement of 30 May 1874.

II. Nineteenth-century Sources

Newspapers and Periodicals

La Gazette des tribunaux, 1870–1880.
L'Événement, 1870–1880.
Le Figaro, 1870–1880
Le Petit Journal, 1870–1880
La Revue des deux mondes, February 1881.

Archives de l'anthropologie criminelle et des sciences pénales, 1886–1926.
Annales médico-psychologiques, 1939.
Revue de droit pénal et criminel, 1930–1937.
Annales de médecine légale de criminologie et de police scientifique, 1924–1926.
Déviance et Société, Geneva, 1981.
Revue d'Hygiène mentale, 1932.
Revue *Romantisme*, 1981.

General Studies

EIGHTEENTH AND NINETEENTH-CENTURY CRIMINOLOGY

Andrieux, L., *Souvenirs d'un préfet de police*, Paris, 1885, 2 volumes.
Bataille, A., *Causes criminelles et mondaines*, Paris, 1887–1898, 18 volumes.
Bellart, *Annales du Barreau moderne*, Paris 1823.
Bourgeois, L.-X., *Les Passions dans leurs rapports avec la santé et les maladies*, Paris, 1861.
Brière de Boismont, *Du suicide et de la folie suicide*, Paris, 1856.
Cabanis, P.-J., *Rapport du physique et du moral*, Paris, 1843.
Caro, J., *Études morales sur le xixe siècle*, Paris, 1876.
Desjardins, A., 'Jury et Avocats', in *Revue des deux mondes*, May–June 1886.
Desmaze, C., *Le Crime et la Débauche, le Divorce*, Paris, 1881.
Durkheim, E., *Le Suicide*, Paris, Alcan, 1897.
Ferri, E., *La Sociologie criminelle*, 3rd edn., Paris, Alcan, 1893.
Garofalo, *Criminologie*, Paris, Alcan, 1888.
Goron, *L'Amour criminel*, Paris, 1897, 4 volumes.
Granier, C., *La Femme criminelle*, Paris, O. Doin, 1906.
Guerry, A.M., *Essai sur la statistique morale de la France*, Paris, 1833.
Joly, H., *Le Crime, étude sociale*, Paris, 1888.
—— 'Les Femmes criminelles passionnelles', in *Archives de l'anthropologie criminelle et des sciences pénales*, 1890.

Jousse, M., *Traité de la justice criminelle*, 1771, 4 volumes.
Krafft-Ebing, *Traité clinique de psychiatrie*, Paris, Maloine, 1897.
—— *Étude médico-légale*, Paris, G. Carré, 1899.
Lombroso, C., *L'Homme criminel*, translated from the Italian, Paris, Alcan, 1887.
—— in collaboration with G. Ferrero, *La Femme criminelle et la Prostituée*, translated from the Italian, Paris, 1896.
—— 'La Bête humaine', in *Les Applications de l'anthropologie criminelle*, Paris, Alcan, 1892.
Lunier, *De la production et de la consommation des boissons alcooliques en France*, Paris, 1877.
Saleilles, R., *L'Individualisation de la peine*, Paris, Alcan, 1898.
Socquet, J., *Statistiques de la criminalité en France de 1826 à 1900*, Paris, 1902.
Tarde, G., *La Criminalité comparée*, Paris, 1886.
—— *L'Évolution de l'idée criminaliste au xix* siècle*, Paris, 1886.
—— *La Philosophie pénale*, Lyon, Masson, 1890.
—— 'L'Amour morbide', *Annales de l'anthropoligie criminelle*, 1890.
Vingtrimier, D., *Examen des comptes de la justice criminelle*, 1864.

Working-Class Conditions

Barberet, J., *Le Travail en France, 1886–1890*, 5 volumes.
Cère, P., *Les Populations dangereuses et les misères sociales*, Paris, Dentu, 1872.
Daubié, J.V., *La Femme pauvre au xix* siècle*, Paris, 1866, 3 volumes.
Duveau, G., *La classe ouvrière sous le Second Empire*, Paris, 1864.
Esquiros, A., *Les Vierges martyres*, Paris, 1840.
Hausonville, 'La Misère et le Vice', *Revue des deux mondes*, 1887.
Leroy-Beaulieu, *Le Travail des femmes au xix* siècle*, Paris, Charpentier, 1873.
Mazerolle, P., *La Misère de Paris, les mauvais gîtes*, Paris, 1875.
Simon, J., *La vie de l'ouvrière*, Paris, 1867.

III. Twentieth-century Sources

Criminology: Studies on Crimes of Passion

Capgras, E., 'Crimes et délires passionnels', *Annales médico-psychologiques*, Paris, 1927.
Courtis, H., *Étude médico-légale des crimes passionels*, Toulouse, 1910.

De Greeff, E. *Amour et crimes d'amour*, 1942 (1973 edn.), Dessart, Bruxelles.
—— *L'État dangereux dans les crimes passionnels*, Paris, 1953.
—— La Structure du drame chez l'assassin, Paris, 1958.
Delain, A., *Le Crime passionnel sous la iiie République*, master's dissertation, Paris, 1979.
Ernest, C., *Les Drames de la passion amoureuse*, Paris, 1907.
Escoffier, P., *Le Crime passionnel devant le jury*, Paris, 1910.
Goodman, Derick, *Crime of passion*, London, Elek Books, 1958.
Holtz, Louis, *Les Crimes passionnels*, Paris, Mellotée, 1904.
Levy-Valensi, 'Les Crimes passionnels', *Annales de médecine légale*, 1931.
Ley, A., 'Jalousie et criminalité', *Annales de médecine légale*, Paris, 1939.
—— 'La Vengeance', *Revue de droit pénal et criminologie*, 1937.
Mitkovitch, R., 'Le Crime passionnel', *Revue de droit pénal et criminologie*, 1910.
Proal, L., *Le Crime et le suicide passionnel*, Paris, 1900.
—— 'La Criminalité féminine', Paris, E. de Sorje, 1890.

Rabinowicz, L., *Le Crime passionnel*, Paris, Rivière, 1931.
Sur, J., *Le Jury et les crimes passionnels*, Poitiers, 1908.

GENERAL CRIMINOLOGY

Abbatecci et Billacois, 'Crimes et criminalité en France sous l'Ancien Régime', *Cahiers des Annales*, 1973.
Bouzat, P. et Pinatel, J., *Traité de droit pénal et de criminologie*, Paris, Dalloz, 1970.
Chaulot, P. et Susini, J., *Le Crime en France*, Paris, 1959.
Granier, C., *La Femme criminelle*, Paris, O. Doin, 1906.
Imbert, J., *Le Pouvoir des juges*, Paris, 1972.
Lagache, D., *La Jalousie amoureuse, psychologie descriptive*, Paris, PUF, 1947, 2 volumes.
—— Contribution à la psychologie de la conduite criminelle', *Revue française de psychiatrie*, 1948.
Lassere, A., *Les Délinquants passionnels*, Paris, 1908.
Léauté, J., *Criminologie et sciences pénitentiaires*, Paris, PUF, 1972.
Lévy, T., *Le Crime en toute humanité*, Paris, Grasset, 1984.
Macé, G., *Les Femmes criminelles, la police parisienne*, Paris, 1904.
Montarron, L., *Histoire des crimes sexuels*, Paris, Plon, 1970.
Pinatel, J., *La Criminologie*, Paris, 1960.
Saillard, P., *Le Rôle de l'avocat en matière criminelle*, Paris, 1905
Tullio, B. Di, *Manuel d'anthropologie*, Paris, Payot, 1951.

PSYCHOLOGY AND CRIMINOLOGY

Ellenberger, H., 'Relations psychologiques entre le criminel et la victime', *Revue internationale de criminologie*, Paris, 1954.
Guttmacher, M., *La Psychologie du meurtrier*, Paris PUF, 1965.
Hesnard, A., *Psychologie du crime*, Paris, Payot, 1963.
Heuyer, G., 'Psychoses et crimes passionnels', *Hygiène mentale*, Paris, 1932.
Klein, R., *L'Amour et la Haine*, Paris, Payot, 1978.
Reik, T., *Le Besoin d'aimer*, Paris, Payot, 1973.

General Studies

Ariès, P., 'Points', *Histoire des populations françaises*, Paris, Seuil, 1979.
Auclair, G., *Le Mana quotidien*, Paris, Anthropos, 1970.
Barthes, R., *Essais critiques*, Paris, 1964.
Blunden, K., *Le Travail et la Vertu*, Paris, Payot, 1982.
Burnan, R., *La vie quotidienne en France de 1870 à 1900*, Paris, Hachette, 1947.
Castan, N. et Y., *Vivre ensemble, ordre et désordre en Languedoc, xviie et xviiie siècles*, collection 'Archives', Paris, Gallimard, 1981.
Chauveau, A. et Faustin, H., *Théorie du code pénal*, Paris, 1887, 2 volumes.
Chesnais, J.-C., *Histoire de la violence en Occident de 1800 à nos jours*, Paris, Laffont, 1981.
Chevalier, L., *Classes laborieuses et Classes dangereuses*, Paris, collection 'Pluriel', Le Livre de poche, 1978.
—— *Montmartre, du plaisir et du crime*, Paris, Laffont, 1980.
Corbin, A., *Les Filles de Noces*, Aubier, Paris, 1979.
Debré, J.-L., *La Justice au xixe siècle*, Paris, 1981, 2 volumes.
Donzelot, J., *La Police des familles*, Ed. de Minuit, Paris, 1975.

Elias, N., *La Dynamique de l'Occident*, translated from the German, Paris, Calmann-Lévy, 1975.

—— *La Civilisation des mœurs*, translated from the German, Paris, collection 'Pluriel', Calmann-Lévy, 1973.

Farge, A. et Foucault, M., *Le Désordre des familles, Lettres de cachet des archives de la Bastille*, collection 'Archives', Paris, Gallimard, 1982.

Foucault, M., 'The notion of the dangerous individual in the 19th century', *Journal of Law and Psychiatry*, 1978.

—— *Surveiller et Punir*, Paris, Gallimard, 1975.

—— *Moi, Pierre Rivière ayant égorgé ma mère, ma sœur, et mon frère*, collection 'Archives', Paris, Seuil, 1977.

Flandrin, J.-L., *Contraception, Mariage et Relations amoureuses dans l'Occident*, Paris, AESS, November–December, 1969.

—— *Le Sexe et l'Occident*, Paris, Seuil, 1981.

Frey, M., *Mariage et Concubinage dans les classes populaires à Paris*, Paris, AESS, July–August 1978.

Garçon, E., *Le Droit pénal, origines, évolution*, Paris, 1922.

Goffman, E., *La Mise en scène quotdienne*, Paris, Ed. de Minuit, 1973.

Imbert, J. et Levasseur G., *Le Pouvoir, les Juges et les Bourreaux*, Paris, Hachette, 1972.

Laingui, A., *La Responsabilité pénal dans l'ancien droit*, Paris, 1970.

Lejeune Xavier-Edouard, *Calicot*, Paris, Arthaud Montalba, 1984.

Ley, A., 'La Vengeance', *Revue du droit pénal et criminel*, 1937.

—— *Les Marginaux et les Exclus dans l'histoire*, Cahiers Jussieu, collection 10/18, 1979.

MacClintock, 'La Violence à l'intérieur de la famille', *Revue des sciences criminelles et de droit pénal comparé*, 1964.

Maffesoli, M., *La Violence fodatrice*, Price, Champ Urbain, 1978.

Merle, R., *De Zola à Lombroso*, RSC, 1964.

Perrot, M., 'L'Affaire Troppmann', *L'Histoire*, 1981.

—— 'Délinquance et système pénitentiaire en France au XIXᶜ siècle', Annales ESC, 1975.

—— 'L'Éloge de la ménagère dans le discours des ouvriers français au XIXᶜ siècle', in *Mythes et Représentations de la femme au XIXᶜ siècle*, Paris, Champion, 1976.

Poulot, D., *Le sublime*, introduced by Alain Cottereau, Paris, Maspéro, 1980.

—— *Les Reporters de l'histoire: La Femme au XIXᶜ siècle*, (1983 edn.), Paris, Levi et Messinger.

Reytier, D., *L'Adultère sous le Second Empire*, master's dissertation, Paris, 1980.

Rom, *Histoire des faits divers*, Paris, 1962.

Seguin, J.-P., *Nouvelles à sensations, canards du XIXᶜ siècle*, Paris, A. Collin, 1959.

Sennet, R., *Les Tyrannies de l'intimité*, Paris, Seuil, 1979.

Shorter, E., 'Points Histoire', *Naissance de la famille moderne*, Paris, Seuil, 1977.

Sleimann, I., *Le Crime passionnel*, Law thesis, Paris, Cujas, 1964.

Sullerot, E., *Histoire et sociologie du travail féminin*, Paris, 1968.

—— *Misérable et Glorieuse, la femme du XIXᶜ siècle*, Paris, Fayard, 1980.

Tarnowsky, *Les femmes homicides*, 1908.

Vimont, J.-C., *La Haute Criminalité populaire dans les premières années de la monarchie de Juillet*, master's dissertation, Nanterre, 1976.

Zeldin, T., *France 1848–1945: Ambition, Love, and Politics*, Oxford, University Press, 1973.

Index

acquittal 171–2, 176
adultery 95–7, 191–2
alcoholism 27, 28, 34, 47, 50, 62–5,
    85, 106, 107–10, 179, 214

Balade, Charles 75–7
Barbot, Louis 46–8, 126, 154
Béal, Célestine 222, 223–6
Bernaux, Charles 151–2
Bessières, Léonie 97–9, 120, 126
Billet, Jacques 34–5, 64, 112
Billoir, Sébastien 64–7, 215–17,
    223
brasseries 75
Breffeil, Thomas 49–54, 119
Breton, Eugène 82–3
Brière, Marie 189–91
Broca, Paul 179

Cabanis, P. J. 179
Capgras, E. 200
Charrier, Marie 110–11
Chesnais, J.-C. 20–1
Common Law (civil code) 17, 203
commune 28, 49
concierges 29–30
Coste, Guillaume 152–3
Courtis, Hélie 195, 196

Couturier, Antoine 81–2
Couzimié, Jean 96
crime (general) 22, 167, 177, 186–8
crimes of passion 167–71, 182–3,
    192, 197, 202–3
  causes *see* adultery; jealousy; money;
    poverty; revenge; separation;
    unemployment
  court procedure 218–23
  extenuating circumstances 69, 108,
    211, 214, 223
  incidence among the bourgeoisie 23
  incidence among the working class
    17, 35
  incidence within the family 21–3
  legal definition 167, 191
  as unpremeditated crime 69
criminal anthropology 178–82
criminologists *see* Ferri; Lombroso

Daudet, Alphonse 149
d'Aurevilly, Barbey 149
Debuyst, C. 199
Dée, Antoine 96–7
Delafosse, Anna 107–8
De Greeff, E. 57, 197–200
Descombes, Claude 80–1
Despine, P. 179

divorce 80
domestic quarrels 21–2, 106
Douard, Aréna 106–7
Dubien, Jean-Baptiste 48–9
Dubourg, Arthur 30, 134–9, 173–6
Duc, François 99–103, 134,
    139–41, 156–7
Du Camps, Maxime 103
Dumas *fils* 176
Dupont, Alphonse 32–4, 127
Durkheim, E. 181

Elias, Norbert 19

family
    middle-class view of 20, 192
    role of 118–19
Féaux, Pierre 158, 223
Ferri, Enrico 69, 95, 179, 180, 181,
    183–4, 185, 199
Forestier, Louis 158–60, 217–18,
    226

Gall, F. J. 179
Garofalo, Raffaello 180
Gassion, Léopold 84–8, 227
Gaudot, Charles 117–20, 128–31
Gautré, Pierre 115, 119, 157–8
Granier, Camille 188
Gras, Eugénie 142–9, 221
Guesde, Jules 114
Guillot, Modeste 126–7, 212–14

Helfrich, Adam 93–4
Heuyer, G. 200
homicide 167
Holtz, Louis 194, 195
honour 23–7, 84

in flagrante delicto 79, 95, 96, 97,
    104, 131, 133, 134, 152, 169,
    174, 177
infanticide *see* Moyaux, Pierre

jealousy 22, 58, 88, 105, 191
Jouault, Louis 74–5, 210
Joly, H. 181

Kemps, Alexis 127
Krafft-Ebing 192, 196

Laccassagne 181
Lafargue, Paul 114
lawyers
    Chopin d'Arnouville 146, 160
    Maître Lachaud 149, 173, 191
    Maître Nicolay 153
Lavater, J. K. 179
Lebersorg, François 30–1, 108–9,
    157
Lecomte, Charles 64
legal aid 80
legal status of women *see* Common
    Law
Lombroso, C. 161, 179, 180, 185,
    186, 187, 192, 199
Lucas, Prosper 179

Marambat, Auguste 123–4
Marié, Jean 68, 116, 120–2, 204
marriage 35
ménage à trois 149–56
Michaud, Emile 58–61
Michel, Jacques 210–11
middle-class women 95, 104, 117,
    118, 134, 141–2
mistresses 103–4, 142–9
Moignon, Pierre 1–12, 154, 222
Morel, B. A. 179
money 73, 116
Monchanin, Etiennette 77–8
Moyaux, Pierre 39–46, 211, 220,
    222

occupations 58

Parizot, Victor 116, 126
Paulmier, Philippe 112
Penal Code
  in France 17, 97, 168, 171–2,
    176, 180
  in Italy 184, 199, 200
Pène, Jean 63, 217
Perbos, Barbe 118, 122
Perdriat, Louis 110, 217
Piplet, Pierre 161–3
poisoning 16, 21, 130
Poulot, Denis 18
Pourcher, Marie 30, 103–5
poverty 17–18, 19, 39, 113
press reactions 1, 12, 97–9, 103,
    111, 152, 155, 160, 173,
    194–5, 227
Prévost, Elisabeth 91–3
Proal, Louis 23, 39, 191, 192, 194
psychiatry 188–9, 190, 195–6,
    200–1
psychology of crime 51, 55, 56–8,
    62, 70

Rabinowicz, Louis 197–8
revenge 24; see also servants

Saleilles, R. 170, 172, 184, 193,
    200, 215
Savary, Médard 55–6, 68, 118,
    204–10
self-justification 60, 68–9, 81
sentencing 46, 171–3, 184, 193, 215
separation 73–4, 80, 81, 85, 101,
    141, 204, 205, 208, 209
servants 102
sexuality 122–3
Shenk, François 96, 119, 131, 203
Smeyers, Frédric 155–6
Solhart, Georges 79–80, 217
stereotypes of women 103–4, 111,
    114, 127, 187; see also women

suicide 17, 27, 56, 88, 107, 114,
    169, 183

Taine 181
Tarde, G. 181, 182
trials 42
Trouvé, Isidore 88–91

unemployment 46

Valensi, Lévy 200
Vallaud, Auguste 125
victims 43, 69, 84, 202, 210, 211
violence 19, 27, 28, 106, 108, 110,
    111, 115, 120, 169, 205
vitriolage 16, 77, 111, 148–9

weapons 50, 63, 68, 69–70, 74, 76,
    79, 80, 82, 83, 84, 92, 93, 94,
    96, 99, 105, 106, 109, 126,
    131, 133, 153, 158, 162,
    175–6, 190, 204, 208, 215,
    217, 223
wives, duty of 80, 211
women
  independence of 113–15, 119–20,
    134
  treatment by men 94, 108, 111
  see also middle-class women;
    stereotypes of women; working
    class women
women's movement 176
working class
  attitude towards 114, 120, 150,
    152, 178, 203
  living conditions 28–9, 149–50,
    153–4
  women 82, 95, 100, 113–15,
    117, 118, 127

Zola, E. 36–7, 95, 120, 153, 161,
    203